AN
AMERICAN
MARTYR
IN PERSIA

ALSO BY REZA ASLAN

No God but God
How to Win a Cosmic War
Zealot
God

ANTHOLOGIES

Tablet & Pen

AN AMERICAN MARTYR IN PERSIA

*The Epic Life and Tragic Death of
Howard Baskerville*

REZA ASLAN

W. W. NORTON & COMPANY
Independent Publishers Since 1923

For information about permission to reproduce selections from this book,
write to Permissions, W. W. Norton & Company, Inc.
500 Fifth Avenue, New York, NY 10110

For information about special discounts for bulk purchases, please contact
W. W. Norton Special Sales at specialsales@wwnorton.com or 800-233-4830

Manufacturing by Lakeside Book Company
Book design by Ellen Cipriano
Production manager: Anna Oler

ISBN 978-1-324-00447-9

W. W. Norton & Company, Inc.
500 Fifth Avenue, New York, N.Y. 10110
www.wwnorton.com

W. W. Norton & Company Ltd.
15 Carlisle Street, London W1D 3BS

1 2 3 4 5 6 7 8 9 0

To everyone, everywhere, fighting for their rights.

Persia much regrets the honorable loss of
your dear son in the cause of liberty, and we give our
parole that future Persia will always preserve his name
in her history, like that of Lafayette in America,
and will respect his venerable tomb.

—Cablegram concerning the death of
Howard Conklin Baskerville, sent to his father, Henry,
by the revolutionary commander,
Sattar Khan. April 1909.

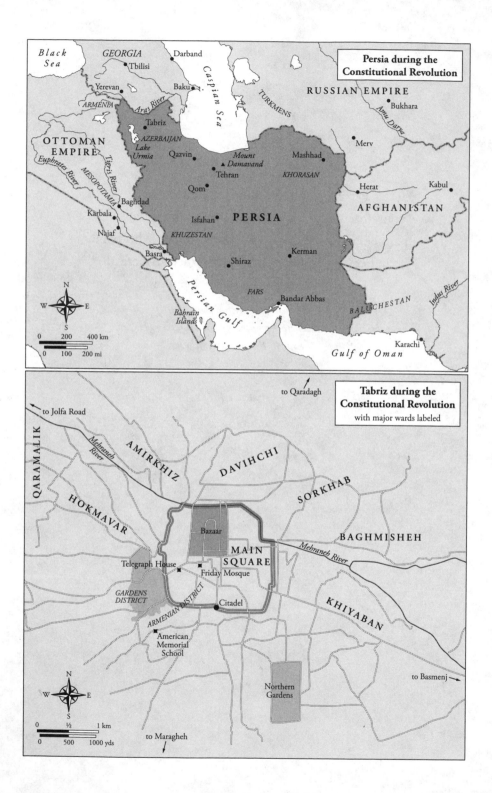

Persia during the Constitutional Revolution

Black Sea
GEORGIA
Darband
Tbilisi
Baku
Yerevan
Caspian Sea
ARMENIA
Aras River
Tabriz
AZERBAIJAN
Lake Urmia
Qazvin
TURKMENS
RUSSIAN EMPIRE
Bukhara
Amu Darya
Merv
OTTOMAN EMPIRE
Euphrates River
Tigris River
MESOPOTAMIA
Mount Damavand
Tehran
Mashhad
KHORASAN
Qom
Herat
Kabul
AFGHANISTAN
Baghdad
Karbala
Najaf
KHUZESTAN
Isfahan
PERSIA
Kerman
Basra
Shiraz
Bahrain Islands
Persian Gulf
FARS
Bandar Abbas
BALUCHESTAN
Indus River
Karachi
Gulf of Oman

N W E S

0   200   400 km
0   100   200 mi

Tabriz during the Constitutional Revolution
with major wards labeled

to Qaradagh
to Jolfa Road
QARAMALIK
AMIRKHIZ
Mehraneh River
DAVIHCHI
SORKHAB
HOKMAVAR
BAGHMISHEH
Mehraneh River
Bazaar
MAIN SQUARE
Telegraph House
Friday Mosque
GARDENS DISTRICT
ARMENIAN DISTRICT
Citadel
KHIYABAN
American Memorial School
Northern Gardens
to Basmenj
to Maragheh

N W E S

0   ½   1 km
0   500   1000 yds

CONTENTS

INTRODUCTION

I HAVE ALWAYS known the name Howard Baskerville. For as long as I can remember, his name was a flash in the corner of my eye. When I was a child growing up in Iran, there were schools named after him. His face, cast in bronze, was prominently displayed in a museum in Tabriz, the city in which he died and was buried. His tomb is still there, pressed up against an overgrown apricot tree, in a long-abandoned cemetery. The edges of the sarcophagus are smooth and worn—not from the elements, but from a century or so of curious hands. People used to come here from all over the country to honor the American who gave his life for Iran. These days, hardly anyone comes at all. Those few who still visit his tomb know little about the man lying inside, save for the bare facts of his life and death.

He was twenty-two years old, a Christian missionary. He came to Persia* in the fall of 1907 to teach English and history and to preach the Gospel. He took up arms and fought alongside his students in a bloody revolution against a ruthless tyrant. He died a martyr in the cause of freedom and democracy.

---

* Although Iranians referred to the country as Iran, it would not officially be known as Iran until 1935.

That is pretty much all I knew about Howard Baskerville. To Iranians of my generation he was simply "the American." The name embodied the country. It was a metonym for the United States: youthful, impassioned, a little bit naïve, perhaps, but earnest in the conviction that freedom is inalienable.

In the run-up to the Iranian Revolution of 1979—the third of three revolutions in my home country over the course of the twentieth century—Baskerville's name surfaced once again. There was an expectation among some Iranians that America, "a nation of Baskervilles," would undoubtedly support the struggle against a dictator that many deemed to be as vile and repressive as the one Baskerville died fighting against seventy years earlier. That would not be the case, of course. America was more concerned with promoting its interests than its principles in Iran.

"If Mr. Baskerville were resurrected today, and still intent on fighting dictators and oppressors," wrote a prominent Persian writer and activist in 1977, "he would find himself shooting his own countrymen."

The metonym, it seemed, had broken.

Afterward, when the American-backed Shah fled to the United States and the Persian monarchy transformed into an Islamic Republic—a different form of tyranny—Baskerville's story was wiped from the country's collective memory. The schools were renamed, the bronze bust tucked into a corner of the museum. His tomb was abandoned, his name forgotten, his self-sacrifice buried beneath decades of anger and animosity between the United States and Iran.

I, too, eventually forgot his name. As an Iranian refugee living in America, I could have made Baskerville my lodestar, my guide and beacon in an unfamiliar country I was suddenly forced to call home. But no American had ever heard of him. He wasn't taught in schools or talked about in politics. In Iran, Baskerville had been erased from our history books. In America, he was never in them to begin with.

Over the years, I found myself occasionally looking for Howard

Baskerville again. I would pour over what little I could find in archives and libraries, trying to piece together a meaningful account of his life and death. I found historical documents casting him as a "pure-hearted youth" whose blood came to a boil at the sight of the suffering that took place around him and read opinion pieces painting him as a reckless "white savior" whose insertion into Persian affairs presaged a century of American interference in Iran. Some called him a hero—"the American Lafayette"!* Others viewed him as naïve and easily manipulated into giving his life for a country that wasn't his, a people he barely knew, a cause he hardly understood. The US government at the time labeled him a traitor and threatened him with imprisonment or worse if he did not desist his revolutionary activities and return to America at once. The Presbyterian Church, which had sent Baskerville to Tabriz to convert the population, disavowed him altogether. He wasn't one of theirs, they claimed—not really.

Yet nothing I read adequately explained how this pious young man from the Black Hills of South Dakota wound up fighting a revolution in turn-of-the-century Persia. It's as though he spent the first twenty years of his life walking a path beaten by generations of Baskervilles before him—including his father and grandfather, his uncle and brother—a path that led directly to the pulpit. And then, for reasons that aren't exactly clear, he suddenly swerved off the path and strode headlong into the wilderness.

It was only in the process of writing this book—the first biography ever written about the young man—that my eyes were finally opened as to who Howard Baskerville truly was, what led him to abandon everything he knew to fight for Persia, and what his death a century ago could mean for all of us today.

I wrote this book because I believe every American and every

---

* Marquis de Lafayette was a French military officer who fought in the American Revolutionary War.

Iranian should know the name Howard Baskerville, and that name should be a reminder of all the two peoples hold in common. My hope is that his heroic life and death can serve in both countries as the model for a future relationship—one based not on mutual animosity but on mutual respect. Perhaps then, America can once more be known as a nation of Baskervilles.

PART ONE

A student without devotion
is a lover without money;
A traveler without knowledge
is a bird without wings;
A scholar without action
is a tree without fruit;
And a devotee without learning
is a house without a door.

—Saadi

CHAPTER 1

The Mohammedan Work

HOWARD BASKERVILLE EXITS the Presbyterian Board of Foreign Missions building on the northwest corner of Fifth Avenue and Twentieth Street in New York City, a one-way ticket on a steamship bound for Europe tucked into his jacket pocket. He drags a small, secondhand steamer trunk packed with a Bible, some books (Thackeray, Dickens), and a few items of clothing. The one "first-class outfit" he owns, he purchased specifically for this trip; he will need a fine suit for preaching. But I like to picture him wearing it on this steamy midsummer morning—perhaps in August or late July; it isn't clear. He'd want to look his best for his final meeting with the general secretary of the missions board, the esteemed Robert E. Speer. It's not that Baskerville thought Speer might change his mind about dispatching him overseas. He had more than demonstrated the "strong Christian character and true missionary spirit" the board expected of those it sent into the field. But after the suffocatingly slow train ride from his family's home in South Dakota, it would have felt good to be clean and proper again, dressed in a white waistcoat and striped tie, a stiff bowler hat perched at an angle on his head.

Even at this early hour, the city would be bustling with activity: horse-drawn carriages and lumbering trollies vying for space with the

odd motor car on the broken cobblestone streets. It is the twilight of
the Gilded Age in America, though, in truth, the gilt peeled off long
ago. In a few short years, the Great War will lay waste to most everything east of the Atlantic. But on this side of the ocean, war will mean
more factories, more shipyards, more coal and steel, and, thus, more
riches for the handful of robber barons who control it all. From where
Baskerville stands on that busy street corner, he could lift his head and
see towers scraping the sky. On the streets below: stoop-shouldered
men; wailing children; cold, unlit tenements.

I doubt the meager travel allowance Baskerville received from the
Presbyterian Church would allow for a carriage ride to the docks—
and, anyway, why deny the ambience of a stroll through the city? Push-
carts piled with fruit as pale as the women selling them. Workmen in
knee-high boots sweeping horse shit off the streets. Blank-faced children shucking oysters on the curb. The stench would only get worse
as Baskerville turns down Fourteenth Street and walks past the blood-
splattered butcher shops of the meat-packing district.

That's when the docks come into view.

In 1907, New York Harbor is the busiest port in the world.
Stretched along its craggy shore are dozens of double-decked
piers crowded with workers unloading cargo, merchants selling their wares, and thousands upon thousands of newly arrived
immigrants—mostly Italians, Poles, and Yiddish-speaking Jews carrying their entire lives in sacks flung over their shoulders. They came
here crammed in the bowels of ships—"steerage class," they called
it: men, women, and children packed into small, lightless compartments, sleeping in beds stacked one above the other, eating gruel
dished out of copper kettles, all for the chance to build Rockefel-
ler's railroads and Vanderbilt's ships. New York is as far as many of
them will go; nearly three-quarters of the city's population are either
newly arrived or the children of immigrants. Some never even leave
the docks; there is plenty of work to do on the piers, helping pas-

sengers like Baskerville board the very same ships they took on their long voyage here.

There is no shortage of ships. The gray waters of the Hudson are choked with hulking ocean liners and state-of-the-art steamships, their engines belching smoke across the harbor. Stiff competition among American, British, and European shipping companies over who can best cater to the needs of the well-heeled traveler has led to a dizzying array of innovations meant to make the journey across the Atlantic safer, faster, and far more extravagant. First-class passengers can expect private commodes wrapped in marble, wood-paneled dining rooms capped with glass-domed ceilings, smoking rooms designed to resemble Italian palazzi, and dining bars that look like French châteaux. The German liner SS *Amerika* features the world's first à la carte restaurant at sea (called the Ritz-Carlton), allowing passengers to dine whenever they wish, instead of during rigidly set mealtimes. On RMS *Adriatic*, recently launched by the Liverpool-based White Star Line—the shipping company that would gain infamy in a few years with the sinking of the pride of its fleet, RMS *Titanic*—one can relax in a Turkish bath, play squash belowdecks in the ship's gleaming gymnasium, or take a dip in the world's first floating swimming pool. The colossal sister ships of the Cunard Line, RMS *Lusitania* and RMS *Mauretania*, both of which would dwarf anything else floating in the harbor, boast never-before-seen turbine steam engines, making them the fastest passenger ships in the world. The *Mauretania*—at the time the largest moving structure ever built—can cross the Atlantic in a record-setting four and half days, thanks to the backbreaking work of the boiler-room crew.

With the outbreak of the Great War, some of these vessels will be seized by their nations and outfitted as troop carriers or hospital ships. Shipping lanes will be cluttered with naval mines and patrolled by German U-boats (one of them sank the *Lusitania* in 1915), and passenger ports will be repurposed as pickup points for soldiers heading to the front. But war is still seven years away. For now, a steady parade of fully laden ships continues to steam west to the New World—their bellies bursting with emigrants huddled inside closed-berth cabins, eating rancid food, breathing rancid air—and then east back toward Europe, their main decks flecked with top hats and parasols.

Baskerville, of course, will experience neither the luxuries of first class nor the inhumanity of steerage. In 1907, a trip from New York to Liverpool could cost anywhere between $50 and $80; on the *Mauretania*, a first-class ticket could cost as much as $150. That's nearly $4,000 in today's prices. But Baskerville could still grab a third-class seat on any one of these ships for about twenty bucks. No sense, then, looking for him in an oak-lined dining bar constructed from Palestinian wood and littered with plush leather chairs. He'll be taking his evening drinks in a dimly lit cafeteria, standing at a metal-topped communal table.

It's hard to imagine the luxuries available to first-class passengers would have mattered much to a pastor's son from South Dakota. After all, Howard Baskerville isn't some new-monied traveler eager to consume the riches of the Old World. He is a 22-year-old Christian missionary en route to the far-flung lands of Persia for a two-year mission in pursuit of what he termed "the Mohammedan work"; that is, the conversion of Muslims to Christ.

❖

HOWARD CONKLIN BASKERVILLE was born in North Platte, Nebraska, on April 13, 1885, the son and grandson of Presbyterian preachers. His father, Henry Coleman Baskerville, was a peripatetic pastor and lifelong seeker of knowledge who had made his public confession of faith at the age of sixteen while kneeling in an old, clapboard box of a church in Nutbush, North Carolina. The elder Baskerville went on to study Christian ministry at Davidson College and the University of Virginia before graduating from the University of Georgia in 1867. Two years at Virginia's Union Seminary resulted in his ordination by the Presbyterian Church, though rather than go immediately into full-time ministry, he chose instead to pursue a law degree, ultimately being admitted to the bar in Baltimore in 1876.

There is no evidence that Henry Baskerville actually practiced law, either in Baltimore or anywhere else for that matter. In 1879, his first wife, Julia Blanton, died unexpectedly, leaving him to raise their daughter on his own. He wouldn't remain a bachelor for long. A year later, he married Emma Reed in a small, private ceremony in Plattsburgh, New York; together they would have one more daughter and then four sons, one after the other. Howard was the second-born son.

In 1883, the family settled in Nebraska, where Henry Baskerville was assigned various preaching positions in small Presbyterian churches across the state. When Howard was five years old, his father moved the family from Nebraska to New Jersey so he could pursue yet another degree, this one from Princeton Theological Seminary, where he would ultimately receive a bachelor of divinity in 1897. Over the next few years, even as he was completing a PhD from Wooster University in Ohio, Henry would bounce from one church assignment to another: first in Spring Mills, Pennsylvania; then Goode's Ferry, Virginia; then back to Princeton for a brief stint teaching; then in Alzada, Montana; and Camp Crook, South Dakota; before finally being named lead pastor of the Presbyterian churches in Spearfish Valley, on the northern edge of the Black Hills, in 1901.

Although Howard would spend only a few years in Spearfish before leaving for college, the Black Hills and Badlands of South Dakota—with their broad prairies, spectacular buttes, and seemingly bottomless gorges—bore into his soul a deep and abiding love for the outdoors. The area had only recently been opened to white settlement; the entirety of the Black Hills region was designated by the US government as the permanent home of the Lakota tribe in the 1868 Treaty of Fort Laramie. Six years later, however, after Gen. George Custer discovered gold in these hills, the US government tore up the treaty and took the land back, herding the Lakota into sparse reservations scattered across the barren lands of western South Dakota.

Amidst the brightly colored spires and wind-ravaged pinnacles that ringed this natural wonderland, Baskerville matured into an adventurous young man in the mold of the naturalist "Rough Rider" who was then president of the United States, and whose face would soon be carved into a mountain just a few miles south of here (actually, with his brown hair, blue eyes, and rosy cheeks, the bespectacled Baskerville bore a faint resemblance to the young Teddy Roosevelt, minus the ever-present mustache). He could hike across the prairie grasslands all the way up to Bear Butte mountain, the path marked with prayer cloths tied to tree branches by the expelled tribe for whom this mount was sacred. He could hunt pheasant, or grouse, or perhaps try his luck picking off one of the countless black-tail prairie dogs whose burrows made these wide-open plains look like a veritable moonscape. He could explore the river-carved canyons or go fishing in the cold waters of Spearfish Creek, which was fed year-round with trout eggs hauled by covered wagon all the way from Yellowstone.

His favorite pastime, however, was riding horses. During his summer vacations, he occasionally worked at a nearby horse ranch where, in exchange for feeding and caring for the animals, he would have the opportunity to ride across the endless pastures of South Dakota, racing alongside wild buffalo, skirting the edge of the surrounding granite cliffs. Baskerville also loved to box and play tennis, both of which were more salutary to pursue in the desert climate of the Black Hills region, where the dry air eased the chronic catarrh from which he suffered all his life, the result of a bout of malaria he contracted as a child.

Like his father, Baskerville was a bookish young man with a thirst for knowledge and a talent for picking up languages. By the time he graduated high school, he was fluent in Latin, Greek, and German. But unlike his father, Baskerville never seemed to have expressed much interest in becoming a country pastor. He wanted to spread the word of Christ to all peoples, in all nations. Ever since he was a child, he had thought about becoming a missionary, "with more or less definitiveness," he wrote in his application to the Presbyterian Board of Foreign Missions. He had taken mission-study courses through his church and served as president of the local chapter of the Young People's Society of Christian Endeavor, an evangelical organization that, at the time, boasted three and half million members in countries as far afield as China and Australia. He was even put in charge of his own mission field by the Black Hills Presbytery, during which he claimed to have "spoken with a number of persons about this Christian life," though with what success he was too modest to say in his application.

When it was time to decide on a college, memories of the year he spent with his father at Princeton returned to his mind. And so, Howard followed in Henry's footsteps, applying to Princeton University for a degree in Christian ministry.

It was the fall of 1903, an auspicious time for Princeton, which was still roiling from a seismic shift in the school's program and priorities. Only a year earlier, the board of trustees had promoted one of its more popular professors, Woodrow Wilson, to be president of the university, and he had wasted little time in remolding the school in his own image.

Young Howard was immediately drawn into Wilson's orbit. It would have been difficult to miss the tall, thin man in the starched white collar, dashing back and forth across The Quad, the rubber tip of his walking cane hovering always a few inches off the ground. Wilson's face, once you glimpsed it, was unforgettable: an almost perfect rectangle framed by a high, flat forehead and an aggressive jaw that jutted out like an admonition.

As a professor, Wilson had a famously low tolerance for fools. He was severely critical of Princeton's student body and battled publicly—and frequently—with both the faculty and the administration. Yet his students adored him. Seven times he was voted Princeton's favorite professor. He routinely filled 300-seat lecture halls, often with students from other classes crowding the hallways, straining to hear his stirring orations about the greatness of American democracy and the need for American leadership abroad. The coiffed-and-preened Princeton men would lean forward in their seats, notebooks open, as Wilson thrilled them with grand proclamations such as "the progress of civilization has obliterated the frontier!" or "the Nation has broken its shell!"

They would stamp their feet and rise in applause.

Even in informal settings, Wilson spoke with ecclesiastical authority, as though he were reading from a script. It was an oratory skill bred into him at a very young age. His father, Joseph Wilson, a fire-and-brimstone Presbyterian preacher, would often force him to memorize the speeches of great men, and then not just recite them on command, but improve upon them. As a child, Wilson practiced giving rousing sermons to empty pews, the expectation being that he would follow his father into the Presbyterian ministry. That is likely why he himself enrolled as a student at Princeton, then known as the College of New Jersey. Princeton was a school founded by Presbyterians, and its chief function in those days seemed to be to churn out a bevy of black-robed ministers to replenish America's pulpits. Nearly a quarter of Wilson's graduating class would go on to become men of the cloth. But, as with Baskerville, the pulpit never held much interest for Woodrow Wilson. His passion was politics.

Wilson entered Princeton as a freshman in 1879, fourteen years after the end of the Civil War. The war had a deep impact on the Wilson family, which fully identified with the Confederacy. Wilson's father was a slaveholder and fervent supporter of the Confederate cause, even after the war's end. A family photo taken in 1892—nearly three decades after Emancipation—depicts the Wilsons smiling and seated together in front of their doorstep in South Carolina; two elderly Black servants in matching white cotton dresses stand at attention behind them, staring uneasily off camera.

As a child, Woodrow Wilson idolized the Confederate general Robert E. Lee. His classmates recall him always taking "the southern side" in debates, and he was never happier than when he was debating. At Princeton, he was a star member of one of the legendary debating clubs, the Whigs and the Clios (Wilson, emulating one of his political heroes, James Madison, joined the Whigs). Yet, when at a prestigious end-of-year debate in 1879, he was randomly chosen to argue the side of universal suffrage, Wilson threw a fit and stormed off the stage, rather than be forced to argue for the right of Black Americans to vote.

Indeed, one cannot speak about any stage of Woodrow Wilson's storied career without acknowledging his unrepentant racism. He was, in the judgment of the Black actor and activist Paul Robeson, "an advocate for democracy for the world and Jim Crow for America." As a professor, Wilson regaled his students with an endless supply of racist jokes about "rustic negroes." In his writings, he lavished praise on the Ku Klux Klan, calling it "a veritable empire of the South" whose role in protecting "the southern country" should be enshrined. As president of Princeton University from 1902 to 1910, he refused to follow the lead of other Ivy League schools and allow admission to Black students, arguing that their presence "would be embarrassing for them and for Princeton University." As president of the United States, he made segregation official government policy, firing Black federal workers and reversing decades of racial progress. He even screened *Birth of a Nation* at the White House.

Wilson could speak with biblical certainty about the inviolability of God-given freedoms. He could, in his speeches, elevate human liberty to a moral prerogative. He could preach "universal sympathy for those who struggle" and claim, without irony, to seek to lift "the unbearable burdens that were upon their backs."

He just didn't mean the backs of Black people.

Still, if you were a young white man of privilege, like Howard Baskerville, Wilson was your paladin. In 1902, Woodrow Wilson was promoted from professor of politics to president of the university. In that role, he helped enact an educational revolution whose reverberations are, to this day, felt by nearly all university students in the United States. He reorganized Princeton's academic departments, enforced higher educational standards for graduates, and reformed the school curriculum to better match the needs of a rapidly changing, increasingly interconnected world. He instituted an "Oxford-style" mentoring program, known as "the preceptorial system," the purpose of which was to shepherd students out of Princeton's high-ceilinged halls and into a more intimate setting, where they could receive personal, one-on-one instruction from their chosen professor. More broadly, he redirected undergraduate education away from its focus on specialized fields and toward "general training," or, as Wilson put it: "a familiarity with principles rather than the acquisition of, imperfect at best, a mass of miscellaneous information." This included overhauling Princeton's electives system in a bid to encourage students to stretch their minds by taking courses outside of their chosen fields.

Wilson's goal was not merely to transform higher education in America. It was to transform university students from cloistered scholars to global citizens, to make of them an army of righteous young men primed for national service. The reforms caused a stir among Princeton's old guard, the alumni, and wealthy donors. But it brought Wilson national notoriety, paving the way for his eventual entrance into politics—first, as governor of New Jersey, and then, as president of the United States.

Once in the White House, Woodrow Wilson would expand his vision of a student body in service to the nation into a policy of a nation in service to the world. He was inaugurated in 1913, a year before the outbreak of the First World War, and while he managed to keep the United States out of that conflict during his first term, by 1917, thousands of American troops were marching into Europe to fight alongside the Allied powers. For better or worse, the Great War forced America out of its isolation, and in its aftermath, Wilson sought to inject what he viewed as America's universal values onto the global stage.

In the rubble and ash the war had left behind, Wilson saw an opportunity to rebuild the world in America's image. He envisioned a new world order composed not of detached, isolated countries in perpetual conflict with one another, but of interdependent nations guided by international norms, governed by international law, and safeguarded by international organizations. In this new world order, America would no longer be "the city on a hill," a shining beacon of liberty for weary travelers yearning for freedom. Rather, it would be a torchlight shined into every dark and shattered corner of the globe by a corps of young, Ivy League graduates trained to preserve democracy at home and defend it abroad.

Howard Baskerville was long dead by the time Wilson's dream of a new world order climaxed in 1920 with the creation of the League of Nations, the precursor to the United Nations. But he was there, at Princeton, as the seed of that idea put out shoots across the campus.

❖

BASKERVILLE SPENT HIS first two years at Princeton with his nose buried in the Bible, mastering the fields of scriptural exegesis and Christian apologetics required of all those studying for the ministry. During his junior year, however, Baskerville took advantage of the university's revamped electives system to enroll in two courses taught by Wilson himself: one on jurisprudence, the other on constitutional government.

The two men—both of them preacher's sons; both of them compelled to follow suit—ought to have gotten along swimmingly. They both had deep southern roots. Howard's great-great-grandfather, John Coleman, owned a sprawling plantation with a large number of slaves. His grandfather, William Baskerville, was a member of the Confederate Congress from Virginia, and his great-uncle, George Baskerville Douglas, was a surgeon for the Confederate army who fought alongside the Georgia Regulars at Bull Run; he was captured by Union forces on Easter Sunday, 1865, and paroled soon after the war's end.

With so much of his family tree having sprouted from Confederate soil, it's fair to wonder whether Baskerville shared his mentor's prejudice toward Black people. The answer is difficult to know. Howard Baskerville was a white man in America at a time in which the scars of the Civil War could still be seen in the burn lines left behind by Sherman in the South. He lived in a state in which the only people of color had been forcibly removed. He attended a university where Black students were not welcomed. How did he feel about all this? Was he even aware of the inequity? Probably not. The only thing that can be said with certainty is that no one who knew Howard Baskerville ever described him as a bigot.

Like Wilson, Baskerville became a passionate debater at Princeton. He won general honors in debating as a freshman and placed third in a university-wide oratorical contest his junior year. He was awarded the prestigious Francis Biddle Sophomore Prize, given to the student who wrote the best essay on English or American literature, neither of which were Baskerville's chosen field of study. By his own admission, he spent between eight and nine hours a day studying; he would go on to graduate *cum laude*. Always a serious, studious boy, he refused to join any of the upper-class eating clubs (Princeton's version of fraternities), which Wilson detested as a waste of valuable time and which he tried yet failed to get rid of during his tenure as university president.

Princeton's newly established preceptorial system was meant to encourage students to seek out mentors from the faculty, and it is not difficult to imagine why Baskerville would have chosen Wilson. Not only were the two men aligned in interest and temperament; they were both devout Presbyterians.

Wilson's piety, and the role of religion in shaping his political views, are matters too often neglected in his biography. "My life would not be worth living if it were not for the driving power of religion,"

Wilson once confessed to a friend. It was his faith in God, his fealty to the Presbyterian church, and his unshakable confidence in Christian ethics that underlay most of the political assumptions that drove him into government.

"If I did not believe that the moral judgment would be the last and final judgment in the minds of men, as well as at the tribunal of God," Wilson wrote, "I could not believe in popular government."

The primary purpose of religion, in Wilson's view, was to draw the believer toward public service. Politics was no mere civic duty; it was a religious obligation. Political involvement was all about "translating principle into social action." And because, for Wilson, the principles that strengthened and sustained American democracy were derived not from men, but from God—"individual salvation is national salvation," he never tired of saying—they could not possibly be reserved for Americans. They must be applied to all peoples, in all parts of the world, regardless of creed, culture, or nationality. They must be planted in the native soils of Europe and Asia, Africa and the Middle East. And who better to do the planting than the pious Princeton graduate, whom Wilson had spent the entirety of his educational career carefully cultivating?

"It is noteworthy how often God-fearing men have been forward in those revolutions which have vindicated rights," Wilson would have reminded Baskerville in his lectures on constitutional government. And then, lest he miss the point: "Revolution was not to be distinguished from duty in Princeton."

The fusing of politics and piety, the belief that our obligations to each other are indistinguishable from our obligation to God, the conviction that popular sovereignty is a divine mandate over all lands at all times—these are the ideas that Baskerville would have picked up from his two courses with Woodrow Wilson. They would ignite the religious and intellectual passions of the young man, setting him on a course he could scarcely have envisioned.

By the time Baskerville returned to Princeton for his senior year, his mind had been made up. Despite enormous pressure from his church and his family to enter seminary immediately after graduation, Baskerville decided to take three years off from his studies to heed the call of his Lord and "go out and make disciples of all nations"—nations that, as his mentor Wilson had taught him, all men should fight to make free. He penned an impassioned letter to the Presbyterian Board of Foreign Missions in New York, declaring his intention to "spend my life in the foreign field" and inquiring whether the church could use him "in any of the mission schools." Asked in the formal application where he wanted to be placed, he wrote "China or Japan." And then, almost as an afterthought, he added ". . . or Persia" in small print, just above the typewritten text.

Baskerville did not really want to go to Persia. His missionary application makes it clear that he felt called by God to preach the Gospel in the Far East. In a separate letter to the missions board, he wrote that, while he'd be willing to go wherever "it will count for the most for the observance of Christ's Kingdom," after much prayer and discernment, he had concluded that his life "can be used to the best advantage in China."

It is possible he had read the colorful missionary dispatches being sent home from long-established missions in China and Japan, boasting of the spectacular successes the faithful were experiencing among the noble savages of the Far East. "One church reports a net increase for the year of two hundred percent," read a dispatch from northern China. "All the schools are crowded, while the demand for Christian education is growing. . . . Training classes for members, in which the Bible and Christian doctrine are taught, are in demand."

The dispatches sent from Tokyo spoke of the striking similarity in climate between the islands of Japan and the British Isles. "Japan may be called the Great Britain of the East," read a report to the missions board. "The skies are clear and beautiful, and nature clothes itself in its brightest robes of green. It is a land of fruits and flowers, and its hills are stored with the choicest minerals."

Compare these reports with the missionary dispatches sent from Persia: "Probably nowhere in the world has deceit been more nearly universal, the state of the family and women more degraded, and the ruins of past achievement more manifest than in Persia," wrote Frances B. Packard, a physician and Presbyterian missionary who served in both Kermanshah and Tabriz.

Even those missionaries who spent a lifetime toiling in Persia and who, as a result, came to love and admire its culture and people seemed incapable of avoiding the most base stereotypes in their dispatches. The Rev. Justin Perkins, the legendary Presbyterian missionary who almost single-handedly built the West Persia Mission, who spent decades living and preaching in Persia, and who buried six of his seven children there, could not help but temper his praise for the Persian people with his own prejudice. "The inhabitants of Persia doubtless surpass all other nations in external ease and artificial politeness; and it is with great propriety that they are often styled 'the French of Asia,'" Perkins wrote in his memoir. "But, sad to tell, Persian politeness is little more than external. Their real character is that of treachery and falsehood in the extreme. . . . And the general degradation of their morals is appalling. Almost all the sins forbidden in the Decalogue are fearfully prevalent among them; and to those many add the yet more abominable sin of Sodom."

Reading these missionary reports, Baskerville could be forgiven for wanting nothing to do with Persia or its "treacherous" population. At the same time, he knew that the Presbyterian Church was actively recruiting missionaries to carry the saving knowledge of Christ to the "lost sheep" of the Middle East. Robert Speer had given numerous speeches at Princeton lamenting the lack of young Christians willing to confront what the church called "the solid wall of Mohammedanism, which, as yet, except in the most general way, has been unyielding."

Speer had formed a particularly close connection with the West Persia Mission, specifically the American Memorial School run by the Rev. Samuel Graham Wilson and his wife, Annie Rhea, in the city of Tabriz, on the northwestern edge of the country. Indeed, he had made it his personal mission to send the school a corps of zealous young men and women ready to win the souls of the students who studied there.

Baskerville was aware of Speer's obsession with Persia and so was willing to consider a post in Tabriz, should there be no room for him in China or Japan. But he could not hide his disappointment when he received his assignment. Nevertheless, he humbly accepted the commission, under one condition. He would commit only to two years in Tabriz, rather than the standard three. If at the end of the two years he felt he could no longer stay in Persia, he would pay for half his own ticket back to the United States.

He would last one year and seven months before being shot in the back, in a bombed-out orchard, in a besieged city, while leading a militia made up of the very same students he had been sent there to teach and, should the opportunity arise, bring to Christ.

He was twenty-four years old.

❖

ATTACHED TO BASKERVILLE'S missionary application is a neatly typed recommendation on Princeton University letterhead: "I have known Mr. Baskerville quite well throughout his college course, and regard him as in every way a most estimable man," it read. "I think, too, that he has developed considerably during his course, and that there is every likelihood that he would fill the position of teacher in the school at Tabriz in a very acceptable manner. I sincerely hope that it will be possible to accord him the appointment."

The letter is signed Woodrow Wilson, March 20, 1907.

When I picture Howard Baskerville in my mind, standing on the prow of a steamship bound for Liverpool or perhaps Glasgow—either destination merely the first leg of a journey that would cover more than ten thousand miles—I like to imagine a copy of that recommendation letter tucked away in the secondhand steamer trunk. There he is: his shoes shit-stained, his brand new breeches flaked with mud; staring at the flat horizon, wondering what's to come.

It is no stretch of the imagination to think of him at that moment repeating to himself Wilson's words about God-fearing men and revolutions. Is it too far a stretch to hear those same words ringing in his ears as he creeps with his students through that ruined orchard in Tabriz, bullets whizzing past his head?

Howard Baskerville in 1907 on the eve of his departure for Persia.

CHAPTER TWO

One Thousand Words for Sword

L IVERPOOL WAS THE LIKELIEST port of entry. In 1907, there was not another seaport on this side of the Atlantic that could compete with its seven-mile stretch of stone-built docks. When Herman Melville first came here with a crew of harpooners aboard the whaling ship *St. Lawrence*, he compared Liverpool's chain of granite-rimmed docks to the Pyramids of Egypt, so grand and mighty were the structures. Of course, unlike those "idle towers of stone," Liverpool's piers and floating roadways were bustling with life. Two of the largest and most lucrative shipping companies in the world—the White Star Line and the Cunard Line—were headquartered here. It's likely the ship Baskerville boarded in New York was launched on the very shores he now slowly approached. Standing on deck, he could look out over the gray dawn and see black smoke rising from the shipyards, the wooden hulls of long-abandoned ships splayed along the banks like the fossils of some great leviathan.

Baskerville's ship would have berthed at one of the south-end docks, perhaps Prince's or Albert or Queen's. Prince's Dock was the one most frequented by steamships arriving from America. From there, he could walk to Riverside Station and board a train directly to London. But why not stay in Liverpool, just for a day or two? He could sleep in one of the evangelical boarding houses Melville wrote about, where missionaries found temporary shelter before heading out into the field. He could take high tea on the waterfront or shop for souvenirs in the elegant, lamp-lit boutiques on Lord Street. After all, he was about to cross an entire continent by train, all the way to Moscow—and this, on the eve of a war that would kill twenty million people in ways no human had yet imagined.

❖

EUROPE, AT THE time of Baskerville's arrival, was, in the indelible words of Barbara Tuchman, "a heap of swords piled as delicately as jack straws; one could not be pulled out without moving the others." Half a century of carefully crafted charters and treaties had created a complex web of alliances that bound together the fates of nearly every European nation; none could go to war without dragging the others along.

It was a shaky balance, to be sure, but it had maintained a measure of peace across the continent. There hadn't been a large-scale war in Europe since Napoleon's *Armée du Nord* shattered against a wall of Anglo-allied forces at Waterloo a century earlier. Back then, soldiers fought each other across short distances—often face to face. Napoleon's feared *grande batterie* involved rolling eight-inch howitzers to the front and concentrating their firepower on the center of the enemy's line so that the French cavalry could rush through the breach swinging swords. Napoleon's infantry carried flintlock muskets tipped with bayonets that could, in the best of circumstances, fire three volleys a minute at an effective distance of about one hundred yards, so long as the muzzle was reloaded after each shot.

In the intervening century, war had become mechanized. Six British soldiers manning a single Vickers machine gun firing five hundred rounds a minute could have sliced through the entirety of Napoleon's fighting force in a matter of minutes. A hundred men in a trench could ward off a thousand on the battlefield. Cavalry charges were obsolete, swords worn mostly for show. Baskerville could have purchased a rusty bayonet blade for a few shillings in any one of the antique shops on Liverpool's Lord Street.

And yet, despite all this, the prospect of a continent-wide war seemed somehow inevitable. Signs of the impending conflict could be felt across Europe. It was a high-frequency pitch lodged in the ear. You couldn't tell where it was coming from, but it was impossible to ignore. And it was only getting louder.

"If this war breaks out, then its duration and its end will be unforeseeable," warned the Prussian field marshal, Helmuth von Moltke, in a speech to the German Reichstag. "Woe to him who sets Europe alight and first throws the match into the powder barrel!"

The match would be thrown in June 1914 by a nineteen-year-old Serbian nationalist named Gavrilo Princip, who happened to be standing across the northern end of Latin Bridge in Sarajevo when an open-air motor car bearing Archduke Franz Ferdinand and his wife took a wrong turn and stopped directly in front of him. Princip pulled out his pistol and lit the powder barrel.

Princip wanted nothing more than to put an end to Austro-Hungarian rule over Bosnia. He ended up pulling the first sword in the heap. The archduke's assassination would lead to the Austro-Hungarian invasion of Serbia. The Austro-Hungarian invasion would awaken the lumbering Russian beast, which had pledged Serbia's safety. Russian mobilization would force Germany's hand, which would then spur France into action. France would inevitably drag the United Kingdom behind it. And once the British joined the fray, the United States would not be far behind—not with Woodrow Wilson at the helm.

"We desire no conquest, no dominion . . . no material compensation for the sacrifices we shall freely make," Wilson would tell Congress in April 1917, urging a declaration of war against Germany. "We are but one of the champions of the rights of mankind. We shall be satisfied when those rights have been made as secure as the faith and freedom of the nations can make them."

No doubt Baskerville could feel the tension building across the continent. But at this moment in 1907, he had more immediate concerns. He was still thousands of miles from his final destination. Before him lay an arduous journey by train, carriage, caravan, and saddle. There were plagues to avert, bandits to outrun. Traveling this close to the end of the stifling summer months meant unending days beneath a merciless sun, followed by nights so cold it froze the marrow. And all of this was before he even arrived in Persia, the thought of which was already setting him on edge. He had been reading about the turmoil taking place in that unfamiliar land. It was in all the papers.

"PERSIA HAS A PARLIAMENT!" shouted the London *Independent*. "Merchants and Mullahs Compel the Shah to Grant Reforms" cheered the *New York Times*.

After two long years of strikes and street protests, a band of young revolutionaries, backed by business and religious groups, had forced the bloated monarch of Persia, Muzaffar ad-Din Shah, to accept a constitution establishing the rule of law and severely limiting his unchecked powers. The Persian Constitutional Revolution, as it would come to be known, was the first of its kind in any Muslim majority state. Its fundamental goal was to marry traditional Islamic principles with modern concepts such as individual rights and popular sovereignty to create a truly indigenous democratic movement. While the revolutionaries lifted some of their language and ideas from Europe and the United States, the movement itself was firmly grounded in a century or more of Persian political thought and promoted by an amalgam of dissident intellectuals, popular preachers, and political activists. Their efforts had resulted not only in a constitution guaranteeing basic rights and freedoms for all Persians; it also led to the creation of an independent parliament, called the National Consultative Assembly, with free elections and the clear separation of powers. Persia was now technically a constitutional monarchy: the Middle Eastern equivalent of the nation upon which Baskerville had just stepped foot.

❖

MUZAFFAR AD-DIN SHAH had signed the Persian Constitution into law on December 31, 1906. Three days later, he died in his bed. The throne was now in the hands of Muzaffar's tyrannical, 35-year-old son, Mohammed Ali.

A pompous, pudgy young man with a ridiculous mustache who enjoyed playing military dress-up, Mohammed Ali Shah was, in the words of one American observer, "the most perverted, cowardly, and vice-ridden monster that had disgraced the throne of Persia in many generations." The new shah was incensed with his father for making his God-given authority suddenly contingent upon the will of the people. From the moment he took the crown in January of 1907, he had been looking for ways to undermine the constitution he had sworn to uphold. Thus far, however, he had been unable to seriously challenge the new constitutional order. It had only been about eight months since his ascension to the throne, but it seemed as though the democratic experiment in Persia was working.

"By an almost bloodless revolution, the centuries-old absolutism of the Persian monarchs had been legally modified by constitutional forms," wrote Morgan Shuster, the American official hired by the National Consultative Assembly to clean up the financial mess left behind by a succession of debauched shahs who had steadily sold off bits of the country to pay for their extravagances. "What was even more important," Shuster continued, "the people had learned something of their real power and were more determined than ever to save their nation from the straight road to disintegration and decay along which it had been for generations skillfully piloted by its hereditary rulers."

The Constitutional Revolution was cheered by the liberal elite across Europe. In England, the eminent scholar and Persophile,

E. G. Browne, became one its most vocal champions. In his many speeches, articles, and books, Browne documented the growing demand among the Persian people for freedom and democratic rights. Through his contacts in-country, he received a steady stream of letters updating him on the daily struggle against the shah—letters he would translate and publish in journals and newspapers across Europe.

Browne grew hoarse trying to convince the British government to throw its support behind Persia's constitutionalists. Yet his calls fell on deaf ears, and he knew why. Britain considered Persia to be "a backward country, which, in the hands of its own people cannot be developed," Browne wrote in the preface of his book, *The Persian Revolution of 1905–1909.* The British government was firm in its belief that "the best thing that can happen is that some European Power, whether England or Russia, should step in and 'develop' it, whether its people like it or not."

In Browne's telling, the English Parliament viewed the Persian Parliament as little more than "a novelty imported from Europe, along with motor-cars, gramophones, and other Western innovations." Persian culture, in English eyes, was unfit for constitutional government. The Persian people were like children; they needed a firm hand to guide them. And the shah provided that. Was he a depraved, self-absorbed tyrant? Yes. But without him, Persia would be in shambles. Besides, the idea of a genuine democracy arising in a place like Persia was laughable. As one sniffy British minister declared, "the vast majority of the people were not yet clear whether constitution was something to eat or something to wear, and although this may be something of an exaggeration, it may be confidently asserted that popular interest in the matter ceased when it became clear that it was neither of these."

Conventional British bigotry aside, there was something else that motivated Britain's imperial policy toward Persia, and that was its stiff opposition to Russia. Anglo-Russian rivalry over Central Asia had been the primary motif of the nineteenth century; it would come to be known as the "Great Game." And by the time the Constitutional Revolution was in full swing, Persia had become the game's principle staging ground.

The Russians had long sought to establish control over northern Persian lands. A century of disastrous wars between the two nations had already stripped Persia of almost all its territories in the Caucasus. But that had only whetted the Russian appetite. "Persia must fall entirely under Russian influence," claimed Aleksandr Izvolskii, the Russian diplomat and adviser to Tsar Nicholas II.

Russia demanded unfettered access to the warm waters of the Persian Gulf, which could only be achieved by running a railway line across the length of the country. Yet such talk from St. Petersburg rang alarm bells in London, which had its own plans to control Persia's railway construction in order to maintain Britain's existing claims over the Persian Gulf coast.

The Great Game shifted suddenly, however, when the Germans began planning their own railway line between Baghdad and Berlin. Baghdad itself was no great prize, but its location—a mere three hundred miles northwest of the port city of Basra—would allow Germany to more easily access the Persian Gulf, and from there the trade routes to India and the Far East. This, in and of itself, was cause for concern. But what truly worried Britain and Russia was what the Berlin-Baghdad railway signified: an emerging alliance between the German and Ottoman Empires.

Despite its stale epithet as the "Sick Man of Europe," the Ottoman Empire was a giant, unignorable force in the region. It controlled all trade throughout the length of its vast empire—from the Austro-Hungarian border to the shores of the Persian Gulf. As the bridge between the Occident and the Orient, its sprawling capital, Constantinople, had become the center of gravity for all economic activity in the Black Sea and the Mediterranean basin. With Europe teetering on the edge of war, there was understandably a mad dash across the continent to curry as much favor as possible with the Ottoman court. And in this race, the Germans had a distinct advantage: the hotheaded emperor, Kaiser Wilhelm II.

Wilhelm was unquestionably a bore and a brute—a tin-pot dictator who mistook shouting for commanding. But he was not the fool historians have portrayed him to be. He possessed a quick intellect and an iron-willed resolve in political matters that, in the full light of history, can easily be interpreted as narcissistic pathology, even madness. A traumatic breech birth had left him with a withered arm, which he spent his entire life trying to hide from others, and there is some truth to the refrain that Wilhelm manifested in his disabled body the inferiority complex felt by the entire German Empire. He did, after all, title himself Caesar.

However, Wilhelm's instinct with regard to the strategic importance of an alliance with the Ottoman Empire was prescient, to say the least. In 1898, he spent several days as a fawning guest in the court of the Ottoman sultan, Abdul Hamid II. The British and French publicly criticized him for consorting with "the blood-stained monster who had slain all the Armenians," but Wilhelm left Constantinople with both an agreement to extend the German-built Anatolian Railway all the way to Baghdad and the eternal friendship of the Caliph of Islam.

Before he returned to Berlin, Wilhelm took a royal tour of the Ottoman realm. In Jerusalem, he donned the gleaming white cloak of a pilgrim and rode a magnificent black charger through the gates of the Holy City. In Damascus, he visited the mausoleum of Saladin, where he gave a moving speech about "standing on the spot where held sway one of the most chivalrous rulers of all times . . . who often taught his adversaries the right conception of knighthood."

When the trip was over, Wilhelm dubbed himself "Hajji Wilhelm"*—the Western protector of Muslims against the infidels. "Let me

---

* The designation *Hajji* indicates completion of the *hajj* pilgrimage in Mecca, which Kaiser Wilhelm II most definitely did not do.

assure His Majesty the Sultan and the three hundred million Moslems [*sic*] who, in whatever corner of the globe they may live, revere in him their Kalif [*sic*], that the German Emperor will ever be their friend."

The kaiser's words sent shockwaves through London and St. Petersburg, both of which held under their colonial rule a rather sizable number of those "three hundred million Moslems." What exactly was Hajji Wilhelm suggesting? Was he attempting to rouse the Mohammedan masses to revolt?

All at once, the bickering stopped between the British and Russians over who would control Persia. All that mattered now was coming up with a counterbalance to the rising German-Ottoman alliance.

In August of 1907, just as Baskerville was arriving in Liverpool, an agreement was formulated in St. Petersburg, known as the Anglo-Russian Convention, whereby Persia was cleanly divided into two spheres of influence: Russia would control the north and Britain the south (the full name of the treaty was "The Convention Between the United Kingdom and Russia Relating to Persia, Afghanistan, and Tibet"). The agreement allowed each country to exploit freely their allotted share of Persia's natural resources. Of course, their plans for Persia would only work if its bothersome population abandoned its unattainable dreams of democracy once and for all.

Persia found out about the Anglo-Russian Convention only after it had been signed. The constitutionalists were understandably in shock. They already loathed the Russian Empire for helping prop up a succession of shahs with hundreds of thousands of rubles in loans that were impossible to repay. But they had assumed Britain would be a natural ally in their struggle against the shah and felt deeply betrayed by the agreement with Russia. Without foreign pressure, there was little expectation that Mohammed Ali would continue to comply with the new constitutional order.

That sentiment was even more pronounced in Tabriz, the city where Mohammed Ali had been born and where he had, as royal

tradition dictated, spent the bulk of his time as crown prince. Tabriz
had served as the epicenter of the Constitutional Revolution, and its
unruly population was familiar enough with Mohammed Ali's character not to trust him. Some of the younger, more radical revolutionaries there had already begun to arm themselves; they were ready to
march on Tehran and pull the shah from his throne if he failed to
abide by the Persian Constitution. In response, the shah was threaten-
ing to send a royal battalion to Tabriz if necessary to pacify his rebellious, former city—the same city that Howard Baskerville was now
reluctantly, inexorably, making his way toward.

Was Baskerville aware of the chaotic situation he was stepping
into? No missionary was sent into the field without first sitting through
some kind of orientation about the assigned country, however brief
or ill-informed. There were lectures and pamphlets and slide shows
providing basic facts about the particular mission field ("Mecca is the
goal of the faithful of all Moslem [sic] lands; the Koran [sic], the sacred
book of the Mohammedans, is believed to have been from all eternity,
co-existent with God himself") sprinkled here and there with some
comically incorrect information ("the Arabic language contains one
thousand words for sword, five hundred for lion, four hundred for misfortune, and two hundred for serpent, but not one word which means
home"), and, of course, all the generalizations one would expect from
missionary propaganda: "a Mohammedan woman knows no heart
happiness because she is unloved, oppressed and degraded. Unwelcomed at her birth, ill-treated during life and unmourned in death, is
the sum of her existence. And Jesus died for her too."

What the orientations failed to adequately cover was the contemporary political situation in the countries where the missionaries were
being sent to serve or the specific dangers they could face once they
arrived there. So while Baskerville may have been briefed on the progress of Persia's Constitutional Revolution during that final meeting at
the Presbyterian Board of Foreign Missions in New York City, what

he could not have known, as he boarded a train from Liverpool to Dover on the southeastern coast, was that Mohammed Ali Shah had already begun formulating an ambitious plan, with the help of the tsar of Russia, to dissolve parliament and tear up the constitution his father had signed.

Mohammed Ali Shah Qajar.

CHAPTER THREE

Liberté, Égalité, Fraternité!

A ONE HOUR FERRY RIDE from Dover to Calais, and Howard Baskerville is now halfway to Persia.

It is hard to imagine a more magical time to have experienced France and its shimmering capital city. These were the final few years of *La Belle Époque*, a period of supreme civilizational confidence for the French: an era that produced the Eiffel Tower, the Grand Palais, the Basilica of Sacré-Cœur. A brisk stroll down the Montmartre and Baskerville could glimpse Monet, Matisse, and Modigliani sipping au laits at a sidewalk café. A stop for tea at the Hôtel Ritz and there's Marcel Proust, who has his own private room, tinkering with *Remembrance of Things Past*. Across the Seine, Marie Curie is giving lectures on physics at the Sorbonne: the first woman ever to teach there. She had just won her first Nobel Prize four years ago; she will win another in four years' time.

Baskerville's arrival in Paris coincided with the end of *La Fête Nationale*, the annual holiday commemorating the Storming of the Bastille on July 14, 1789, the act that precipitated the French Revolution. He would have just missed the raucous celebrations that engulfed the country, the fireworks and military parades, the lofty speeches extolling the virtues of constitutionalism and parliamentary democracy.

The French Revolution loomed large in Baskerville's imagination. France was considered the supreme constitutional model on the continent; all other parliamentary democracies in Europe were deemed to have followed in France's footsteps. Beyond the writings of the Founding Fathers, it was the French Revolution that most clearly shaped Woodrow Wilson's doctrine of "national self-determination"—the idea that people should be free to form their own state and choose their own government. His course on constitutional government at Princeton would have spent hours discussing Rousseau and Robespierre. And surely Wilson would not have let his students lose sight of the fact that France's Constitution, like America's, was acquired through revolutionary means.

What might have come as a surprise, even to Woodrow Wilson, was that the romantic ideals of the French Revolution were, at that moment, being revived by a wave of democratic movements sweeping the globe. The first two decades of the twentieth century would witness populations around the world rising up against their rulers to demand a voice in the decisions that governed their lives. In China, a series of popular political reforms begun in 1905 to transition the Qing Empire into a constitutional monarchy would end with the downfall of the dynasty and the rise of the republic in 1912. In Mexico, a conflict over presidential succession in 1910 would result in a national revolution that united the middle class, the peasantry, and organized labor under the common goal of crafting a constitution to enshrine individual rights in the country. In Turkey, the so-called Young Turk revolution, led by members of the bureaucratic and military elite, would soon push the kaiser's friend, Sultan Abdul Hamid II, off his throne, ultimately replacing the Ottoman Empire with the Turkish Republic. And, of course, in Persia, a revolution that began with a series of strikes and protests had led, in 1906, to the Middle East's first constitutional monarchy.

What all of these revolutions had in common was the call for constitutionalism, which had become shorthand for freedom and self-determination. The word itself remained vague and undefined, but that was precisely its appeal: it could mean different things to different people. For peasants and the poor, constitutionalism meant economic equality and an end to unfair taxation. For the downtrodden, it meant equity and social justice. For the middle class, constitutionalism implied upward mobility. For merchants and unions, it was a means to protect local markets from foreign domination. The goals may have been different, the grievances unique, but in each of these countries the solution was the same: the transfer of power from the monarch to the nation; from the few to the many. And in each of these countries, the French Revolution formed the paradigm for popular protest.

Whether in Persia or Turkey, China or Mexico, the French Revolution occupied a privileged place in the consciousness of the revolutionaries. In Persia, constitutionalists marched through the streets of Tehran and Tabriz chanting *liberté, égalité, fraternité*. At the height of the Young Turk movement, books about the French Revolution were being published in Constantinople at an expeditious rate. China's revolutionaries studied the Storming of the Bastille extensively, picking up valuable lessons in their conflict with the Qing. Mexico's revolutionaries quoted the words of Voltaire, Diderot, and Condorcet in calling for the shared sovereignty of all citizens in the country. But nowhere was the legacy of the French Revolution more forcefully felt than in Russia, whose glorious capital, St. Petersburg, had only two years earlier been washed in the blood of its peasant population.

❖

THE RUSSIAN REVOLUTION of 1905 began on Sunday, January 22: "Bloody Sunday." That morning, a large group of peasant workers, together with their wives and children—some 150,000 souls, in all—had gathered at the gates of the Winter Palace in order to hand-deliver a petition to Russia's young emperor, Tsar Nicholas II, begging him to improve worker conditions in Russia.

"Sire," the text read. "We, the workers and inhabitants of St. Petersburg, of various estates, our wives, our children, and our aged, helpless parents, come to thee, O Sire, to seek justice and protection. We are impoverished; we are oppressed, overburdened with excessive toil, contemptuously treated. . . . We are suffocating in despotism and lawlessness."

The workers did not blame the tsar for their terrible plight. On the contrary, they held what could only be described as religious devotion to Nicholas. They had been taught to view the tsar as God's representative on Earth. It was a belief pressed upon them by the Orthodox Church, for which Russia was the "Holy Land," designated by God for humanity's salvation, and the tsar a divinely ordained ruler who must be loved and obeyed as the father of the nation. Indeed, the tsar *was* the nation! He was Russia incarnate.

"The Tsar stands to the people as their highest conception of the destiny and ideals of the nation," wrote one court propagandist.

The problem wasn't the tsar; it was the people around him. The workers truly believed that, were it not for the bungling bureaucrats and corrupt officials dominating his court, the tsar would surely satisfy their demands. He would hand over to them the lands they toiled upon six days a week, if only he knew how they suffered under the boot of his self-serving governors and murderous police force. That is why they had marched to the Winter Palace, to bypass the tsar's intermediaries and take their appeal directly to Nicholas.

Yet, when the workers arrived at the threshold of the Winter Palace, they were confronted by twelve thousand heavily armed troops. Seeing the rifles pointed at them, the workers and their families knelt in supplication and waited for the tsar to exit the gates and come to their rescue. Instead, the troops opened fire. The workers barely had time to rise from their knees before being butchered in a hail of bullets. When the smoke cleared, two thousand unarmed men, women, and children had been killed, another three thousand wounded. And the tsar wasn't even home.

Knowing that the workers were planning to march to his Winter Palace, Nicholas had taken his wife and children to the country for a quiet weekend of pleasant morning walks and evening games of dominoes. By the time he returned from his restful holiday, a general strike had been ordered across Russia in response to the massacre in St. Petersburg.

At first, the tsar tried to tamp down the revolutionary fires by granting the workers some of the basic rights they were demanding and by placing some meaningful limitations on his limitless rule. He even agreed to a constitution and the establishment of a parliament, or *Duma*. Yet these reforms only sparked the people's demands for more. Russia's liberal elite and wealthy aristocrats began talking openly about transforming the country into a constitutional monarchy. Russian socialists urged a complete upending of the old social order: a rapid transition from a "bourgeois" state to a "proletarian" one. Both drew on the French Revolution for inspiration. (Indeed, between 1905 and 1917, the French Revolution became the most popular period of world history in Russia—more popular even than Russian history.)

The clashes in St. Petersburg soon spread to Moscow. Store owners boarded up their shops, and public transportation came to a halt. The entire city went dark. "Processions in the streets appeared, one with the portrait of the sovereign, the other with red flags," recalled Moscow's acting governor, Vladimir Dzhubkovsky; "one group sang the national anthem, the other revolutionary songs."

The tsar responded with unrestrained violence. Workers' children were rounded up and beaten in front of their parents. Russian troops, drunk on vodka, raped women and girls and then hanged them from lampposts. Whole villages were razed and tens of thousands arrested. When the prisons ran out of space, the soldiers were ordered to shoot those they detained. As many as twelve thousand were executed. Thus, the revolution, which began with unarmed protesters in St. Petersburg, came to a bloody end in Moscow. By the time Baskerville arrived in

Paris, Nicholas had somewhat resettled himself on his shaky throne. But the myth of the tsar as God's anointed and father of the nation had utterly collapsed.

Nevertheless, now that Nicholas had, for the time being, survived the challenge to his throne, he had learned a valuable lesson, one he was eager to share with his fellow monarch in Persia. Nicholas believed he had given the people what they wanted: a constitution and a parliament. And look what it got him: civil war on the streets. He had managed to stem the chaos in his own empire only by bathing it in blood; he wasn't going to let the same thing happen on his southern border.

This was more than just strategic thinking on the part of the tsar. The truth was that Nicholas Romanov and Mohammed Ali Qajar had much in common. Both were young and inexperienced. Both had been ignored by their fathers and thrust onto the throne with no preparation. Both believed themselves to be anointed by God. And both were feeling horribly treated by their unruly peasants. Thus, when the shah appealed to the tsar for help in pushing back against the constitutionalists who were assailing his God-given right to rule Persia, the tsar responded with a simple piece of advice: "The Shah can save Persia and his throne only by immediately dispersing [parliament] and the other revolutionary mobs."

The advice would be followed, and with devastating consequences. To help enforce it, however, Nicholas sent Persia one of his most trusted military commanders, a fervent nationalist and loyal servant of the tsar whose name would forever be linked to Howard Baskerville's: Col. Vladimir Platonovich Liakhov.

Standing six feet and four inches tall, with a bullet-shaped head, deep-set eyes, full black beard, and perfectly twirled mustache, Liakhov looked like a cartoon villain, and he played the part well. Before being sent to Persia, he served on the General Staff in Tiflis (modern day Tbilisi, the capital of Georgia), where he earned a reputation as a fierce defender of Mother Russia by helping to violently suppress the revolutionary activities in the city. As reward for his service, Nicholas shipped Liakhov to Tehran to take command of the shah's dreaded Cossack Brigade, a cavalry force composed of about three thousand Persian soldiers, most of them émigrés from the Caucasus, and commanded by Russian officers. But Liakhov's primary mission in Persia was to keep the shah on his throne. And the best way to do that, as Nicholas himself had learned from his own recent experience in Russia, was to put an end to the Persian Constitutional Revolution, no matter the cost.

❖

COLONEL LIAKHOV LEFT Russia for Persia in September of 1906. Almost exactly one year later, Baskerville arrived in Russia on the famed Nord Express, a luxury sleeper that ran twice a week between Paris and St. Petersburg. The entire journey would have taken a brisk forty-eight hours, but what a trip it would have been for the unassuming boy from the Black Hills of South Dakota: afternoons spent inside a luxurious sleeping car wrapped with blue upholstery and leather-lined walls, his nose pressed against the window, his breath fogging up the glass; glamorous meals in the company of exotic foreigners speaking strange tongues, the waiters dressed in tuxedoes and lurching from table to table; long, quiet nights tucked in a plushly made bed, a delicate tulip-shaped reading lamp perched above his head. Those two days in which the pine and beech trees of France slowly gave way to the firs and marshes of Russia would have covered a lifetime. And then, at dawn on the third day, the full glory of St. Petersburg: a glimmering city of high-end European shops, marble statues, and churches painted pink and blue.

The final leg of Baskerville's journey by rail would be from St. Petersburg to Moscow, and then down into Yerevan, the modern-day capital of Armenia. This is as far south as any train went back then. There would be no more leather-lined sleeping compartments, no wide-windowed dining cars, no cozy feather-filled pillows. From Yerevan to the Russian-Persian border would take two days by carriage or caravan, the only means by which one could traverse the broken mountain paths that link the highlands of Armenia to the plains of Azerbaijan.

The city of Yerevan sits at the foot of Mount Ararat, where legend claims Noah's Ark came to rest once the flood waters receded. The locals say it's still there, buried somewhere near the peak, hidden by the clouds. For Christians, Noah is the paragon of faith. He heard God's warning. He believed God's word. He acted on God's command. This is faith as the Bible speaks of it: "the assurance of things hoped for, the conviction of things not seen" (Hebrews 11:1).

Howard Baskerville, too, had heard God's call. He had acted on God's command. He stood now at the precipice of things not seen.

Colonel Vladimir Platonovich Liakhov,
the Russian commander of the Persian Cossack Brigade.

CHAPTER FOUR

Be Faithful unto Death

THE BORDER BETWEEN Russia and Persia is cut by the Aras River, which rises in Turkey and empties into the Caspian Sea. In winter months the river is ravenous; it sweeps away footbridges and embankments, swallowing entire villages in its path. The poet Virgil, who knew it by the ancient name, *Araxes*, called this "the stream intolerant of any span." Yet, by summer's end, when Howard Baskerville arrived at its banks, the water would be calm and brown and easily fordable.

The few foreign travelers who had passed through these parts published harrowing tales of being chased by bandits or robbed by some black-cowled figure creeping up to their camp in the dead of night. More than one missionary sent to Persia by the Presbyterian Church never returned. Just a few months before Baskerville's arrival, a Presbyterian missionary and Canadian citizen named Mooshie Daniel was robbed and murdered in Urmia, a city located about ninety miles west of Tabriz. Three years earlier, Benjamin Labaree, a prominent American missionary stationed in a village called Seir, was kidnapped by Kurdish bandits, taken out into the desert, and tortured to death. The missionary orientation lectures rarely mentioned these martyrs for Christ, but everyone knew their stories. They spread across the mission field with such reverence that one would think they had been eaten by lions in the Colosseum.

No doubt Baskerville had heard these martyrdom stories. But now that he was standing at the Aras River, Persia staring at him from across the muddy waters, there was one story in particular that would have been difficult to shake: the tragic tale of Justin Perkins and his wife, Charlotte Bass, both of whom had stood at this exact spot precisely seventy-three years earlier. They had arrived in 1834: young, newly married, and full of zeal for the Lord; the very first American missionaries ever assigned to preach the Gospel in Persia. They left two decades later: Charlotte, feeble and broken; Justin, an empty shell of a man.

❖

BORN IN 1805 on a small family farm in Springfield, Massachusetts, Justin Perkins came of age in the peak years of the Second Great Awakening, a period of Protestant revival that would ultimately birth what is known today as Evangelical Christianity, the dominant religious expression in America. All across New England, bands of mostly young, mostly white, mostly female Christians had begun abandoning the chapels of their parents and congregating instead in large, outdoor "camp meetings," where they cast off the staid formality of a traditional church service in favor of an emotionally charged, intensely personal religious experience. Travel was no small matter in those days, and so these young worshippers were often forced to stay at the gatherings for days at a time. They arrived in wagons and carriages and slept in tents pitched in clearings or by a river—hence, the term "tent revival." Freed from their labors back home, they plunged into an uninterrupted frenzy of worship and exultation, as one sweat-soaked preacher after another strode upon a makeshift stage, hollering at them to repent and rejoice.

Those wild worshippers who gathered in the thickets of New England were convinced that the End Times were near, that Christ was about to return at any moment. The clock was ticking, and it was their duty as faithful Christians to do whatever it took to carry the Gospel to the unreached masses in the Far East and Central Asia, Africa and the Middle East, to convert both the ignorant heathen untouched by the Good News and the halfhearted believer unwilling to abandon everything for Christ.

Even as a young boy, Justin felt this urgent need to "Christianize the world." He dreamed of traveling to the farthest reaches of the globe, bringing salvation to whatever dark and savage land needed it the most. After graduating with honors from Amherst College in 1829, he entered the Theological Seminary at Andover, where he was ordained as a minister in preparation for a life as a missionary.

While Justin Perkins was completing his degree at Andover, Charlotte Bass was doing the same about twenty miles west of him at Ipswich Female Seminary in Massachusetts. One of the most fascinating aspects of the Second Great Awakening is that it was an overwhelmingly female affair. The vast majority of tent revivalists in New England were young, single women; by most counts, there were at least three female converts for every two males.

Evangelical Christianity's extreme emphasis on individual salvation offered women of the time a sense of independence and autonomy that they simply did not experience in other aspects of their lives. Tent revivals gave young women the opportunity to express publicly, and without fear of judgment, their fears and anxieties, their sins and shortcomings, and to receive not just forgiveness but also sympathy and support from their peers. And because the evangelical ideal compelled converts to signify their conversion through action (in the words of one historian, it made "each proselyte a proselytizer as well"), it encouraged women to pursue other avenues of work beyond spinning, weaving, and needlework—the chief means of female employment in the early nineteenth century. Evangelical women became teachers, preachers, and public servants. They established schools, universities, and benevolent organizations. They even enjoyed nominal leadership roles in the church as "Sunday School" teachers, an evangelical innovation created by and almost wholly staffed by women.

Teaching led evangelical women to more public activities and a larger role in propagating the faith beyond America's borders. There was a sudden influx of missionary applications filed by young, unmarried women who saw in the mission field an opportunity to travel and pursue goals and activities that were closed off to them at home. An urgent need arose to establish schools of higher learning that could train such women for the important work of spreading the Gospel to all nations. Ipswich Female Seminary, founded by two pioneers of female education, Zilpah Grant and Mary Lyon, was one of the earliest and most influential of these all-female seminaries.

Charlotte Bass entered Ipswich in 1832. Twenty-four years old and still unmarried, she was among the first class of students at the seminary, which had been founded only four years earlier. The primary focus of the school was to prepare women for careers as teachers and missionaries: the curriculum included a heavy emphasis on grammar, rhetoric, and composition, as well as advanced arithmetic, geography, history, and the natural sciences. Students were encouraged to think critically, to question and debate. Yet they were also forced to adhere to the strict ideals of womanhood that were still prevalent at the time. Piety and domesticity were key. The women were required to perform all housekeeping functions at the school and were purposely given almost no free time on their own. They were not allowed, in the words of Mary Lyon, "to make themselves prominent in any public place" or to "expose themselves at windows & doors."

Still, this was freedom, for it allowed women like Charlotte to cast off the expectations of their families, to challenge the traditional gender roles imposed upon them by their communities, and, most of all, to pursue a life of meaning and adventure.

Justin Perkins and Charlotte Bass were married on July 21, 1833.

Nearly two months later, the newlyweds sat together on a wooden pew in the Andover chapel, having accepted a commission from the American Board of Commissioners for Foreign Missions (ABCFM)—an independent Protestant missions society established nearly three decades before the denominational Presbyterian Board of Foreign Missions—to become the first American missionaries assigned to Persia.

Christianity, of course, had long had a foothold in Persia, having first been brought there, according to legend, by the Apostles Thomas and Bartholomew. By the second century AD, it was already firmly established as the largest religious minority in the overwhelmingly Zoroastrian empire. But it wasn't until the arrival of Portuguese Jesuits in the sixteenth century that Persia became fertile mission ground. For the next two hundred years, Catholic missionaries maintained a monopoly on the region. The first Protestants did not show up until 1747, when two young missionaries from Germany crossed the Black Sea into Persia. They did not last long. They were robbed twice and badly beaten before reaching their final destination. After a few days, they gave up and returned to Germany, having barely escaped with their lives.

The most successful Protestant missionary in Persia was Henry Martyn, a member of the British Church Missionary Society, who traveled on his own initiative to the country in 1811 from his post in India. Martyn made the conversion of Muslims his primary goal. Considering that such conversions were technically punishable by death under Islamic law, he did not have a great deal of success. Nevertheless, he was the first person to translate the New Testament into Persian, completing the task a year after his arrival, just before he died of disease, an all too common fate for foreign missionaries in the Middle East.

In contrast to Martyn, Justin and Charlotte were specifically instructed not to evangelize to Persia's Muslim community; it still wasn't feasible at the time. Instead, their efforts would be focused on what the ABCFM referred to as "the degenerate churches of the

East"—Armenians in Constantinople, the Greek Orthodox in Smyrna and Athens, Syrian Arabs in Beirut—ancient Christian communities, many of which traced their lineage to the apostles themselves. These Christians, living in lands from which the very religion of Christianity as we know it evolved, were thought by Americans to be misguided and unsaved. Their rituals were primitive and obsolete, their beliefs peppered with "superstitions." In short, they weren't really Christians, not according to the spirit-filled evangelicals of the Second Great Awakening. What they needed was spiritual instruction from the New World. What they needed was *revival*.

In Persia, the "degenerates" were known as Nestorians, followers of the fifth century bishop of Constantinople, Nestorius, who was branded a heretic and exiled by the early church councils for his heterodox views on the dual nature of Christ. This was all part of an early theological controversy that, while quite literally a matter of life and death at the time, has been rendered purely academic today. The argument hinged on whether Christ had a single nature that was simultaneously human and divine or two separate and distinct natures: one human, the other divine. The former viewed Christ as a vessel containing water and wine, mixed together to form a single substance; the latter viewed the vessel as containing water and oil—two separate substances sharing the same space, mingling but not mixing.

Nestorius was punished by his fellow bishops for aligning himself with the latter view. After his exile in AD 431, his followers, fleeing persecution, scattered across the lands of the Middle East, the largest bloc settling in northwest Persia, where they remain active to this day.

The existence of the Nestorians—who refer to themselves as "Assyrian Christians"—was completely unknown to the ABCFM until the spring of 1830, when two American missionaries, H. G. Dwight and Eli Smith, happened to make a stop in Urmia while on a missionary tour through Armenia. No American missionary had ever ventured this far east before; there were no Americans at all, and very few Westerners, east of Constantinople. To avoid undue attention, Dwight and Smith dressed in robes and wore turbans. They shared one packhorse between them and were at times forced to eat bread cooked over dried cow dung and crawling with vermin. Smith caught cholera and nearly died twice. Yet their hardships paid off when, in Urmia, they were surprised to find a large community of Christians who welcomed them with open arms.

Encouraged by the response, Dwight and Smith sent a report back to the ABCFM, asking it to dispatch full-time missionaries to live and work among the Nestorians of Persia. "This field is white and ready for the harvest," Smith wrote. "In all my journeys I have seen no people as willing to accept the gospel."

It took three years to find the right couple for the job.

On the night of September 8, 1833, Justin and Charlotte—their bags already packed, their hearts bursting with excitement—received their final instructions at the Andover chapel. "Your particular field of inquiry and labor is to be the Syrian church, and especially that part of it, denominated Nestorian," the eager couple were told, "and your residence, for the present, will be in Oroomiah [*sic*], just within the western borders of Persia."

Although Justin and Charlotte were expressly told to focus their activities solely on converting Persia's Nestorians, the ABCFM made it absolutely clear that these efforts were designed to serve as a backdoor to the primary goal of converting Persia's Muslims. "[Y]our main object will be to enable the Nestorian church, through the grace of God, to exert a commanding influence in the spiritual regeneration of Asia." In other words, the conversion of the Nestorians was part of a long-term strategy to create indigenous missionaries who could evangelize to their Muslim countrymen throughout the region.

Having received their final instructions, Justin and Charlotte bowed their heads for God's blessing. "May you and your beloved partner be long spared for the work on which you are about to enter," the board members prayed. "It is self-denying, but delightful and glorious work. Be faithful unto death; then will you never regret your self-consecration to the missionary service, nor the solemn designation of this evening, nor the parting scenes of the approaching embarkation, nor the residence for life in countries remote from home and native land. Nor will you be forgotten."

Imagine the thrill the young couple felt walking out of the chapel that sabbath evening, drunk with images of lost souls brought to Christ. For Justin, who probably never thought he'd be anything but a small-plot farmer with a sixth-grade education, and Charlotte, who had shaken loose the chains of her gender to pursue a life of her own making, the night was electric. They would leave for Boston the next morning and board a ship bound for Constantinople, the first leg of a romantic adventure into the unknown that would also double as their honeymoon. They had already said their goodbyes to loved ones. In those days, a journey of such magnitude could very likely be permanent. They were fully prepared never to see their friends or families again, not in this life anyway. So full of zeal was Justin that he found he could barely walk back to his lodgings. He collapsed onto his bed, burning with the spirit of the Lord.

It wasn't the spirit.

The following morning, Justin awoke with a violent fever. He was semiconscious and shaking, unable to rise from his bed. The ship remained docked in Boston for a couple of days, but the fever would not break. It was finally decided that they would sail without him; the mission to Persia would be abandoned. When Justin heard the news, he forced his doctors to lift him out of bed, dress him, and dump him in a wagon headed for Boston. Charlotte was worried and evidently tried to talk her husband into returning home. But he was steadfast and encouraged her to be so, too. "Her fortitude, which was destined to encounter still severer tests, was adequate to the trial," he recounted in his memoirs.

At the dock, Justin was carried aboard half-dead and placed in a tiny cabin in the belly of the ship along with Charlotte and the afore-mentioned Eli Smith and his wife, who were returning to their mission work in Syria. When the ship's captain saw Justin's condition he told his first mate, "we shall very soon have to throw that man overboard."

The voyage lasted a little over two months. Justin's fever eventually broke, though even then the couple spent much of the journey prostrate and wracked with seasickness, huddled belowdecks in a tiny, crowded cabin (Justin uses the term "prison") that they were forced to share with several fellow passengers, including the Smiths.

"The last vestige of romance will soon be expelled," Justin wrote in his diary.

The ship docked in Constantinople on December 21, 1833. Yet the hardships of the journey had only begun. After a delay of five months for winter to pass and the passage east to reopen, Justin and Charlotte said goodbye to the Smiths and booked an English vessel across the Black Sea to Trabzon in northeast Turkey; Charlotte became the first American woman to cross those waters. From there, they began a 700-mile journey on horseback across rugged mountainous roads, dodging thieves and bandits along the way, everywhere pursued by plagues and pestilence. The first third of the journey led across mountain paths so steep and narrow that Charlotte could barely stay seated in her saddle (she rode sidesaddle, as decorum dictated). One wrong step would have plunged them into a bottomless chasm. At night they pitched their tent on the cliff's edge, high enough to watch the clouds drift lazily beneath them. They used their travel trunks as tables and chairs but, more often than not, ate upon the same hard ground upon which they slept. It seemed never to stop raining; the roads were dark and slick with mud.

When they finally reached the Aras River at the Russian-Persian border, they were detained by greedy Russian border guards who seized all their possessions as contraband and informed them that their passports were no longer valid. Unable to proceed across the river to Persia or retreat back into Russia, they pitched their tent on a sandbank and waited.

A week passed. It was August, the hottest month of the year. The temperature rose to 110 degrees in the day. At night, the hot winds from the Caspian Sea filled their flea-ridden tent with fine grains of sand. They were kept under constant watch by border guards, forbidden from venturing out in search of provisions. On the verge of starvation, they had to barter for bread and melons, bought from a village four miles away. They both grew gaunt and frail. Charlotte fell ill.

One day, Justin glimpsed what looked like a government courier crossing the river into Persia. He burst out of his tent and flagged the man down. He begged him to deliver a letter to the British consul stationed at Tabriz informing him of their dreadful plight (there was no American government presence in Persia at the time). The man agreed. A few days later, help arrived, but not before Charlotte had lost consciousness.

She was ferried across the river, placed in a litter, and carried all the way to Tabriz, where a doctor informed Justin there was no hope of recovery. She would not wake except to vomit and shake with convulsions. And then, to the surprise of everyone, Charlotte, still in a daze, gave birth to a daughter. The young couple had no idea she was pregnant. Charlotte herself was unaware she had given birth until three days later, when she suddenly awoke.

They named their first child Charlotte Nisbet Perkins. She was born August 26, 1834. She died a few months later. Two years later, Justin and Charlotte welcomed their second child, a son named William; he died before his fourth birthday, likely of cholera. So did their next child, Justin, who survived a mere eleven months. Another daughter, Fidelia, named after Charlotte's mother, made it just past her first birthday. A third son, Jonathan, lived barely two months. Judith Perkins, their third daughter, was born in 1840 and grew into a beautiful, inquisitive young woman—a "Persian flower," Justin proudly called her. She was the light in her father's eyes: a wild girl who absolutely thrived in the wilderness of Persia. She made it to her twelfth birthday before dying of cholera.

In all, Justin and Charlotte buried six of their seven children in Persia. The grief became too much to bear for Charlotte. She had never really recovered from that original illness in Tabriz, but the experience of watching one child after another die in her arms left her in pieces. In a letter to the ABCFM, Justin claims his wife was suffering from epilepsy. That was probably a polite euphemism: a medical term to couch what was, reasonably, her descent into madness.

"My pen refuses to tell the desolation of our home," Justin wrote.

After more than two decades of toiling in Persia, Charlotte at last abandoned her missionary life and returned to America with their sole surviving son, Henry, in 1857; Justin followed one year later. But he would not stay long. The mission field kept beckoning, and he simply could not refuse the call. Four years later, he set out for Persia again, this time by himself. Charlotte was too fragile to be left on her own, so Justin had her committed to the McLean Asylum for the Insane in Somerville, Massachusetts, where she spent the next few years pleading with her doctors to be released.

Just how long Charlotte was kept in the asylum is difficult to know. But she was out and waiting at the docks when Justin returned from Persia for the final time in 1869, frail, sick, and on the verge of death. And she was by his side when he passed soon afterward, gripping his hand, just as she had that warm sabbath night in 1833, inside the old, stone chapel at Andover, when they were bright-eyed newlyweds about to embark on a lifetime of adventure.

Charlotte lived for another twenty-eight years after Justin's death. Born when Thomas Jefferson was president, she passed away at the age of ninety, with Henry and her beloved granddaughter, Judith (named after the "Persian flower" she had tragically lost), at her bedside. Her legacy as the first female missionary in Persia lived even longer: by Baskerville's time, female missionaries outnumbered their male counterparts in Persia by four to one, and nearly half of all missionary doctors there were single women.

❖

DIETRICH BONHOEFFER, THE celebrated Lutheran theologian hanged in 1945 by the Nazis, once wrote: "It is not the religious act that makes the Christian, but participation in the sufferings of God in the secular life." During their more than two decades in Persia, Justin and Charlotte experienced more than their fair share of suffering. Together, they built a flourishing mission from the ground up, one that Baskerville was about to take full advantage of seven decades later. Indeed, were it not for their work, there would be no Persian mission, no American Memorial School, no memory of Howard Baskerville.

Before their arrival, not a single Nestorian woman in Persia could read or write. By the time they left, proud Nestorian mothers walked their daughters to school—one of twelve Justin and Charlotte opened in West Persia just in their first three years—often lingering by the entrance for a moment to hear them read aloud from their common texts.

The Nestorians, though technically a protected group, were brutalized by the broader Persian population and ignored, or worse, by the state. They were miserably poor and terribly oppressed. Their lands were repeatedly stolen from them, their homes plundered for sport. Justin and Charlotte not only documented the crimes perpetrated against this community but also fought an unsympathetic government in hopes that some measure of justice would prevail.

Urmia was a provincial town at the edge of the Turkish border. It was a dangerous, isolated place, and on more than one occasion Charlotte and Justin came close to being violently killed. Yet they never hesitated to enter the wildest, most mountainous parts of the region, repeatedly putting their lives at risk in order to serve the people. Again and again cholera swept through the area. The year after they arrived, it killed three thousand people in Tabriz in a single month. The year 1840 became known as the "children's holocaust" because of the large number of cholera cases that took the lives of the young and enfeebled. Justin and Charlotte, together with their fellow missionaries, helped build hospitals and clinics to provide free medical services for the sick and dying, even as their own children succumbed to the disease one by one.

Yet, despite all the good they did in Persia, one cannot lose sight of why they were there in the first place: to save souls. Justin and Charlotte believed that this world and all its concerns were transient; the real world was the one to come. They believed they were privy to a wondrous truth, without knowledge of which people would be doomed to an eternity of pain and suffering. And they believed that the time to share this truth with the world was running out. This belief filled them with such compassion for the souls of strangers living thousands of miles away that, to save them from this wretched fate, they were willing to sacrifice not only their own lives but also the lives of their children.

One can ask whether their sacrifice was worth it. But perhaps the more important question—the one all missionaries must ask themselves—is this: What is worth sacrificing everything for? How far should one go to rescue someone, either from the presumed torments of the next life or from the actual hell of this one?

Howard Baskerville may not have faced this question yet, but he was about to. Why else had he come all this way? He was the great-great-grandchild of the Second Great Awakening, heir to the American evangelical tradition that had sent thousands of fresh-faced missionaries like him to every corner of the globe. He had left his home driven by the same conviction that drove Justin and Charlotte—that distant strangers deserved salvation. He could have been back in South Dakota, working in a small farmhouse church, prepping a sermon for a few dozen ranchers and their families to ponder as they toiled away on their dry patches of prairie land. Instead, he had journeyed ten thousand miles. He had crossed the Atlantic, experienced Liverpool and London, Paris and St. Petersburg, witnessed things he'd never dreamt of, met people so peculiar they could have been from distant planets. From the comfort of his seat on a ship, a train, a camel, a carriage, he had watched this extraordinary moment in history slowly unspool before him as though it were painted on a giant panorama. Now that he had arrived at the same river that Justin and Charlotte had crossed more than seventy years earlier, a carriage sent by the American Memorial School waiting for him on other side, it was time to stop merely witnessing history. It was time to start making it.

PART TWO

The earth is a church floor whereupon
In the middle of a glorious night
Walks a slave, weeping, tied to a rope behind a horse,
With a speechless rider
Taking him toward the unknown.

Several times with all of his might the slave
Tries to break free,
Feeling he is being returned to captivity.
The rider stops, dismounts—brings his eyes
Near the prisoner's eyes.

A deep kindness there communicates an unbelievable hope.
The rider motions—soon, soon you will be free.
Tears roll down from the rider's cheeks
In happiness for this man.

—Hafez

CHAPTER FIVE

The Shadow of God on Earth

WHEN, IN JANUARY OF 1907, Mohammed Ali Shah became the first king in the more than 2,000-year history of Persia to be forced to swear an oath "to preserve and observe the Fundamental Laws of the Iranian Constitution, and rule in accordance with the established Laws of Sovereignty," he could barely spit out the words. At least he'd made sure no one from parliament witnessed it. He'd forbidden the newly elected delegates from attending his coronation. Thirty-five years he had waited for his turn on the throne. Now that the crown was finally his, he had no intention of allowing a small band of puffed-up commoners to ruin it for him with their unintelligible talk of freedom and self-determination.

Over the first few months of his reign, the new shah had repeatedly been forced to pledge his allegiance to the constitution. He had little choice in the matter. The revolutionaries remained immensely popular throughout the country, while he himself was loathed by nearly everyone. His greatest fear was that parliament would throw its support to one of his younger (and far more genial) brothers to replace him on the throne, which is why he had gone out of his way to make public statements affirming his support for the constitutional cause—at least, at first.

He bit his tongue when parliament negated a loan of £400,000 he had personally negotiated from Britain. When a law was passed banning the shah from securing any future foreign loans without parliament's permission, he seethed on the inside but publicly relented. He even dismissed some of his more unpopular advisers, though he scoffed at parliament's demand to fire his beloved Russian tutor, Seraya Shapshal. That was not going to happen. Shapshal was not just Mohammed Ali's tutor; he was his closest companion. They'd been together since 1901, when Shapshal came to Tabriz to teach him Russian, back when he was just the crown prince. After his ascent to the throne, Mohammed Ali had elevated Shapshal to court minister, giving him the honorific *Khan*, a title the Russian wore as proudly as he did the ersatz medals his benefactor kept pinning to his chest.

Parliament never trusted Shapshal Khan, viewing him as too closely aligned with Russian interests. Nevertheless, they were willing to drop the matter of his dismissal from court, so long as the shah continued to comply with parliament's other demands. Some delegates simply wanted to avoid an open confrontation with the crown. But most members seemed to truly believe that, given enough time and effort, the young shah could be persuaded to lead the country's historic transition from autocracy to constitutional monarchy.

Tabriz knew better. The city of his birth understood exactly who Mohammed Ali was: a vile and violent despot who genuinely hated his people and cared for no one but himself. Not long after his coronation, the revolutionaries in Tabriz began sending frantic letters to Tehran, warning parliament not to trust the new shah. He was a snake, laying low, waiting for the opportunity to strike. But their warnings went unheeded. "The Shah is giving his utmost support and assistance to the National Consultative Assembly," parliament wrote back. "Your worries are all unfounded. It would be better for all of you to go back to your work and occupations."

Tabriz was right, of course. From the start, Mohammed Ali Shah had been looking for ways to subvert the new constitutional order. Soon after taking the throne, he decreed that all newspapers critiquing his rule be shut down and all popular orators speaking against him silenced. When reminded that the constitution his father had signed guaranteed both a free press and the right of individuals to criticize the government, he hired his own orators to give rousing speeches defending his God-given authority and lambasting parliament. Early in his reign he tried replacing all the provincial governors with people loyal only to him. Most of his new appointments were simply ignored by the provinces; some were sent packing back to Tehran. In a desperate attempt to rally the people to his side, the shah began secretly funding a series of counterrevolutionary demonstrations, including one composed of prostitutes he had personally paid to march unveiled through the streets of Tehran chanting: "The Constitution has given us freedom to abandon our religious obligations and live as we wish!" It was a hamhanded and obvious ploy that had little effect on popular sentiment.

The shah's biggest concern was the so-called *anjomans*. These were local governing councils that had spontaneously popped up across the country at the start of the Constitutional Revolution. One of parliament's first acts was to formalize the anjomans, giving them vast responsibilities to conduct the public affairs of their provinces and to ensure that the dictates of the constitution reached even the most distant city. The anjomans were charged with collecting taxes (hitherto the purview of the shah's corrupt cronies) and with curbing the arbitrary rule of the country's autocratic governors, many of whom had purchased their offices directly from the court. As a result, these local councils quickly became the most trusted face of the new constitutional government in every city—a place where people could go to make direct appeals to the rule of law, now that the law had actually been written down in the form of a constitution.

Mohammed Ali reviled the anjomans, viewing them as treading upon his power as shah. But he had a special loathing for the anjoman in Tabriz that went all the way back to his time as crown prince in residence. He remembered well the day his father finally acquiesced to the constitutionalists. He was home, cowering behind the walls of his princely palace, as jubilant crowds marched past his gates, waving flags, throwing sweets and flowers, shouting slogans and singing songs of freedom.

On the same day that parliament opened its doors in Tehran in 1906, the Tabriz Anjoman took over the administration of the city. The council's membership consisted of committed constitutionalists and low-level clerics, along with a mix of representatives from the city's trade guilds: fruit sellers, clothiers, tobacco and sugar merchants, and so on. The anjoman assumed all responsibilities of governance throughout Azerbaijan—the province encompassing Tabriz. It formed a network of committees to deal directly with local issues in and around the city. A once-daily session, open to all, tackled residents' grievances, while a twice-weekly session, closed to the public, met on Sundays and Wednesdays to draft solutions to the larger problems plaguing the province. The anjoman set up a court of appeals in Tabriz (the first such institution ever created in Persia) and established public schools in a handful of wards where students could receive a secular education grounded in Enlightenment principles.

When residents began complaining about the high cost of basic goods, the anjoman established price ceilings, and then punished the wealthy merchants who defied it by seizing their goods and selling them directly to the public at the correct price. When some of the more conservative clerics in town began agitating the people against the constitution, the anjoman forcibly expelled them from the city, then handed their mosques to popular street preachers who gave rousing sermons extolling the merits of constitutionalism.

Such actions infuriated Mohammed Ali, who was forced to watch an unruly band of merchants, mullahs, and pointy-headed intellectuals brazenly usurp his authority as crown prince in Tabriz. The anjoman had even gone so far as to confiscate some of his own farmlands, a consequence of his refusal to abide by the new price ceilings.

After he became shah in 1907 and moved to Tehran, Mohammed Ali decreed that every anjoman in the country be disbanded at once. But, by then, the councils had become too popular and powerful; they simply ignored the shah's order and carried on with their work.

It seemed like no matter how hard he tried, the shah could not escape the new political reality in Persia. He did receive a boost at the end of August with the signing of the Anglo-Russian Convention. But his hope that the agreement between the two empires would somehow chasten the constitutionalists, making them realize they had no hope of garnering foreign support, failed to materialize. Instead, the agreement had the opposite effect, hardening their revolutionary resolve and leading to renewed calls for sovereignty and self-reliance.

Then, in October of 1907, just around the time Howard Baskerville was arriving in Tabriz, the shah finally got a break. That month, parliament ratified the Supplementary Fundamental Laws, a kind of Bill of Rights meant to lay out the principles upon which the country would thenceforth operate. The laws not only severely curtailed the shah's authority to those powers specifically granted him by the constitution—"The Royal prerogatives and powers are only those explicitly mentioned in the present Constitutional Law"—it also expressly defined all "powers of the realm" as being derived solely "from the people."

This was the opportunity the shah had been awaiting. By placing all powers of the state in the hands of the people (that is, popular sovereignty), the constitution seemed to be taking those powers away from God—or rather, from God's representatives on Earth: the ayatollahs.

❖

ONE OF THE most surprising aspects of the Persian Constitutional Revolution was the overwhelming support it initially received from the country's all-powerful clerical class. A significant number of the first representatives elected to parliament were members of the Shi'ah clergy. A commemorative photo of the first parliamentary class in 1906 depicts nearly half the delegates wearing turbans—and a majority of those are the distinctive black turbans reserved for *sayyids*, regarded as descendants of the Prophet Muhammad. Two of the most compelling voices in the early days of the Constitutional Revolution belonged to the esteemed Ayatollahs Abdollah Behbehani and Mohammed Tabatabai, both of whom would play crucial roles in the conflicts to come. On more than one occasion, the city of Najaf, in modern-day Iraq—then, as now, the theological center of Shi'ah Islam—sent out *fatwas* (religious edicts) declaring parliament "a religious necessity," and claiming that opposition to the Persian Constitution was tantamount to rejecting the justice of God. "The ulama [Islamic clergy] have noticed that this sort of assembly [parliament] is based on the limitation of oppression and protection of the Islamic territory," declared one of Najaf's grand ayatollahs. "Hence, they have declared obligatory the support of such an assembly, and unlawful any action which might result in its weakness or extinction."

The reasons for clerical support of the constitution were complex and varied, but they more or less tracked with the revolutionary goals of ending corruption in the court, curbing the shah's unchecked powers, and pushing back against foreign domination. "Our aim in taking such trouble," wrote Shaykh Ismail Mahallati, one of the first and most vocal of the constitutional clerics, "is to bring a comfortable life for the people, to remove oppression, to support the oppressed, and to give aid to troubled persons."

There was, to be sure, a robust debate in clerical circles regarding what the constitution should actually look like; just because the clergy overwhelmingly supported its creation did not mean they believed it should be a purely secular document that was based on European models. Most expected the constitution to reflect Islamic norms and values and to be grounded upon fourteen centuries of consensus regarding

Islamic law, or *Sharia*. In this regard, the ayatollahs would have agreed with Woodrow Wilson that popular sovereignty is a divine mandate, that our obligations as citizens are indistinguishable from our obligation to God.

However, the dire social and economic situation in Persia had forced the clerical establishment to temporarily table such debates and to unite as one body on the side of the revolutionaries. Persia's natural resources were being sold to the British and Russians, its textile and manufacturing industries subsumed by unchecked imports from Europe. The people had been left to starve, while the shahs had only grown fatter. It was an intolerable situation. Indeed, it was heretical. On this point the Holy Quran couldn't be clearer: "Have you seen him who denies the Day of Judgment? It is he who pushes the orphan away, and does not induce others to feed the needy" (Surah 107:1–3).

For Mohammed Ali Shah, the Day of Judgment was at hand.

But now that the Supplementary Fundamental Laws had been ratified, an unexpected wedge began to divide the clergy. Powerful clerics, such as the Ayatollah Fazlullah Nuri, who had once stood alongside Behbehani and Tabatabai as an early supporter of the revolution, suddenly turned their backs on the constitution. Nuri specifically took umbrage at the notion of popular sovereignty. Sovereignty belongs to God alone, he argued. God is the sole lawmaker. The people could claim no right to such authority.

Nuri's main complaint, however, was with Article 8 of the Fundamental Laws, which established equality for all citizens, regardless of race, class, or creed: "The People of the Persian Empire are to enjoy equal rights before the Law."

Equality before the law was, of course, the entire point, as Ayatollah Tabatabai eloquently argued. "In this [parliament], justice will be given to all the people, and the king and the poor [will be] treated equally."

But for Nuri, the question of equality was a trap: If all people were equal, did that mean their religions were also equal?

The constitution repeatedly affirmed the supremacy of Shi'ism in the land and called for all legal enactments to be in accordance with "the sacred principles of Islam." It even offered a role for the clergy to act as arbiters of the laws passed by parliament, to determine whether they met such principles. But that was not good enough for Nuri and his followers. They demanded that the Fundamental Laws be scrapped altogether, that the constitution specify that all laws be based on Sharia, not just "the principles of Islam"; that only Muslims be allowed to serve in parliament; and that all references to freedom of religion and freedom of speech—both of which Nuri regarded as anathema to Islam—be stripped from the document at once.

"Freedom is heretical to Islam," Nuri declared.

The members of parliament unanimously rejected Nuri's demands, and some members called for his arrest. A few of the younger, more radical delegates wanted him dragged into the public square and flogged. Behbehani and Tabatabai tried to calm the situation and talk sense to their former ally, but it was no use. Nuri's followers revolted. They took sanctuary in the shrine of Shah Abdol Azim, a ninth century Shi'ah saint. From there they began distributing leaflets opposing the constitution. Nuri's religious standing was far lower than either Behbehani or Tabatabai, and he had nowhere near the spiritual authority of the grand ayatollahs in Najaf. But he was a charismatic preacher and managed to gather nearly one thousand high- and mid-ranking clerics to his side. As the historian Ahmed Kasravi, who was a sixteen-year-old resident of Tabriz during the Constitutional Revolution, put it: "Many of the mullahs who had thought that constitutionalism meant handing over the affairs of the country to them were gradually realizing that it was to be otherwise."

For the first time since the revolution began there was real, substantial, grassroots opposition to the constitution. It was time for the snake to strike.

On December 15, 1907, nearly one year into his reign, Mohammed Ali Shah formally declared the constitution to be against Islam. He unilaterally shut down parliament, dismissed all the representatives, and had the prime minister thrown into prison. When a handful of delegates came to the palace to try to peacefully resolve the situation, the shah had them beaten and arrested. For a moment, the crown had the upper hand. Persia's brief experiment with democracy appeared to be over.

But as the shah was contemplating his next move, the revolutionaries regrouped and struck back. They collected what weapons they could muster and barricaded themselves inside the parliament building. Over the next few days they were joined by some four thousand supporters. They slept on the floor and camped out on the surrounding streets. Soon, the merchants followed. The bazaar shut down, halting economic activity, as all of Tehran went on strike. The shah, it seemed, had overplayed his hand. With momentum firmly back on the side of the constitutionalists, and Nuri and his band of followers still holed up in the shrine, Mohammed Ali had no choice but to reopen parliament, restore the prime minister, release the imprisoned delegates, and retreat back to his palace in disgrace.

❖

HOW HAD IT come to this? Mohammed Ali Shah had been raised to believe the throne was his by right. He was a Qajar, part of a dynasty that had ruled Persia for more than a century, ever since his great-great-great-granduncle, Agha Mohammed Shah, united the country under his rule in 1779. Before the Qajar Dynasty came to power, Persia was a fractured country riven by tribal feuds and facing steep economic and cultural decline. The Qajars loosened tribal loyalties and built a strong, stable, centralized government that fostered an incredible revival of Persian culture, religion, and politics.

Agha Mohammed Shah transformed Tehran—at the time, a wasteland in the southern foothills of the Elburz Mountains—into a sprawling capital of magnificent palaces, citadels, military barracks, and mosques. But it was his nephew and successor, Fath Ali Shah, widely regarded as one the greatest rulers to have ever graced the throne, who completed Persia's transition to full-fledged autocracy.

Fath Ali Shah created a court so extravagant that it baffles description. His Golestan Palace remains, to this day, a masterpiece of Persian architecture. Originally built during the Safavid Dynasty (1501–1736), it was expanded under the Qajars into a spectacular showcase of imperial power: intricately carved walls and ceilings covered with brilliant shards of glass; light-filled rooms awash in a kaleidoscope of colors; lush gardens shaded by elm and ash trees and scented with lilac, jasmine, and rose bushes. There were marble tiles running the entire length of the complex, from the entrance gate all the way to the steps of the throne room, where distinguished guests would be ushered beneath a trellis of palace guards into the presence of the shah.

Fath Ali called himself *Shahanshah*, "King of Kings," a title derived from the legendary founder of the Persian Empire, Cyrus the Great. The connection was deliberate. Perched on his Sun Throne (a magnificent marble platform etched with the Lion and the Sun, the ancient symbols of Persian kingship), his head capped with a jeweled turban, his royal beard black and glossy and flowing down to his waist, Fath Ali Shah cloaked himself, both literally and figuratively, in the trappings of ancient Persia. In doing so, he consciously tapped into the primordial Persian concept of *farr*, or "kingly glory": a kind of divine radiance bestowed by God that sanctions the shah's reign and which flows through him to the people, guaranteeing blessings and good fortune upon the land.

The dynasty reached its peak with the ascension of the fourth Qajar shah, Nasir ad-Din, Mohammed Ali's grandfather and one of the longest serving monarchs in Persian history. Having taken the throne at the age of seventeen, Nasir ad-Din Shah spent the next fifty years solidifying Qajar rule over Persia. Called "The Shadow of God on Earth" and "The Pivot of the Universe," he presented himself as the defender of the faith in a bid to marry state and religion under his sole custodianship. He mollified the clergy by bringing them into court and showering them with money and patronage in exchange for their acquiescence.

It was Nasir ad-Din Shah who opened Persia to the world. Throughout his long reign, he took regular tours across the European continent, flanked by his extravagant entourage, to hobnob with his fellow kings and queens (the shah paid for these trips by borrowing money from the very courts he visited). While on a visit to Russia in 1878 to meet with Nicholas II's surly grandfather, Tsar Alexander II, the shah first set eyes upon the mighty Russian army. So impressed was he with the professional fighting force—the uniforms, the precision drills, the modern equipment—that he begged the tsar to help create a similar force in Persia. And thus, the Cossack Brigade was born.

Yet the true innovation of Nasir ad-Din Shah's long reign was the establishment of an entirely new bureaucratic class made up of secretaries, legal scholars, advisers, officials, and professional bootlickers— all with their own competing interests and privileges, and all utterly dependent on the crown. The shah maintained control over this unruly crew by pitting them against each other and by doling out lands and titles to those who pleased him. Plum positions in government were auctioned off to the highest bidder, with the winner forced to recoup the cost by indiscriminately taxing the people over whom he'd been given charge. It was, in the words of historian Abbas Amanat, "an institutionalized form of corruption at every level of government."

The result was a bloated bureaucracy, a stagnant economy, and a widening wealth gap between the fabulously rich and the indigent poor. With no stable means of tax collection, and thus no way to improve or expand upon government services, hunger and homelessness spiked throughout the country. A series of natural disasters, including a horrible famine in 1869 that killed approximately one-sixth of the entire population, only cemented the perception that the government was incapable of caring for those under its rule.

At the end of the nineteenth century, popular discontent began to boil over onto the streets. There were bread riots in Tehran as government officials began hoarding basic goods in order to boost prices. The shah's newly minted Cossack Brigade responded to the disorder with public beatings, arrests, torture, and executions. But while these actions muted much of the internal criticism directed at the shah, a cadre of empowered liberals and Western-educated intellectuals, many of them expelled from the country because of their political activities, began to clamor from abroad for what had hitherto been unimaginable: *revolution*. From the relative safety of their exiles in London, Paris, and Constantinople, they began writing tracts and publishing newspapers denouncing the shah and his cronies and enlightening their fellow citizens of the court's many crimes against the Persian people.

The most influential voice among these exiled dissidents belonged to the famed political activist and father of Islamic modernism, Sayyid Jamal ad-Din Asadabadi, known to everyone as *al-Afghani*: "the Afghan." Born in Persia in 1838, al-Afghani spent most of his adult life in exile. He was a prolific essayist who wrote wildly popular tracts denouncing Western encroachment on Muslim societies. His primary concern was to transform Islam into an ideology for social transformation, to push back against not only the ignorance and rigidity of the clergy but also the tyranny and despotism of the sultans and shahs who supported them.

From his base in Constantinople, al-Afghani began writing a series of tracts assailing Nasir ad-Din Shah's avarice and debauchery and decrying his "dereliction of duty in guarding his subjects against injustice." He accused the shah of treating state revenue as his own personal spoils, taking out loans he had no means of repaying and granting concessions over Persian exports to Europeans for his sole benefit.

It was this last issue—the granting of concessions—that finally lit the match of revolution in Persia.

In March of 1890, Nasir ad-Din Shah granted a British company a complete monopoly over the production, purchase, sale, and distribution of Persian tobacco. The terms of the concession were generous to the extreme: In exchange for a paltry sum of £15,000 a year and one-quarter of its net annual profits—both paid directly to the shah himself—the company was granted an exemption from all customs and entry fees. The money from the concession would go to feeding, not the people, but the excesses of a court bloated with princes, wives, and sycophantic hangers-on.

In some ways, the British tobacco concession was just the latest in a series of disastrous concessions the shah had made to foreign companies on such wide-ranging products as railroads and caviar. Yet this one affected the nation in a way the others had not. A quarter of the Persian population were regular smokers. With the possible exception of opium, tobacco was Persia's primary crop. It dominated the export market. Indeed, it's no exaggeration to say that the production and sale of tobacco was what kept the country's fragile economy from total collapse.

Persia's tobacco merchants sent a petition to the shah begging him to cancel the concession. The shah responded with a stark choice: either find some other line of work or become an employee of the British company.

This was a grave mistake. The Persian people were willing to suffer a great many privations, but not when it came to their cigarettes and water pipes. As soon as the concession went into effect, an uncoordinated mass movement erupted across the country. A coalition of tobacco merchants issued a statement refusing to comply with the concession. Unable to sell their products on the market, they began distributing it for free to the poor. One merchant set fire to his entire stockpile rather than deliver it to the British company. When the shah ordered that merchant publicly flogged, the entire bazaar rallied to his cause by going on strike. In response, the shah sent his Cossack Brigade to the bazaar with the explicit threat that every closed shop would be given to plunder. But the move backfired, rallying the population to the side of the merchants and escalating the struggle beyond the single issue of this latest concession into a popular protest against Nasir ad-Din himself.

The shah, it seemed, had lost his *farr*.

With nowhere else to turn for help, the tobacco merchants appealed to the clergy. Up to this point in Persian history, the clerical establishment had remained fairly divorced from affairs of the state. Most of the ayatollahs had been bought off and silenced by the court. But not even they were immune from the consequences of the tobacco concession. Gradually, they began to throw their weight behind the protestors. Sermons were given denouncing the shah's concession as a monopoly, something expressly forbidden in Islam (Islamic law forbids the infringement of an individual's free exercise over his or her own property or business). Fatwas were written forbidding the use of tobacco in any form until the concession was canceled. The people responded by shattering their water pipes in the streets. Even in the shah's own harem, the pipes were left unlit.

Over the next few weeks, the protesters—nerve-wracked and angry from extreme tobacco withdrawal—grew increasingly violent. Buoyed by appeals from al-Afghani to use this moment to rise up against the entire Qajar Dynasty (the first open call in Persian history for the overthrow of the monarchy), they stormed Golestan Palace. A badly shaken Nasir ad-Din had no choice but to withdraw the concession, and at a devastating cost to the treasury. The price for canceling the contract with the British firm was a staggering £500,000 (about $75 million today), which the shah was forced to borrow from the British themselves at 6 percent interest for a span of forty years.

The tobacco protests may have come to a successful end, but the experience awakened the national consciousness of the people. Never before in Persian history had a popular protest achieved its stated goal. People suddenly understood the power they possessed. Political activities became more pronounced. There were sporadic strikes every few months all over the country. Secret societies began forming to strategize ways to affect permanent, large-scale change. Most important, the tobacco protests marked the first time that the clergy, the merchant class, and liberal intellectuals had united together under a common cause.

It would not be the last. Indeed, the seed of what would become the Constitutional Revolution of 1905 was planted during the popular protests against the shah's tobacco concession. All it required now was a little watering.

On May 1, 1896, Nasir ad-Din Shah traveled to the shrine of Shah Abdol Azim—the very same shrine that Ayatollah Nuri would seek sanctuary in eleven years later—in order to celebrate his fiftieth year on the Sun Throne. After he had finished his prayers, he was approached by an impoverished, petty merchant named Mirza Reza Kermani, a disciple of al-Afghani. Kermani handed the shah a petition scroll. He then pulled out a pistol and shot the Shadow of God in the heart.

Fearing panic in the streets, the Cossack Brigade rushed the shah's body to his carriage. They arranged his limbs to make it seem like he was alive and waving at the crowd as they raced back to the palace.

Kermani was taken to Tehran where he was hanged. His final words were, "I have rendered a service to all creatures, and to the nation and the state alike. I have watered this seed, and it is beginning to sprout. All men were asleep, and they are now awakening."

After some backroom maneuvering by the British and Russian envoys, Nasir ad-Din's mild-mannered and woefully unprepared, 43-year-old son, Muzaffar ad-Din, was chosen as successor. He departed Tabriz for Tehran, leaving his own son, Mohammed Ali, behind as crown prince in command of the city. In gratitude, the new crown prince rounded up Kermani's presumed supporters in Tabriz, cut off their heads, scooped out their brains, stuffed the heads with cotton and wood chips, and sent them as a coronation gift to his newly crowned father in Tehran.

Muzaffar ad-Din Shah's reign would be short-lived and fraught with conflict. The previous shah had left him an empty treasury and massive amounts of foreign debt, which Muzaffar paid by taking out even more loans. The government was forced to impose higher taxes on basic goods such as sugar and wheat. An emboldened populace showed its discontent by repeatedly pouring into the streets, demanding not just lower prices and higher wages but also an overhaul in how the country was run. These disturbances continued right up to the day that a frail, bedridden Muzaffar ad-Din signed the Persian Constitution into law, and then took his last breath, leaving his son and successor to deal with the consequences.

❖

HAD MOHAMMED ALI Shah exhibited the strength of Agha Mohammed, or the majesty of Fath Ali, or the cunning of Nasir ad-Din, or even the placation of his father, Muzaffar, perhaps he could have been the man to lead this moment in Persia's history. But he had none of those traits. There was nothing to him but cruelty and bluster, both of which served only to mask a fearful and indecisive nature. Now that his bungled attempt to shut down parliament had failed, even the most conciliatory delegate had been disabused of the hope that the new shah could be trusted to uphold the constitution. The mask had been removed. Tabriz was proven right.

After parliament reopened, Mohammed Ali Shah fell into a deep depression. His advisers tried desperately to rouse him to action, but he was too distracted by his humiliating defeat. Shapshal Khan argued forcefully for a decisive blow against the constitutionalists. It was now or never, he warned. The revolutionaries, smelling blood, were becoming bolder in their calls for the shah to abdicate his throne. Peasants were refusing to pay their rents. Workers were going on strike with impunity. The anjomans were ignoring direct orders from the crown. Tabriz had fallen almost completely beyond Tehran's control. It was imperative for the shah to re-exert his authority over the country at once. Parliament may have the people, but the shah had the canons.

Perhaps, Shapshal slyly suggested, it was time to place the matter in the hands of Colonel Liakhov, the newly appointed commander of the shah's Cossack Brigade. Had not the tsar sent him to Persia for this very reason, to secure the shah's throne? Why not allow him to do so?

Liakhov had only recently arrived in Persia from his post in Tbilisi. But he was already a constant presence at court, flanking the throne with Shapshal Khan—the two men always whispering over the shah's head in Russian. Liakhov had wasted little time in publicizing his views about the revolution. "Anyone who knows the Persians as closely as I do cannot help laughing at a Constitution in a country where the very government has no idea as to what the word *constitution* means," he told the *Manchester Guardian*. In fact, he had arrived at court with a plan already in place for dealing with, in his words, "the nest of robbers that is here grandiloquently called a parliament."

When the shah heard Liakhov's plan, he panicked. What the Russian was proposing amounted to nothing less than a coup d'etat: a declaration of war against both parliament and the constitution. How would the people react? They nearly took over the capital when he shut down parliament for a few weeks. What would they do if he tried to abolish it altogether? How would the British respond? What would his friend the tsar say?

Liakhov calmly explained that his plan had been formulated in St. Petersburg; the tsar himself had personally signed off on it. Still, the shah hesitated. He was feeling humbled and despondent, in no mood for a fight.

Having anticipated the shah's reluctance, Liakhov informed His Majesty that the plan he had been presented was accompanied by a personal message from the tsar. "If the Shah is not willing to agree to [the plan]," the message read, "Russia will refuse him all [future] support."

The threat sealed it. War it would be.

Seraya Shapshal Khan, tutor and chief adviser to Mohammed Ali Shah.

CHAPTER SIX

Teach Them What You Have Taught Me

BASKERVILLE'S FIRST IMPRESSION of Tabriz, as his carriage came rumbling down the Armenian mountains and onto the salt-whitened valley, could not have been reassuring. If he had anticipated a cityscape matching the Orientalist fantasies he'd seen emblazoned on those brightly painted posters advertising travel to the Middle East—onion domes and minarets sketched in gold; a white adventurer in a pith helmet standing in the foreground, admiring the view from a safe distance—he would have been sorely disappointed. There were no lofty towers in Tabriz, no Moresque monuments to fawn over, no glazed-tile palaces or grand mosques glimmering with multicolored façades. The Tabriz that Baskerville first laid eyes upon was a squat city, densely packed with flat-roofed homes made of clay and mud plaster and painted the same dull yellow-brown as the hills surrounding the city.

There was a time when this was one of the greatest cities in the world, the crossroads between East and West, the seat of long-forgotten kingdoms. Alexander the Great knew the city by its ancient name, *Tauris*. The Mongols made Tabriz the administrative capital of an empire that stretched nearly the length of Asia. When Marco Polo passed through in 1275, he described beautiful gardens and fabulous riches. "Merchants of the faraway countries come to Tabriz purchasing goods and fulfilling huge deals of precious and dear stones which are plenty in the city," he wrote in his *Travels*.

From what Baskerville could view in his carriage, Tabriz looked like an old clay vessel that had been repeatedly shattered and put back together again, the cracks and fissures no longer concealable.

The city had, in fact, been shattered several times. The basin upon which Tabriz sits is prone to earthquakes; throughout its long history, it has been repeatedly razed and rebuilt. One earthquake, in 1780, reduced all of Tabriz to rubble, killing practically the entire population (some two hundred thousand people). The city had also seen its share of invading armies, having constantly changed hands from the Russians to the Persians and back again during a century of war between the two empires over control of the Caucasus. Most of its architectural treasures, including the famed Blue Mosque, built in 1465, were now just piles of colored rock. The only prominent surviving landmark was the Citadel: a huge compound left behind by the Mongols containing a mosque, a library, a mausoleum, and a courtyard with an enormous reflecting pool—all of it encircled by a wall a hundred feet high and twenty-five feet thick.

The Citadel could be seen from any point in town. For years, criminals condemned to execution were cast off its summit. To this day, Tabrizis repeat the story of the young woman who, condemned to death, was pushed off the Citadel, only to have her skirt billow out beneath her like a parachute. She landed gently at the bottom. That was the last time the Citadel was used for executions (Persians, as Baskerville would soon discover, are intensely superstitious people). Yet even this majestic monument was, by the time Baskerville saw it, a neglected ruin, its crumbling walls a metaphor for the city itself: broken, deprived, still standing.

Whatever anxiety Baskerville may have felt upon seeing Tabriz from a distance would only have increased once his carriage passed through the city gates. Tabriz looked, for all intents and purposes, like a frontier town in the old Wild West. Bands of armed gangs, their chests crisscrossed with ammunition, roamed across the city's main square. Everywhere he looked there were elegantly dressed, musta-chioed men wearing six shooters and lounging atop horses or leaning against the sides of buildings. These men were bandits, brutes, and thieves: unschooled and unbreakable; defiant of all authority; loyal to none but their own. In America, they would be called cowboys. In Per-sia, they were known as *lootis*.

The looti was a gentleman outlaw, someone who made a living as a hired gun. Some lootis worked as personal retainers for wealthy noble-men, protecting property, settling disputes, collecting debts. Others acted as intermediaries between citizens and the local government, somewhat akin to a neighborhood council, albeit a heavily armed one. Lootis were boisterous and fearless and notoriously difficult to control. They drank and gambled and fought duels to the death. They com-peted with each other in public feats of strength. And, for a while, they more or less ran Tabriz.

What set the looti apart from the common thug or hooligan was his adherence to a strict code of conduct, steeped in ancient Persian ideals of manliness and social justice. The looti was sworn, in all his actions, to the protection of the poor and dispossessed. He was the champion of women, children, and the elderly. He acted as judge and jury in disputes involving people the courts deemed unworthy of atten-tion. He was the law in lawless times.

It was easy to pick out the looti from a crowd, for he distinguished himself by his dapper appearance. A looti always wore a crisp suit and knitted slippers, a black fez perched on his head, a long silver chain dangling from his pants pocket. His hair was greased back, his mus-tache waxed to perfection. No looti would be caught dead without a fine silk handkerchief tucked in his vest pocket; it was as essential to the guise as the rifle slung over his shoulder. His style of dress was matched by his repartee; the looti was expected to be as quick with his wit as he was with a trigger. Most lootis could neither read nor write; but even the most uneducated among them could recite the great Persian poets by heart.

Lootis could be found in every Persian city, but the revolution had elevated their role in Tabriz into a kind of unofficial police force. The Tabriz Anjoman posted them in strategic locations around the city, guns at the ready, ears attuned to any hint of royalist sentiment among the population. Seeing the sunburnt, bespectacled youth who had just rolled into town in a carriage—dust-covered and clearly out of place—would have immediately raised their suspicions. The young man could be a spy for the shah. Worse, he could be Russian.

Baskerville would have been wise to keep his head down and not stare back at the dark faces turned menacingly toward him. Besides, there was so much more for his eyes to see: the gaggle of women covered head-to-toe in black, picnicking in the middle of the street; the baker taking thin sheets of bread out of an earthen oven and draping it over a rod for sale; the wandering barber, scissors tucked in his girdle, calling out for customers to squat before him for a quick shave and cut. Every sight a spectacle: new and exotic and wondrous.

The city of Tabriz runs only about twelve miles long. It was, at one time, completely encircled by walls. But as the city grew, it burst its borders, swallowing up the surrounding fields and farmlands, gardens and vineyards—and these became the new walls in some sections of the city. The entire western edge of town was now just a massive orchard, though the original wall still covered much of the eastern edge.

The streets in Tabriz are narrow; they snake through neighborhoods, leading the unwary traveler on a course that, more often than not, ends abruptly at a wall. The sidewalks can be perilous. Every few feet there are holes in the cobblestone so that residents can dip a bucket or a bag of skin into the precious waterways that flow beneath the city. The water comes from nearby Lake Urmia and from the snowmelt on

Mount Sahand, south of the city. It is carried underground in chan-
nels and distributed across Tabriz through clay pipes plugged here and
there with rags. Once a day, the city's waterman removes the rags, filling public tanks for the poor or private reservoirs for the rich. The lion's
share of the water, however, is reserved for the fabled gardens of Tabriz.
So wrote Hafez, the greatest of all Persian poets:

> *With wine beside a gently flowing brook—this is the best*
> *Withdrawn from sorrow in some quiet nook—this is the best.*

Baskerville didn't know it yet, but he would spend many hours in
the quiet nooks of Tabriz's gardens, lounging in the shade of a sweet-
smelling tree, watching the sun dip below the low-lying hills. He would
also be buried in one.

Tabriz, at the time, was divided into twelve wards, separated
primarily along ethnic and religious lines. Each ward was managed
by a magistrate (often the head of the particular community), who
answered to the mayor (a position elected by the residents), who
reported to the governor (usually some well-fed nobleman from Tehran), who purchased the job directly from the shah. In the center of
the city was the main square. This was the location of Tabriz's historic bazaar, perhaps the finest in the Middle East: a huge, labyrinthine
structure evenly divided into two narrow passageways and roofed over
with vaulted arches made of brick and masonry (holes in the arched
roof allowed light and air to seep through). Here, Baskerville would
get his first glimpse of the kaleidoscopic character of Tabriz. Turkish
traders weighing foreign coins. Georgians wearing sheepskin hats and
puffing water pipes. The Armenian silver merchant admiring his fine
filigree. The Jewish cap-maker and his son, knitting a fine felt hat for
the dignified looti waiting patiently in his shop.

The largest building in Tabriz was the crown prince's palace: a circular building with a marble fountain at its heart and crowned with a

cupola. Tucked inside a 170-acre garden called *Bagh-e Shomal,* or the Northern Gardens, the residence had been empty for nearly a year, ever since Mohammed Ali succeeded his father on the throne and moved his entire household to Tehran. Although custom dictated that the new shah's ten-year-old son, Ahmed, be named the crown prince in residence in Tabriz, Mohammed Ali was not so foolish as to entrust the safety of his heir to the residents of a town who would like nothing more than to string up his entire family from the nearest lamppost. He, therefore, secretly transferred his wife and sons to Tehran and shuttered the Northern Gardens.

To the east of the bazaar lay the government buildings: an old courthouse, the customs office, and the newly built Telegraph House, which connected Tehran directly to Tabriz, and Tabriz to the rest of the world. There was also the armory, which was attached to the Citadel, and the stables, crammed with thick-hoofed stallions that must have flooded Baskerville's mind with dreams of taking long horse rides across the wild river valley.

Opposite the government buildings, at the southwest corner of the bazaar, was the Armenian district, a section of the city reserved primarily for Christians and foreigners. This is where Baskerville's 10,000-mile journey would come to an end as his carriage pulled up to the front gates of the American Memorial School. There to meet him at the entrance was the school's headmaster, the Rev. Samuel Graham Wilson, alongside his wife, Annie Rhea.

❖

SAMUEL WILSON WAS the rare foreigner in Persia who could boast no enemies: a man respected by the mullah and the Marxist alike. He had been living in Tabriz for twenty-seven years when Baskerville arrived; he would live there ten more years after Baskerville was gone. The author of numerous well-received books on the people, faiths, and customs of the land of the Lion and the Sun, Samuel Wilson genuinely loved Persia. Indeed, it is impossible to find a single negative word written about him in any of the Persian journals, diaries, dispatches, or histories of the time. Under his leadership, the American Memorial School became an island of tranquility, set apart and protected from the political tempests roiling the city, respected by all.

And yet, it was Annie Rhea who was the true child of Persia. She was born in a small village not far from Tabriz, called Seir, where her mother and father had served as missionaries. Along with her brother, Foster, and her baby sister, Sophie, Annie spent her early years roaming the surrounding countryside, pretending to be pilgrims exploring the New World. The mission in Seir was one of the first in Persia; Annie's family lived in a small adobe house in a compound full of missionary families. There were more boys than girls at the time, and so her closest friends became the Labaree boys, sons of the Rev. Benjamin Labaree, who would, some years later, be kidnapped and tortured to death by Kurdish bandits.

After Annie's father died of cholera, her mother decided it was time to leave Persia. They booked passage on the next available ship back to the United States. The year was 1869. There were seven missionaries in their party, including a frail, old man who had founded the American mission in Seir and who was himself leaving Persia for the final time in order to see his wife before he died: Justin Perkins. Annie called him grandpa.

Back in the United States, Annie's family settled in Lake Forest, Illinois, where she attended Ferry Hall, a school for the privileged daughters of the midwestern elite. After graduating valedictorian, she enrolled in Wellesley College to study Greek and Latin. She was back in Lake Forest, teaching Latin at Ferry Hall, when she met Samuel Wilson: "a handsome young man," Annie wrote in her unpublished memoir, "whose youth was belied by a full beard."

Samuel was born in 1858, just outside of Pittsburgh, Pennsylvania. Like Baskerville, he attended Princeton University, then received his theological training at Western Theological Seminary in Allegheny. He had already served in Tabriz for six years when he returned to the States for a brief furlough in the spring of 1886. That's when he first set eyes upon Annie, at a missionary conference sponsored by the Presbyterian Board of Foreign Missions.

Annie asked him where he was serving. Samuel replied, *Persia*. It was meant to be.

The next time they saw each other, Samuel Wilson proposed. A few months later, they were on a ship, setting sail back to the land of Annie's birth.

The Wilsons moved into a small home in Tabriz with a tiny, two-room schoolhouse in the back. Annie taught the equivalent of kindergarten. Samuel maintained day-to-day operations. Their little school offered basic classes in arithmetic and geometry, astronomy and geography. It even taught calligraphy, a cherished art form in Persia. All the classes were co-ed, and the students were almost all Armenian Christians.

Over the course of a few years, their little schoolhouse became enormously popular. Yet their ambition could not be contained by its two small rooms. They wanted to build a real campus, with multiple grade levels and a huge, international faculty—a school that would be open to both Christian and Muslim students.

Residents told the couple their plan would never work. "Moslems [*sic*] and Armenian boys can't be together," Annie remembers the locals warning. "They will be at each other's throats."

"That's just the reason they will become friends as school-mates," Samuel replied.

One day, Samuel came upon a large, private garden for sale not far from their home. It was perfect. He wrote frantic letters back home to his community in Pittsburgh, begging for a few thousand dollars to buy the property. He ended up raising $10,000.

The money was used to build a massive, two-story, red-brick building with classrooms on the first floor and a large assembly hall on the second for school gatherings and Sunday services. They even built a bell tower, something that was expressly forbidden by law to Christians in Persia (usually, a servant would go house to house on Sundays, knocking on doors to announce it was time to gather for church). It is a testament to the esteem in which the Wilsons were held, even by the governing officials and the religious authorities in Tabriz, that there were no complaints about the bell being rung on Sunday mornings.

When the school was finally finished, Samuel and Annie invited the entire town to a feast on campus. Standing before the crowd in his black cassock and white collar, a broadbrim hat protecting his head from the sun, Samuel dedicated the American Memorial School as a gift from the people of America to the people of Persia in the name of Jesus Christ.

In the spring of 1890, four years after their arrival together in Persia, the Wilsons welcomed their first child—a son they named Samuel Rhea. "Never was a baby more enthusiastically welcomed," Annie recalled in her memoir. "Little Rhea," as he was called, was a beautiful boy "with a mass of golden curls and big blue eyes." He died of diphtheria before his second birthday. Tragedy struck again with the death of their second son, Andrew, who also died of diphtheria, and their daughter, Esther, who died of sunstroke. Yet, the couple persisted, and four of the seven Wilson children survived into adulthood: three daughters—Agnes, born in 1892; Rose, who arrived two years later; and Annie Rhea, named after her mother—and one son, Robert Graham, who was four years old when Baskerville arrived.

Agnes, the eldest, was the pride of the family. Stubborn, strident, and absolutely irrepressible, she was Tabrizi, through and through. Fluent in the city's many tongues, her first word was spoken in Turkish. She was a precocious one-year-old, wearing a pretty new dress. She stood up suddenly, fanned out her skirt, and shouted, *Bakh!* "Look!"

The locals were amazed. "She is ours," they told her mother. "Her tongue opened in our language."

Under the guidance of the Wilsons, the American Memorial School quickly became the center of activity in Tabriz. The student body ballooned to around eight hundred full- and part-time students. Faculty came from all over the world. Classes were taught in Persian, Arabic, Turkish, Armenian, French, German, and English. There were courses in history and government, Bible and ethics, as well as advanced training in the field of Christian ministry. The female students, including the Wilson girls, were taught sewing and cooking, as was expected; but they were also offered courses in business and economics, as well as industrial and agricultural training. Special emphasis was placed on mathematics and the physical sciences, particularly algebra and geometry, for the Presbyterian mission believed that such subjects had "a high degree of disciplinary value, [helping] to develop accuracy and logical reasoning, two things sadly needed in this country."

There were also extracurricular activities, including team sports for both girls and boys, with the principle rule being that teams could not be divided by nationality or religion. Samuel preached sermons and conducted weddings, baptisms, and funerals. Annie gave music lessons on a piano—one of only two in Tabriz—shipped all the way from Pennsylvania as a wedding gift from Samuel's father.

The couple started a literary club for both men and women to read Persian literature in translation; the satirical folk tales of Mullah Nasruddin were a favorite of the group. With few temporary lodging options in Tabriz, the school became a kind of hotel for European adventurers passing through town. Dignitaries paid their respects. In January 1907, William Doty became the first US consul general assigned to Tabriz, and he would spend much of his free time on campus, regaling the students about the differences between Persia and his previous post in Tahiti.

Robert Speer, the head of the Presbyterian Board of Foreign Missions in New York, came to visit with his wife. So impressed was he by what the Wilsons had built that he vowed to help them populate the faculty with a crop of faithful Princeton men. And now, here was Howard Baskerville, pulling up to the entrance gate, fulfilling Speer's promise.

The Wilsons, for their part, were delighted to have the young man. They moved him into a spare room in their home, and Samuel gave him a tour of the campus.

One of the first students Baskerville met was a fifteen-year-old, part-time pupil named Sadeq Rezazadeh Shafaq, who was there study-ing English. In his recollections, published fifty years later, Sadeq describes Samuel Wilson stopping him as he walked across the school-yard to introduce "a handsome young man with bright blue eyes smil-ing behind his glasses."

"This is the new teacher," Samuel said. "His name is Baskerville."

Sadeq was one of a growing number of bright, well-to-do Muslim students at the American Memorial School (there was only one other educational institution in all of Tabriz where Christians and Muslims studied together, and that was the French Catholic School across town). When the Wilsons first opened the school, the majority of their Mus-lim students came from poor families, lured with the promise of a free (or nearly free) education. After a few years, however, wealthy Muslim families with dreams of one day sending their children to European universities began looking to the American Memorial School as a place for them to gain the English skills necessary to study abroad. They may have been wary of the evangelical nature of missionary education, but they understood its value, and so began enrolling their privileged sons and daughters in ever greater numbers.

Sadeq was one of these upper-class students. He came from a pious, traditional family, but he was smart and ambitious and desperate to improve his raw yet passable English skills. A day would come when Sadeq Shafaq will graduate from the American Memorial School, leave Persia to study in Constantinople and Berlin, receive a PhD in western philosophy, and begin a long academic career as a distinguished man of letters fluent in six languages. He will become a founding member of the Iranian Academy, a senator in the Iranian Parliament, and a delegate representing Iran at the signing of the United Nations Charter in 1945. Yet, before he enrolled at the Christian school as a shy, sheltered young man, he did not even know there were other religions in the world besides Islam.

Baskerville's fellow faculty members ran the gamut from clerics to communists, royalists to revolutionaries, Christians and Muslims, men and women. Most of the teachers were, unsurprisingly, American missionaries. There was, for instance, a Mrs. Van Hook, who ran the Girls' School, and the Rev. Charles Pittman and his wife, Lucille Drake, who met and were married on campus, inside the school's assembly hall: "a regular American wedding," Annie gushed. Their first son, a one-year-old boy named Clement, would be buried in a grave next to little Samuel Rhea.

Another recent Princeton graduate, Frederick Jessup—himself the son of Presbyterian missionaries in Syria—had been teaching at the school since 1903, along with his wife Helen Grove, a fellow missionary whom he met in Tabriz. John and Mattie Wright were Presbyterian missionaries who moved to Tabriz from their previous post in Salmas; they had four children, the eldest of whom, fifteen-year-old Sarah, was close friends with the Wilson girls. Sarah's adolescent diary, in which she jotted down her thoughts on her favorite school subjects or made gossip about cute boys in town—"Oh! he looked so nice and so like a villain!"—would, inadvertently, become the most detailed eyewitness account of the devastating siege of Tabriz by the shah's troops in 1909.

The Europeans included a Protestant missionary from France name Monsieur Vauthier, who taught courses in French. There was also a sizable number of Armenian and Persian instructors, most of them bright, young scholars barely in their twenties, like Mirza Ansari, a devout constitutionalist who taught international law at the school.

But among the indigenous faculty, the one who left the biggest mark on Baskerville was Hassan Sharifzadeh: a 27-year-old scholar and orator known for his high-mindedness and unsullied morals; a man who had dedicated himself body and soul to the dismantling of tyranny, not just in Persia, but in every corner of the world.

A self-described humanist and progressive, Hassan was born in 1880 to a prominent clerical family in Tabriz. His father was a respected sayyid who had groomed his son from an early age to follow family tradition and become a member of the Shi'ah clergy. As a young man Hassan studied Arabic and the Quran, Islamic theology, discourse, and debate. But when the Constitutional Revolution started, he lost all interest in becoming a cleric and began focusing his energies instead on the constitutional cause.

Unable to reveal his ambitions to his father, Hassan came to the American Memorial School to study English in secret. He begged Samuel Wilson to conceal his presence in the school, and Samuel, who was struck by the young man's passion and intelligence, agreed. Already knowledgeable in Arabic and French, Hassan quickly mastered English. He also formed a close bond with Samuel, who became a kind of surrogate father to the young man.

A few months into the program, Hassan showed up at the school with his mother and sister in tow. "Teach them what you have taught me," he implored.

After graduation, Hassan returned to the school, this time as a teacher giving lessons in Arabic. No longer the timid student hiding his studies from his father, Hassan was now one of Persia's most popular and compelling supporters of the constitution: an intellectual genius with a unique ability to communicate the revolution's goals to the masses in terms they could understand and get behind. He'd gained national fame both for his fiery speeches in defense of parliament and for his fearless attacks on the shah and the mullahs who supported him. Standing atop a crate in front of the Telegraph House, in the middle of Tabriz's main square, he would raise his voice above the din. "People!" he'd shout. "As the dog drinks blood it becomes rabid! [So] these Mullahs have drunk your heart's blood and become mad!"

As a member of the faculty of the American Memorial School, Hassan founded the Union of Students. They met regularly to discuss the revolution and to give speeches on campus in support of the constitution. He was known to be a compassionate teacher who always tried to amplify the political consciousness of his students. And his students worshipped him for it.

Every story ever told about Howard Baskerville mentions Hassan Sharifzadeh. His was the defining friendship in Baskerville's short but meaningful life. The two had a lot in common. They were both young and passionate, from similar backgrounds, with similar views. Each had defied his father in favor of blazing his own path through the world. Baskerville taught Hassan about America, and Hassan became Baskerville's mentor, instructing him in Persia's politics, and introducing him to the other young revolutionaries in Tabriz. He also served as his translator and tour guide. Walking hand-in-hand together through the bazaar—as was the habit among male friends in Persia—Hassan initiated Baskerville into a world that was as far away from South Dakota, as South Dakota was from the moon.

See the fine silk brought by camel train from Kashan? See how smooth the fabric feels to the touch. There is an old rug merchant from Khurasan, smoking his pipe, feigning disinterest in our approach. Here, a sweetshop full of delicacies tinged with rose water and brought all the way from Isfahan: Shall we stop for a taste? Look out for the nobleman's carriage! Press your body against the cold brick wall to let him pass.

This is how Howard Baskerville spent those first few months in Tabriz. His days in the classroom, teaching English and history—the latter course quickly becoming the most popular in the school, with students of all ages and academic backgrounds clamoring to attend. His afternoons lounging in a garden with a tight inner circle of students led by Sadeq, who quickly became the teacher's pet. His evenings with the Wilsons, taking turns reading aloud from *Bleak House* or *Vanity Fair*, singing duets with Annie at the piano, or lounging with Agnes by the fireplace, swapping stories about life "back home" (the color in both their cheeks slowly rising). And his late nights with Hassan, sitting cross-legged on the floor of a café, sipping bitter, black tea through a block of sugar lodged in his teeth in the Persian manner, discussing politics and revolution. He even got to ride horses, thanks to Sadeq's wealthy father, who, having grown fond of his son's "good American teacher," managed to procure a couple of steeds for them to take out and explore the surrounding wilderness. He was, in short, having the time of his life.

But he had not come to Persia to enjoy himself. He had come here to save souls. And that part of his mission was not going so well.

❖

THE PRIMARY PURPOSE of the American Memorial School was, unambiguously, the evangelization of Persia's population. Educating young Persians was vital work and the Wilsons took the task seriously, committing their entire lives to it. But Samuel's community in Pittsburgh had not sent him $10,000 so he could teach poor Persian children how to read. The money was meant to help him preach the word of Christ. On this point, the records of the Presbyterian Board of Foreign Missions could not be more clear: the goal of missionary education was to lay "the bait with which we attract the Musselmans [Muslims]."

The American Memorial School's clock, calendar, and curriculum were centered on the salvation of Persia. Each morning began promptly at 8:00 a.m., with all students gathered in the assembly hall for hymns and morning prayers, usually led by Samuel Wilson. Sunday morning church services were attended by the families of both Muslim and Christian students: a screen separated the men and women in the congregation, and all women, regardless of religion, wore headscarves (Annie would often skip these services and instead go door to door to the homes of students who couldn't make it to church). Sunday afternoons, the older students would visit the Wilsons for lessons on individual books of the Bible. Thursday evenings were reserved for "tea and games" at the Wilson home: the male guests entered through the front door, the women came through the back, as dictated by Persian custom. Once a week, Annie hosted a women's night at the house, a chance to talk about life and faith without men around.

The only optional courses at the school were in the language arts, meaning every student took required courses in the Bible and Christian ethics, both of which were viewed as essential in meeting "the moral and spiritual need" of Persia. As with most other Presbyterian schools in the country, smoking, swearing, drinking, or breaking the Christian sabbath were strictly forbidden (the Muslim sabbath falls on Fridays, which seems to have been treated as a normal school day). Every action and decision at the American Memorial School was predicated on furthering "the diffusion of Christian ideas and influences, the conversion of pupils, and the development of the Christian community."

In some ways, Tabriz was the ideal city for this kind of missionary work. Sitting at the crossroads of Europe and Asia, connected to Russia and the Ottoman Empire by rail and land routes, with easy access to the Mediterranean Sea and the Black Sea, Tabriz had historically been the most populous and prosperous city in all of Persia, a place of dynamic cultural exchange since the early days of its founding. It was precisely this international character that drew the first missionaries here. As one Episcopalian pastor put it: "Tebriz [sic] is the most eligible point in Persia for commencing an effort at [missionary] education. It has been more frequently visited by foreigners than any other city, and has been more affected by the introduction of European arts and manners."

And yet, the same cosmopolitanism that drew missionaries to Tabriz also made their work here far more difficult than in other Persian cities. Tabriz was an extremely religious city, but eclectically so.

Practically every major Middle Eastern religion had a foothold here, including a wide variety of indigenous Christianities—Armenian, Assyrian, Nestorian—as well as a rapidly expanding Catholic parish and a small but thriving Jewish community. The long presence of Zoroastrians in the city is evidenced by the large number of fire temples scattered around the vicinity of Lake Urmia. Nearby Mount Sabalan was thought to be the mountain where the prophet Zarathustra communed with his god, *Ahura Mazda*. Tabriz was also a stronghold for Persian Buddhism, whose adherents traced their religious lineage all the way back to the Mongols. And it had become one of the principle centers of Persia's two newest religions: *Babism*, a short-lived, messianic movement founded in 1844 by Sayyed Ali Muhammad, a 25-year-old merchant from Shiraz who called himself "the Bab"* and who preached the coming of a savior at the End of Days; and *Baha'ism*, which arose in 1863, when Mirza Husain Ali Nuri—known as *Baha'ullah*, "the Splendor of God"—claimed to be the savior the Bab had prophesied.

Of course, the majority religion in Tabriz was Islam. Yet, even here, there existed a wide range of sects and schisms in the city. There was the Islam of the pious women weeping inside the tomb of some saint, grasping for the cloth-covered coffin in hopes of becoming pregnant; and the Islam of the stuffy black beards who preached duty to state in government-run mosques. There was the Islam of the wild-eyed dervish dancing half-naked in the streets; and the Islam of the young street preacher, who calls the people to cast off the yoke of tyranny, whatever the cost.

Most of all, there was the Islam of Imam Husain, grandson of the Prophet Muhammad, and the progenitor of Shi'ism, the largest sect of Islam and the majority religion of Persia. Shi'ism began as little more than a political rift in the early Muslim community over who should succeed the Prophet Muhammad as caliph. While the majority wanted

---

* "Bab" in Persian means "gate" or "door."

leadership to fall into the hands of Muhammad's friend and father-in-law, Abu Bakr, a small but powerful contingent of Muslims supported Muhammad's son-in-law, Ali. This latter faction became known as *Shi'atu Ali*: "the partisans of Ali."

The Shi'ah eventually got their way when Ali was named caliph in AD 656. But it was a short-lived victory. Five years later, Ali was assassinated. The result was civil war within the Muslim community. When the fighting was over, the partisans of Ali had been reduced to little more than a tiny protest movement inside what had grown into a massive empire centered not in the Arabian Peninsula, where Islam was born, but in Syria.

In AD 680, Ali's son, Husain, led an ill-fated rebellion meant to restore leadership of the community back to the Prophet Muhammad's family. On his way to Syria, however, he and his small band of followers were intercepted in the city of Karbala, in modern day Iraq, and slaughtered by the forces of the Syrian caliph, Yazid. Husain's martyrdom at Karbala transformed Shi'ism from a purely political movement bent on reclaiming power for the family of the Prophet Muhammad into a wholly new and distinct sect of Islam. At the heart of that sect was the notion of the lone, righteous believer who, following in the footsteps of the martyrs at Karbala, willingly sacrifices himself in the struggle for justice against oppression. So central is the concept of self-sacrifice to Shi'ah identity that the massacre at Karbala is reenacted very year, on the tenth day in the month of Muharram, in a somber passion play called *Taziyeh*, with professional actors playing the parts of the reluctant hero Husain and the villainous Syrian general, Shimr.

And therein lies the difficulty with traditional evangelism in Tabriz. It's not just that the city's multi-religious landscape makes claims to absolute truth difficult to sustain. It's that religion in Tabriz, and especially the majority religion, Shi'ism, has long been viewed as a form of protest, a vehicle for dissent, a call to *action*. Evangelical Christianity, as it was preached by the "awakened" American missionaries in Persia, was all about personal piety and individual salvation. Certainly, good works were emphasized. But good works could not save the soul. Only Christ could do that.

As with most Presbyterian missions across the world, the West Persia Mission—which encompassed the cities of Urmia, Tabriz, Salmas, and Mosul—was concerned, first and foremost, with the conversion of the native communities. Providing humanitarian services, building hospitals and schools, feeding and caring for poor populations—all of these were secondary to preaching the Gospel. And while missionaries undertook numerous philanthropic projects that, on the surface, seemed to have little to do directly with evangelization, even these actions were meant to serve the primary goal of converting unbelievers.

This is why the West Persia Mission was so careful to avoid any hint of political activity. It refused to engage in any action that could jeopardize its primary work, which was to bring souls to Christ. The mission was aggressively neutral throughout the Constitutional Revolution, though always with arms open, ready to take in those who needed healing: spiritual or physical. Otherwise, they had been given instructions by the Presbyterian Board of Foreign Missions to "put aside their concern for the civil and temporal conditions of the proselyte community and focus instead upon the work of evangelization."

The problem was that this revivalist, apolitical, individualistic brand of Christianity was a wholly foreign concept in Persia, even among its Christians. Religion, as it was preached by American missionaries, was a personal preference: a cloak one could simply choose to wear. Not satisfied with the cloak you're wearing? Exchange it for another!

But for the vast majority of Persians, and especially Tabrizis, religion wasn't an individual choice. It was a communal identity. In Persia, "Christian" was an ethnicity, not a denomination—or, more precisely, ethnicity and denomination were considered one and the same. Religion was less about the things you believed and more a matter of who you were. How, then, could it possibly be divorced from politics? Religion *was* politics.

If Baskerville ever doubted this fundamental truth about the country in which he was preaching, he had only to glimpse the pockmarked façade of the courthouse in the center of the city's main square. Tabriz was the site of the Bab's execution.

On July 9, 1850, the founder of Babism was charged with blasphemy and treason (in Persia, they meant the same thing) and dragged in chains to the courthouse to be executed by firing squad. Along with one of his disciples, he was hoisted in midair in front of a regiment of soldiers and given the opportunity to recant his claims before a large crowd of his followers. He refused, of course. In the six short years the Bab had been preaching in Persia, he had attracted tens of thousands of disciples from all walks of life. These were people of different classes and with different loyalties who were nevertheless united in their belief that the country's clerics had been corrupted by the crown. They longed for a new era of justice and equality for all—one free from the imperial boot.

Now that the boot was pressed on the neck of the Bab himself, the authorities had hoped his execution would put an end to the movement. But the Bab's self-sacrifice served only to amplify his calls for change. Babism survived his execution, and not just in the form of its offshoot, Baha'ism. The Bab's vision of a new kind of Persian identity— one independent of the state and the clergy, in proud opposition to both—provided the spiritual bedrock upon which the Constitutional Revolution would eventually be constructed. The Bab's emphasis on equality and egalitarianism, his elevation of women's status in society and his insistence on female education, his pursuit of a free and unfettered press accessible to all citizens, his calls to protect and preserve the country's environment and natural resources—all of these ideals would be fully adopted by Persia's revolutionaries a generation after his death. Indeed, it was the Bab who had first conceived of the idea of a "House of Justice" in Persia, a place to protect the people from the arbitrary justice of the shah—the precursor to Persia's National Consultative Assembly.

Fifty-eight years after the Bab's execution, the pockmarked courthouse wall was still there for all to see: a reminder to some that the state always wins; to others that, without self-sacrifice, there would be no Persian Constitution.

The lesson to learn from the fate of the Bab is that the true test of salvation in Persia lies not in the acceptance of one set of beliefs or another. It lies in the willingness to sacrifice everything for those beliefs. That is why Justin and Charlotte Perkins were so successful for so many years. It wasn't just the good they did. It was the terrible sacrifice they were willing to make to fulfill their mission. They were the Bab, strung up before the courthouse, willingly baring his chest before the firing squad. They were Husain and his companions, watching helplessly as their children died in their arms, never wavering in their conviction, refusing to surrender the cause.

During his time in Tabriz, Howard Baskerville made every effort expected of him in performing his obligation to evangelize the population. He attended every Sunday service and every chapel prayer meeting at the school, including those conducted in Turkish, even though he could not understand the language (he simply wished to be, in his words, "among God's people"). He always had a Bible on his desk and never shied away from sharing his faith openly with his students and the wider community. He regularly went out of his way to have religious conversations with his class and would often boast to the Wilsons of what a "good talk" he'd had with this student or that one. "He has never been unChristian in word or deed," Annie recalled. "His faith and spiritual longings and love for souls were an inspiration."

However, in reading the recollections of those who knew him in

Tabriz, one finds little evidence that he was even remotely successful in converting anyone in his orbit to his faith. His dearest friend, Hassan, and his favorite student, Sadeq, both remained faithful Muslims, and not for lack of evangelizing on Baskerville's part.

The truth is, it probably wouldn't have mattered how hard he had tried to convert the people of Tabriz. In this city—in this country— nothing he said would have made much of an impression. If he had any hope of reaching those whose souls he'd come here to save, he would have to think of some way to *show* his faith, to put it into action for all to see.

Samuel Graham Wilson, head of the American Memorial School in Tabriz.

CHAPTER SEVEN

Oath-Breaker

WITH THE ARRIVAL of winter, the bare yellow hills surrounding Tabriz appear white and shimmery. The salt-and-sulfur valley floor is buried in snow. Snow blankets the homes, the mosques, the schools. It leaves smooth white mounds over the piles of garbage, the discarded bricks, and the broken pieces of concrete that somehow always seem to accumulate in the streets. In this city, no mess is ever cleaned up unless some rich nobleman complains about it.

Tabriz is not a place of great architectural wonders, but the natural scenery surrounding the city can take the breath away. Stand atop any of the flat-roofed homes and you can see for miles around. There, in the south, is the broad dome of Mount Sahand. In the north, the high ridges and defiant valleys of the Qaradagh. And, in between, a sweeping view of the flat valley, bursting here and there with groves and orchards that appear from this distance like a mirage. In a couple of months, when the snow finally melts, the valley will be overrun with daffodils.

For Howard Baskerville, the fall semester had been filled with glee and wonder. He'd been told Persia was a land of treachery and falsehood, its people deceitful and degraded, its achievements negligible and ruined. It had only been a few months but, so far, his experience in

Tabriz had put the lie to those dispiriting missionary reports. He loved his students, and they loved him. He had made one or two dear friends among the faculty. He was taking courses in French and Turkish and was slowly picking up Persian. He read entire volumes of books on topics as eclectic as systematic theology and the lives of English poets. He stayed up at all hours, drinking tea in cafés and talking politics with the locals. He gorged himself on Persian cuisine. He boxed and played tennis and occasionally rode horses. All in all, Persia was shaping up as precisely the grand adventure he had dreamed of when he filled out his missionary application.

With winter now upon them, the excitement of those early months in Tabriz was, like the January chill creeping into the valley, beginning to settle into a recognizable routine. The first two classes Baskerville was assigned to teach at the American Memorial School were English and history, and he poured all his energy into being the best instructor he could be. He was sober and serious, yet always patient and kind, even when his students stumped him with some vaguely worded question posed in unintelligible English.

This was Baskerville's first teaching experience, but he'd had one or two formidable teachers of his own back at Princeton, and he strove to apply the lessons he had learned from them in his own classroom. In fact, he created his own version of Princeton's preceptorial system in Tabriz, supplementing his class instructions with personal, one-on-one mentorships with a handful of students, with whom he formed a tight bond. He tried not only to teach his students but also to encourage and inspire them, to foster within them a love of learning. Sadeq Rezazadeh Shafaq, who enrolled in both of Baskerville's classes, called him one of the best teachers he'd ever had. "He always gave us hope that gradually we were going to understand more and more," Sadeq recalled, "and, in fact, his pleasant demeanor and attractive personality awoke in us a real desire to learn more and work harder."

The missionary teachers at the school were a close-knit bunch.

Along with Samuel Wilson, Frederick Jessup, Charles Pittman, and John Wright, Howard Baskerville was one of only five American men teaching at the school—all of them proud Princetonians. Even William Doty, the new American consul general in Tabriz, was a Princeton man. He and Jessup were old friends; they'd both graduated from Lawrenceville Preparatory in New Jersey, an elite boarding school that was, at the time, almost wholly composed of missionary children sent home by their parents to receive a high school education before inevitably matriculating at Princeton.

Doty, of course, was not a missionary but a diplomat, though, in his mind, there wasn't much of a difference between the two roles. He was a devout Presbyterian with a seminary degree who seemed genuinely to believe that his duty as consul general was to promote the work of the West Persia Mission, rather than, say, issue visas or fill out birth certificates. On more than one occasion he was reprimanded by the State Department for trying to "extend his consular jurisdiction over the morals of naturalized American citizens residing in his district." That is to say, *evangelizing.*

William Doty was the first to serve as the US consul general in Tabriz. Despite the city's strategic importance, it had never before had an American consulate. When he arrived in January of 1907—sun-kissed and bronze from his previous post in Tahiti—he was escorted directly to the Citadel. The ancient, crumbling structure, which sat in the center of the city like an anchor in the desert, would be the new American consulate office. With its high, thick walls and towering summit, this was not only the most secure location in Tabriz; it was, by far, the tallest. Now, no matter where in the city you were, you could always see the Stars and Stripes, waving in the wind.

Doty had been in Tabriz less than a year when Baskerville arrived, but he was already a fixture at the Wilson home. He spent most of his nights there, dining with the family, singing at the piano, telling tall tales by the fire. Baskerville would have had no choice but to sit with him at the Wilson table, patiently listening to his adventures among "the savages" of Tahiti. But there was little chance the two men would become friends. They had vastly different views on what was taking place in Persia. Doty fully endorsed the American government's position that the Persian Constitutional Revolution had no hope of succeeding; such a quixotic venture could not be supported by the United States. The State Department had said as much in a memo it recently sent to Persia: "This government can take no cognizance of any subversive movement unless it should succeed to actual power."

Doty was also, by all accounts, a bit of a boob. He was earnest and gregarious, but also wide-eyed and overly dramatic, eager to insert himself in everyone's affairs. He approached Persia with undisguised exuberance—an easy mark for the city's merchants and hustlers. His comedic attempts to exert his authority over the native population were a constant source of ridicule in Tabriz. The children especially had great fun over Doty's mangling of the local tongues. "Mr. Doty's nervousness and his tendency to exaggeration are so great that he has become a kind of joke to other foreign residents," reported the American legate in Tehran, John B. Jackson.*

Baskerville had a better chance of forming a friendship with Frederick Jessup. The two shared similar interests, including a passion for tennis (Jessup was a two-time men's singles champion back in New Jersey). Like Baskerville, Jessup came from a family of preachers, although his were titans in the Presbyterian Church. Frederick's father, Henry Harris Jessup, spent fifty-three years spreading the Gospel in Syria and was a world-renowned theologian. He was equally renowned for his contemptuous views about the people he served: in "the conflict between civilization and barbarism, Islam must be the loser," he famously wrote in his masterwork, *The Mohammadan Missionary Problem.*

---

* A legate is a diplomatic office of lower rank than that of ambassador. Iran would not have a US embassy or ambassador until 1944.

Frederick Jessup had a deep and abiding commitment to the people of Tabriz he served and was among the more vocal pro-constitutional missionaries at the American Memorial School. But he, too, dismissed Persia as "a fanatical Moslem [sic] land," tarred the religion of Islam as "the strongest and bitterest enemy of Christianity in the world," and considered nearly the entire population of the country to be "under bondage to every form of sin."

Besides, Jessup may have been the American closest in age to Baskerville at the school; but he was still ten years older. And he was married. In fact, every male missionary at the school was married, and they all had children. Baskerville was the sole single American man in the entire school. So it's no surprise that he would spend most of his free time with members of the mission community who were closer to his age, especially the fifteen-year-old diarist, Sarah Wright, and the eldest Wilson girl, Agnes, often taking them out on shopping excursions or for horse-riding lessons in the countryside. Sarah's diary contains many entries in which Baskerville would show up at her house unannounced, horse reins in hand, wanting to know if she'd like to "take a ride." She would grab her mother's fur coat, and off they'd go.

It's difficult to know exactly when his friendship with Agnes began raising eyebrows. Agnes had matured into a wise and worldly woman: a politically conscious, socially active sixteen-year-old with a strident feminist streak and passionate opinions about the country of her birth. "All that is needed to redeem Persia is to teach the nation how to help itself along the lines of modern civilization," Agnes once told an American reporter. "Foreign nations must not be content to take all they can get from Persia and give nothing in return."

Howard and Agnes spent a lot of time together. They lived under the same roof. They shared most meals. They sat with each other at church. They stayed up late singing songs and telling stories. They exchanged books and secrets. It was only a matter of time before Samuel Wilson started to notice the romance budding between them. This may be why, at some point early in the new year, Howard Baskerville was asked to find other lodgings in town. He moved out of the Wilson home and into a cramped room on campus reserved for visiting faculty.

❖

THE MOVE MAY have pulled Baskerville away from Agnes, but it also pushed him toward Hassan Sharifzadeh and his fellow revolutionaries, with whom he could now spend even more of his free time. Under Hassan's protection, Baskerville was given entry into Tabriz's so-called secret societies. These were unofficial councils formed by young Social Democrats who were more strident in their views of the revolution and more uncompromising in their tactics. They gathered clandestinely at night to discuss ways to fight corruption and tyranny and to awaken the people to the cause of liberty. Members read speeches, created pamphlets, formulated demands, debated the articles of the new constitution, and strategized ways to defend the democratic rights they had already won.

Can you see Baskerville in one of these dark, smoke-filled rooms, listening to those fresh-faced revolutionaries arguing about popular sovereignty and inalienable rights, his mind harkening back to another band of revolutionaries who also had no chance of succeeding yet, nevertheless, did?

The secret societies tended to attract members who were more radical, more progressive, and more secular-minded than most other constitutionalists in Tabriz. Some members served in the anjoman; a handful had been elected to parliament. In both organizations, they were already the loudest, most unyielding voices urging forceful opposition to the crown. But the shah's failed attempt to shut down parliament the previous December had pushed many of them past the point of compromise. As far as they were concerned, the curtain had been pulled back; everyone could now see Mohammed Ali for what he was. What more doubt could there be as to his true intentions or his true character? Had he not stood before the nation, placed his hand upon the Holy Quran, and sworn to uphold the constitution during his coronation? What kind of ruler would so brazenly break a solemn vow made before God and men?

An "oath-breaker," that's who. That is what the shah was called in the secret society meetings Baskerville attended. What did it matter that the shah was forced to retreat? What difference did it make that he had apologized for his actions against parliament and once again pledged to uphold the constitution? His word was forfeit, and so, therefore, was his reign.

The secret society members held enormous sway over the anjoman in Tabriz, and it was under their pressure and influence that the council began sending telegrams to other anjomans across Persia demanding the shah's immediate abdication. "The Shah swore an oath to accept the constitutional law and has now broken his oath," the telegrams read. "For this crime, the people of Azerbaijan remove him from power. . . . You, too, remove him and inform the embassy."

This was a jaw-dropping declaration. Never before in Persian history had the people claimed the right to legally remove the shah. The notion that God had placed the shah on the throne and thus only God could remove him from power had been baked into the Persian psyche for thousands of years. It was a belief that could be traced back to the first "King of Kings," Cyrus the Great.

But the constitution had fundamentally challenged that view, not by denying the divine authority of the throne, but by reimagining that authority as a trust given by God to the people, and then by the people to the shah. Article 35 of the Supplementary Fundamental Laws stated in no uncertain terms that "the sovereignty is a trust confided (as a Divine gift) by the people to the person of the King."

If the people could, on behalf of God, gift the throne to the shah, then the people could, on behalf of God, take the gift away.

"Has His Majesty forgotten that . . . he does not have a deed to absolute rule from the skies and the God of the Universe?" read a collective statement from the country's leading anjomans. "No doubt that if he pondered for a moment he would realize that his monarchy is dependent upon the acceptance or rejection of the nation. He would realize that the same people who have raised him to this high level and recognized him as shah are quite capable of removing him and choosing another to replace him."

In the end, all these telegrams and declarations amounted to nothing. Mohammed Ali had publicly apologized for trying to shut parliament down and vowed not to do so again (a lie, as he was, at that moment, scheming with Shapshal and Liakhov to do just that). An agreement was reached whereby the shah swore to abandon his opposition to the constitution once and for all, and parliament promised to put an end to "outrageous acts" such as the brazen calls for his abdication. The agreement calmed the waters somewhat in Tehran.

But Tabriz would not move on. The shah's attack on parliament had radicalized the city. If anything, the calls for his abdication were growing louder, and not just among the secret societies. What had seemed like an impossible idea just a few months ago—the removal of the shah by the will of the people—was becoming an increasingly accepted possibility on the streets of Tabriz. Mohammed Ali's reign was polarizing the city. It was splitting the most ethnically and religiously diverse province in all of Persia into two opposing camps: the royalists, who supported the shah; and the nationalists, who supported parliament and the constitution.

Ironically, the growing polarization in Tabriz only strengthened the shah's hand. What Mohammed Ali understood about the city of his birth is that its traditional divides could be manipulated to his advantage, given enough money and resources. His cause was bolstered by some of the more extreme actions taken by the anjoman in Tabriz. Its attacks against the city's large landowners and wealthy merchants (not to mention its forceful expulsion of anti-constitutional clerics) had created potent enemies among the city's rich and powerful. The more the new political order came into focus, the more those with vested interests in the status quo began to turn against it.

Long before his bungled attempt to shut down parliament, Mohammed Ali Shah had been sending carriages filled with money and weapons to his allies in Tabriz. He had purchased the services of hundreds of lootis from all over the province of Azerbaijan and shipped them off to secure his interests in the city. He had even urged his backers in Tabriz to launch their own rival anjoman—which they did in the summer of 1907, giving it the strategic name of *Eslamiyeh* ("the Islamic Anjoman"), a blatant attempt to pull the city's pious poor away from the constitutional cause.

With the city now bitterly divided and teetering on the edge of civil war, the American Memorial School became neutral ground. Samuel Wilson was diligent in trying to keep the chaos engulfing the city from penetrating the tranquility of the school. No doubt he was worried about the country's future. But he had spent years building a reputation in Tabriz as a trusted figure, a man beholden to no one, in favor of no faction. He could not be seen as taking sides in Persia's political affairs, regardless of what was at stake.

Early in the revolution, the Wilsons had made a conscious decision to maintain the school schedule no matter what else was happening outside of campus. Yet there was only so much they could do to tamp down the rising revolutionary fervor among the student body. It certainly didn't help matters that two of the city's most prominent revolutionaries happened to be members of the faculty. Mirza Ansari, the school's youthful international law teacher, was spending the bulk of his time giving rousing speeches in front of the Telegraph House, extolling the virtues of the constitutional cause, while Baskerville's friend, Hassan Sharifzadeh, was conducting daily campus meetings of the Union of Students, discussing ways to bolster the defense of the constitution among the people.

In Baskerville's English and history classes, the conflict with the shah dominated discussions. How could it not? The students may have been shielded somewhat from the events roiling the city, but their friends and families were mired in it. Tabriz had the feel of a small, provincial town. Everyone knew everyone else; many of the residents were related to each other in one way or another. The fighting on the streets was as much a family feud as it was a civil conflict. So then, how was Baskerville expected to keep the conflict from intruding into his classroom?

It would have been natural for his students to assume their young American teacher was an ally to the cause, and there was no reason to think Baskerville wasn't. He may very well have been deeply invested in the success of the Constitutional Revolution. After all, his closest friend was one of its most vocal proponents. And it could not have been lost on him that the principles he had just studied at Princeton— principles he had abandoned his family legacy to pursue; principles he would ultimately give his life to defend—were being battled over just outside his classroom window.

But he had been in the country barely four months, and in that time, he had been repeatedly instructed by both Samuel Wilson and William Doty not to engage in any activity outside of his responsibilities as a missionary and teacher, in accordance with the US government's explicit mandate of neutrality for the West Persia Mission.

This must have come as something of a shock to the people of Tabriz. The long presence in the city of American missionaries like the Perkinses and the Wilsons had given the population an impression of America as a benevolent power. What little most Persians knew about American history had primarily to do with its own fight for independence against a corrupt and out-of-touch monarch. Wasn't this fact reason enough for America to find common cause with the Persian Constitutional Revolution?

The US government, however, wanted nothing to do with Persia or its struggle for independence. Not only did the United States have no interest in antagonizing the British and Russians; it had no faith in Persia's revolutionaries. Doty's superiors in Washington had concluded that Persians were too ignorant of constitutional government, too uneducated and uninformed, too *backward* to be able to create anything approaching a real democracy. "History does not record a single instance of a successful constitutional government in a country where the Mussulman religion is the state religion," read an internal State Department memo. "Islam seems to imply autocracy."

There's no way Baskerville would have agreed with that statement. He had been taught by Woodrow Wilson to believe that the rights of the individual were absolute and nonnegotiable. This was no mere political philosophy. It was a religious conviction. Democracy was a gift granted by God to all peoples everywhere. What difference did it make by what name you called that God? Democracy was either inalienable or it wasn't. It was either universal or confined solely to Christians. The US government may have believed the latter. But not Howard Baskerville.

Still, there was simply nothing he could do about it, not without abandoning his missionary work, being stripped of his teaching position, possibly even losing his citizenship. He had no choice but to put his head down and do the job the Presbyterian Board of Foreign Missions had sent him here to do. He would ignore the tempest brewing in his chest whenever he watched Hassan stand before a crowd and urge them never to surrender the fight for freedom. He would bite his tongue when one of his students looked him in the eyes to ask what he could do to help the country. He would shut his ears to the occasional whiz-bang of bullets being exchanged in the streets, the dull thud of a body hitting the pavement.

He would teach his classes, read his books, ride his horse whenever he could, and try his best to pretend that none of it was happening.

Hassan Sharifzadeh.

CHAPTER EIGHT

The People's Commander

I T WAS NOT UNUSUAL to spy a camel ambling down the unpaved streets of Tabriz, not even one as garishly outfitted as this one. Those crotchety beasts are as common as flies when you're this close to the Caucasus. However, this particular camel, on this particular day, had been expressly forbidden. Its presence in the city's main square was a deliberate act of defiance, not only against the Tabriz Anjoman but also against the very constitutional order the anjoman represented in the city.

It was the Islamic feast of sacrifice, *Eid al-Adha*, a day in which Muslims all over the world commemorate the Prophet Abraham's near-sacrifice of his eldest son, Ismael (in Judaism, it is Abraham's younger son, Isaac, who is almost sacrificed). Across Persia, people adorn camels with colorful beads and cloths and then parade them through towns and villages for all to see. They then slit the camel's throat and distribute the meat to the poor. In some cities, it is customary to present the camel's head as an offering to the most esteemed resident. In Tehran that was the shah. In Tabriz, it would have been the crown prince, had he still resided there.

The feast of sacrifice occurs on the tenth day of *Dhul-Hijjah*, the last month of the Islamic lunar calendar, which, in the year 1908, fell on January 17. It was a precarious time in Tabriz—barely a month had passed since Mohammed Ali Shah tried and failed to shut down parliament in December. The heavy winter snow had curbed some of the conflict on the streets, but the city remained bitterly divided between the nationalist wards controlled by the Tabriz Anjoman—Amirkhiz, Khiyaban, and some smaller neighborhoods in the south of the city inhabited mostly by merchants, workshop owners, craftsmen, and tradesmen—and the royalist wards under the influence of the so-called Islamic Anjoman: Davehchi, Sorkhab, and a handful of neighborhoods in the northeast, crowded with dyers, weavers, laborers, and muleteers. Much of the population was caught in the middle: loyal to one side or the other, yet unwilling to die for either. The camel was meant to push them over.

The whole thing was a clever ploy by the newly designated leader of the Islamic Anjoman, an influential cleric and wealthy resident of the Davehchi ward named Mir Hashem, who had personally paid for the camel and its adornments. The plan was to parade the beast through the royalist wards, gathering a crowd, then sacrifice it in front of the Hamzeh shrine, which was located just east of the main square, where all things worth witnessing took place.

However, the Tabriz Anjoman, for reasons that are not entirely clear, had forbidden the feast of sacrifice from taking place in the city that year. Perhaps it was a means of steering the populace away from what many constitutionalists believed to be barbaric rituals that no longer had a place in the new, modern Persia. Perhaps it was nothing more than an attempt to flex its muscle, to demonstrate that its authority over Tabriz stretched beyond the wards under its direct control. Either way, the plan backfired.

Surrounded by a mob of royalists and under the protection of a horde of anti-constitutionalist lootis paid for by the shah himself, the camel was brought before the Hamzeh shrine and prepped for sacrifice. The Tabriz Anjoman could do nothing but watch the spectacle take place at its expense.

The camel came in, resplendent and draped with garlands and tassels, its hind legs painted red and green, its snout encased in a soft mesh muzzle. The sword moved like a whisper. The animal buckled at the knees, then slowly dropped to its stomach, legs splayed, a pool of red swelling beneath its body. The head was delivered to Mir Hashem.

For Baskerville and the other Americans, the bloody pageant was little more than a curiosity: the kind of exotic cultural celebration that made serving in faraway lands so exciting. They could not understand the tension in the air. Perhaps they recognized that the sacrifice had taken place against the wishes of the Tabriz Anjoman. The council was the official governing body of the city, democratically elected and charged with managing the people's affairs. It had every right to expect its orders to be followed by everyone under its jurisdiction, not just those who happened to be in the same political camp. This other anjoman— the *Islamic* Anjoman—was, as far as the Americans understood, nothing more than a club. It didn't have any real authority. It couldn't pass laws or collect taxes. So it sacrificed a camel? Why the fuss?

Tabrizis, however, understood precisely what it was that had been sacrificed at the Hamzeh shrine. The feast was no mere act of defiance by the Islamic Anjoman; it was an expression of the true state of affairs in Tabriz. How would the city's governing body respond?

Some among the Tabriz Anjoman wanted to punish Mir Hashem for ignoring the council's demands. But he was too wealthy to fine and too powerful to arrest. Others thought it best to ignore the entire affair and move on. But what would happen the next time he challenged their authority? The elected members were stuck, the council thrown into disarray. The camel had done its job.

Having so brazenly defied the orders of the Tabriz Anjoman, and without consequence, Mir Hashem began sending his lootis into nationalist wards. They ransacked homes, pillaged "disloyal" businesses, and attacked religious minorities with impunity. The city was thrown into panic. People felt vulnerable, unprotected, and they naturally blamed the Tabriz Anjoman. What sort of government was incapable of performing its most basic function: protecting citizens from harm? Who really controlled this city anyway?

It was at this moment of chaos and uncertainty, when the future of the Tabriz Anjoman—indeed, the future of the Constitutional Revolution—was suddenly in doubt, that a new figure took the stage, a poor, illiterate horse trader and hired gun who had no education, no real skills save with a gun, and no experience in combat: Sattar Khan, the man who would one day be known as the "People's Commander."

❖

SATTAR KHAN WAS born sometime between the years 1867 and 1869; no one knows for sure. So much of his life is shrouded in legend. As with most heroes cast in bronze, he has become more myth than man.

He was the third son of Hajji Hasan Bazzaz from Qaradagh (modern-day Arasbaran), a broad mountainous region lying just south of the Aras River. Baskerville almost certainly traveled past Sattar's childhood village on his way to Tabriz, though no one can say for certain which of the villages tucked between the mist-covered mountains was his. Some of them aren't even named. Others look empty and abandoned, save for the clotheslines quivering in the wind.

The people of Qaradagh are as stubborn as the mountains. They carve their homes into the face of a cliff or perch them on the lip of a gorge so deep you would think it was scooped from the earth by some giant's hand. This is, in fact, a land of giants, some fabled, some very real: a place of ghosts and witches and supernatural beings who dwell in caves and trees. They say there are as many *jinn* in Qaradagh as there are people; their homes are marked by stone pillars and offerings of bread and cheese.

Sattar never spent a day in school. He and his brothers made their living raiding the caravans that passed through the region en route to Tabriz. It was after one such raid that Sattar's eldest brother, Ismael, was caught and executed by the Qajar authorities for the crime of highway robbery. Sattar was just a child when it happened, but the image of his brother swinging from a noose stamped upon his soul a lifelong hatred for the entire Qajar line and everything it represented.

At the age of seventeen, Sattar's family moved to Tabriz. There, he quickly came into conflict with the law after his father gave shelter to two men from his hometown who had killed a muleteer during a dispute. Sattar hid the two fugitives in a garden just outside the city walls, but they were discovered. The men were executed, but Sattar, who had been injured during the arrest, was sent to the notorious Narin Ghaleh prison in Ardabil, a brutal penitentiary located about one hundred forty miles east of Tabriz that was reserved for violent criminals and the occasional rebellious prince.

The prison was actually a converted castle complete with battlements, parapets, and a moat requiring a wooden bridge to cross. The walls were so tall they would block out the sun in the middle of the day, plunging the prisoners into darkness. In winter, the sun never reached them. In summer, the air was so hot that many would suffocate and die.

For two years, Sattar languished in these insufferable conditions. He spent months in solitary confinement, unable to speak to another soul. Yet, if you asked him, he'd probably say that those months alone, wrapped in silence, were preferable to the time he spent with his fellow prisoners—or, at least, with one prisoner in particular. His name was Rahim Khan and he was the leader of the Shahsevan tribe.

The Shahsevan were a seminomadic tribe from northwest Persia. Their name means "those who love the shah," a tribute to their centuries-long devotion to the Persian throne, regardless of who sat upon it. It should not come as a shock, therefore, to learn that the Shahsevan was loyal to the crown and hostile to the constitutionalists. Yet it wasn't politics that forged a burning and soon to be historic hatred between Sattar and Rahim. At the time in which he languished in the Narin Ghaleh prison, Sattar had likely never heard the word *constitution* before. It was something far more mundane.

Every morning, Rahim Khan would rise before the sun and begin shouting his prayers at the top of his lungs, begging God to set him free, swearing on the life of his son that he would change his ways, if only God would release him from his bonds. Sattar, who at that point had probably never prayed a day in his life, repeatedly asked Rahim to keep it down. But it did no good. Then, one morning, while Rahim was howling his prayers to the heavens, Sattar picked up a brick and threw it as his head.

"You idiot!" Sattar cried. "You shout and hullabaloo as if God is deaf."

A brawl broke out between the two. They were eventually separated into more distant cells. But the fight that began in that prison yard would not be finished until some years later, when the two men would face each other on opposite sides of the battlefield in Tabriz.

A few months after the fight with Rahim Khan, Sattar was given a new cellmate named Hashem, a young, impressionable tribesman who almost immediately fell under Sattar's influence. The two of them would stay up all hours of the night, chatting, making plans for their release, trying to escape their misery with company. One night before bed, Hashem whispered to Sattar that he should stay awake until dawn.

"Why?" Sattar asked.

"Perhaps tonight God will send us some means of rescue," Hashem replied.

Sattar paid no attention to his friend and went to sleep. In the middle of the night, Hashem shook him awake. "Get up," he said, "we have no time to spare."

Sattar stood and followed Hashem until they reached the foot of the castle's exterior wall. There they found a rope hanging from the parapet. Hashem told him to take it. Sattar grabbed the rope and was pulled up and over the wall by invisible hands on the other side. Waiting across the moat was a group of horsemen from Hashem's tribe.

After his escape from prison, Sattar tried his best to abandon his lawless ways, but it was no use. He soon returned to a life of highway robbery and was arrested again. And again. Eventually, his ferocity, and his proficiency with a gun, caught the attention of Muzaffar ad-Din when he was crown prince in residence in Tabriz. It was Muzaffar's practice to pay groups of armed thugs and troublemakers to act as his bodyguards and to perform whatever violent tasks he might require around town. Sattar was hired, first as one of the crown prince's riflemen, and then as part of his personal armed escort. He became, in other words, a looti.

It was a lifestyle that served Sattar well. Even as an impoverished villager he'd had a sense of style. He was tall, slender, and slightly built, with a dark, handsome complexion, bushy eyebrows, and a nose as long and as sharp as an arrow. In the dozens of photographs of him that have survived the period, even those taken in the midst of the war, he is always wearing a perfectly pressed suit and matching felt hat, his mustache elegantly waxed and draped into two long strands past his cleanly shaven chin.

It was during his time under the crown prince's employ that he was given the honorific *Khan*. Yet every time he looked upon the well-fed cheeks of the Qajar prince he protected, he saw the ashen face of his older brother, swinging by his neck from a tree. The memory was enough for him to abandon his new life and stable career and return to highway robbery. Once again, he found himself on the run from the law.

By 1901, Sattar Khan had grown weary of his life as a criminal. Never a pious man, he nevertheless decided to make a pilgrimage to the holy city of Najaf in order to visit the shrine of Imam Ali, the Prophet Muhammad's son-in-law. There, in a display of raw, unfettered emotion, he vowed to mend his deviant ways, to lead a life of honor and justice.

Sattar Khan returned to Tabriz a new man. He moved into the Amirkhiz ward in the northwestern part of town and started his own modest business raising and selling horses, all the while continuing to use his muscle to defend the people in his neighborhood against both local marauders and the arbitrary cruelty of the government. And then, the revolution broke out.

The Tabriz Anjoman, recognizing that its authority would ultimately be measured by the strength of its arms, started recruiting a large number of lootis to enforce its orders in town. These were the men that Baskerville had seen in the main square when his carriage came through the gates of Tabriz. Sattar was hired to maintain order on behalf of the Tabriz Anjoman in his Amirkhiz ward, while a friend of his, a stonemason by the name of Baqer Khan, performed a similar function in the Khiyaban ward, a large neighborhood located in the southeast.

In the aftermath of the feast of sacrifice debacle, as the legitimacy of the Tabriz Anjoman was being openly called into question and royalist lootis were wantonly attacking nationalists on the streets, Sattar Khan took it upon himself to set things right. With Baqer by his side, he launched a daring assault on the royalists. The shooting lasted through much of the night, with numerous deaths on both sides. But when it was all over, Sattar and Baqer had rid the nationalist wards of the royalist thugs. The city was still divided—more so than ever. But power was firmly back in the hands of the Tabriz Anjoman. Both Sattar and Baqer were feted as heroes.

The nationalists had learned a valuable lesson from the whole affair. It was not enough to merely pay a bunch of lootis to act as muscle for the movement. A legitimate government needed a legitimate protection force. It needed an army. And now they knew exactly who would command it.

Sattar Khan's first act as the People's Commander was to break open the armory housed within the Citadel and scoop up the shah's massive arsenal inside. Armed with a huge cache of weapons and ammunition, and with Baqer Khan as his second-in-command, Sattar began training the citizenry, giving shooting lessons to farmers and merchants. He created a true people's army, composed of a mishmash of lootis and tradesmen, peasants and laborers, the young and the old—all of them volunteers. Some had fought in the Perso-Russian wars; others had never fired a weapon before. Sattar even encouraged women to join the ranks. Hundreds signed up. They threw off their veils, put on pants and vests, cropped their hair short, picked up rifles, and fought shoulder to shoulder with the men. One of the best-known stories of the era concerned the time Sattar Khan went to the hospital to have a wound dressed. There, he came upon one of his fighters stubbornly resisting a nurse's attempts to undress him. Sattar intervened, ordering the young man to remove his clothes at once so that the doctors could examine him. The young man looked up at Sattar, tears in his eyes, and said, "I can't undress here, sir. I am a girl."

In a short amount of time, Sattar's home in Amirkhiz became a makeshift barracks, his small courtyard crowded at all hours with fighters taking turns sleeping on the floor. Sattar, it seemed, never slept. If he wasn't building barricades in the nationalist wards, he was drilling volunteers, reminding them always what they were fighting for: "It's right that peace is better than war, but what peace?" he'd shout. "True peace is one devoid of dishonor and impoverishment."

It did not take long for the legend of Sattar Khan to wind its way through the crooked alleys of Tabriz. Inside the American Memorial School, his name was on every student's lips. In Baskerville's classroom, Sattar was all anyone wanted to talk about. Sadeq Rezazadeh Shafaq had tried to rally a group of fellow students together to join the fight, but the People's Commander had laughed and sent them back to school. "We are fighting for you," he said. "Instead of being armed with weapons, better you get armed with knowledge."

Every history lecture Baskerville delivered would inevitably devolve into a debate over whether this or that historical figure was or was not like Sattar Khan. Maybe he was George Washington? Hardly. More like Claude Duval! Or perhaps a Persian Garibaldi!

A teacher couldn't have asked for better engagement. Baskerville's students were living through a truly historic moment in time, and he completely understood their infatuation with Sattar Khan. Indeed, he shared it! He was living alone at the time, in a small, one-room dormitory, having recently been asked to leave the Wilson home. He still spent most of his time with the missionary community: he still shared most dinners with the Wilsons; still nodded along to William Doty's meandering stories; still took Agnes and Sarah on horse rides. But he now had greater freedom to come and go as he wished.

He started spending more of his evenings at the homes of his students, especially Sadeq, who lived in a spacious house with a large garden blooming with roses, tulips, and geraniums. He also began exploring more of the city. Late nights sitting with Hassan Sharifzadeh and his friends on a flat, wooden bench in one café or another—the wood draped with a carpet for comfort—a steaming cup of tea in his hands for warmth, Baskerville would have heard all there was to know about Sattar Khan: his criminal past; his humble rise from an uneducated peasant to a successful horse trader; his sudden ascent from an illiterate looti to commander of the constitutional army.

Hassan and his friends spoke of Sattar Khan with a reverence usually reserved for saints. They were already calling him "Father of the Nation." Was that so preposterous?

Where was the harm in leaning back on a rough pillow, sipping tea, and letting his imagination run wild? Perhaps one day Sattar would indeed be known as the Persian George Washington. And if Baskerville were willing to make that leap, could he not go one step further and picture himself as Marquis de Lafayette—the foreigner caught in another country's fight for freedom? Why not? It was just a group of friends, hanging out at night, dreaming about what might be.

And, in all likelihood, it would have remained just that: a dream. Baskerville would have finished his tea and bid goodnight to his friends. He would have returned to his dorm room and gone to sleep, woken up and taught his classes, graded his papers and gone to chapel, finished his mission and returned home; and all of this—Tabriz, Hassan, Sattar Khan—would have been nothing more than a thrilling adventure he'd had as a youth, a story he could tell his grandchildren. That very likely would have been Howard Baskerville's fate—had not someone tried to kill the shah.

Baqer Kahn (left) and Sattar Khan (right).

CHAPTER NINE

Long Live the Just King of Kings!

THE FEAST OF SACRIFICE was an entirely different affair in the capital city. By the time the sun rose over Tehran on January 17, 1908, the streets were already slick with blood. Hundreds of sheep had been crammed into makeshift pens near the city center, most of them donated by the shah's wealthy loyalists, and in his name. One by one they were pulled out, splayed between trees, and sliced cleanly down the middle. The meat would be distributed among the city's hungry masses. On this day of charity at least, the people could thank the shah for a full belly.

Inside Golestan Palace, preparations had been made for a grand banquet in honor of the occasion. The vast gardens surrounding the palace were festooned with lamps and colorful banners waving in the wind. All that was missing was the camel. It came through the palace gates in mid-afternoon, escorted by a parade of costumed dancers and lively musicians. The camel was draped in a silk blanket the color of blood, two naked sabers attached to either side of its saddle. An old mullah at the front of the procession carried the spear with which the poor beast would be pierced.

The parade came to a stop in front of the large rectangular fountain at the entrance to the throne room. The musicians fell silent as the mullah lifted his head to the tinted windows above and waited. The camel swayed back and forth on its toes. Nothing could happen until the shah appeared. This was all for his benefit.

Finally, there he was, in silhouette, framed by the window. He wore his usual attire: silk slippers, a long, black lapel skirt, wide trousers. Perched on his head was the Kiani Crown—the symbol of Qajar rule: a tall, weighty hat made of red velvet and stitched with pearls, emeralds, and rubies. His face was full and round, his eyes concealed behind gold-rimmed glasses. He stood motionless at the window, his posture less a gesture of command than a sign of uncertainty. A simple nod was all that was needed to proceed. The camel's head would be cleaned, stuffed, and delivered to the throne room within the hour.

It was an inconvenient time for such a grand celebration. The palace was still reeling from the failed attempt to shut down parliament the previous month. The shah was feeling chastened and embarrassed. Worse, he was broke. Parliament had just slashed the crown's bloated budget by a staggering 4 million tomans,* leaving the court with an annual stipend of about 500,000 tomans, of which only 30,000 was designated for the shah's personal expenses, with the rest set aside to pay the salaries of the court's employees: janitors, muleteers, attendants, and so forth. True, the shah had pocketed most of the money and had informed his employees that their wages had been cut by parliament. But even that amount would barely cover a lavish banquet like this.

Still, there were protocols to adhere to, customs to consider, an image to maintain. And so dozens of officials, dignitaries, clergymen, diplomats, and governors were now awkwardly milling about the throne room, drinking tea and smoking cigarettes, eyeing the mountains of food spread out before them, awaiting the signal to dig in. Shapshal Khan was there, of course. As was Colonel Liakhov. I

---

* In 1908, 1 toman roughly equaled 1 US dollar.

can see the two men conspiring in a corner, their heads practically pressed together.

The plan that had been prepped in St. Petersburg was moving along nicely. Regular shipments of money and arms were being sent to Tabriz to prop up Mir Hashem and the Islamic Anjoman. A few of the more loyal tribes had been lured down from their hovels in the mountains of Qaradagh with the promise of a handsome reward should they be willing to act as the shah's advance troops. And, in an absolutely inspired move, the Shahsevan leader, Rahim Khan, had been freed from prison and was now comfortably ensconced in Tehran, awaiting orders.

So far, everything was progressing smoothly. The only trouble the two Russians faced was with the shah himself. Despite the tsar's threat to cut off all support, Mohammed Ali was still not fully convinced by Liakhov's plan to topple parliament. What if the coup failed? What would happen to him and his family then? Perhaps they should take more time to see if the new agreement he had struck with the delegates would hold. Maybe he should go on holiday for a little while, let things with parliament settle down a bit. Then they could revisit the coup plans in the summer.

A holiday was a terrible idea, as far as Shapshal and Liakhov were concerned. It would leave a vacuum of power in the capital at a time in which the crown needed to exert itself. Tabriz was slipping from their control; Tehran could be next. They had already lost the streets; they were now in danger of losing the mosques. Having failed to rouse the pious masses against the constitution, Ayatollah Nuri and his band of anti-constitutionalist clerics were hiding out in the shrine of Shah Abdol Azim, worried that if they left the sanctuary they'd be pilloried in the streets. The two Russians were in agreement with St. Petersburg that the shah's holiday could not be permitted under any circumstance. Shapshal would make sure of it.

There was a third Russian in the throne room that day. He stood apart from the festivities, near the entrance, patiently awaiting the shah's attention. His name was Konstantin Nikolaevich Smirnov, and he was there to present the shah with the crown prince's report card.

Now that the shah's son and successor, the ten-year-old Prince Ahmed, was safely stashed away inside Golestan Palace, rather than in the Northern Gardens in Tabriz, as custom demanded, Mohammed Ali was directly responsible for his education and upbringing. Perhaps because he had grown up with his own Russian tutor, the shah thought it best for his son to have one, too. He asked Liakhov for a recommendation. Liakhov reached out to the Russian Ministry of War, and the ministry chose Konstantin Smirnov, who was, at the time, serving as an intelligence officer in the Imperial Armed Forces. Captain Smirnov was swiftly retired from his military duties and sent packing to Tehran.

Unlike the two other Russians at court, Smirnov was a passionate Persophile. A tall, thick-set, handsome man with kind eyes and a bushy salt-and-pepper mustache, he was born in 1878 in modern-day Dagestan to a family of minor nobility. He had graduated with honors from the Russian military's school for oriental languages, specializing in Turkish and Persian. Even before he'd taken his post as the crown prince's tutor, he had written a number of well-received books about Persian language, history, and culture, including one on the history of missionaries in Persia, and another on the Perso-Russian wars of the nineteenth century. His two-volume opus, *Persi*, published in 1914 and 1916, respectively, was an ethnographic study of the country and a meditation on Persia's many religions. He even helped translate and publish the memoirs of the personal secretary to the second Qajar king, Fath Ali Shah.

Still, Smirnov was Russian and thus automatically viewed with suspicion by parliament. As one Persian delegate put it years later: "It was completely obvious that the matter of K.N. Smirnov did not concern the prince's education so much as the maximization of Russian influence in the Shah's Court."

The delegate wasn't wrong. An intercepted letter written by the Russian minister of foreign affairs to the head of the General Staff made clear that Smirnov's primary responsibility was to exercise direct influence on the future shah on behalf of the tsar. Smirnov himself understood that a large part of his job as the crown prince's tutor would require sending St. Petersburg detailed reports of the young man's proclivities toward Russia, its allies, and its enemies (the crown prince, Smirnov dutifully reported, does not much care for the British, he respects the Germans, is indifferent when it comes to the Turks, and has very warm feelings for the tsar).

But while it is true that Smirnov was a loyal Russian soldier, his love for Persia was sincere. He may have reported directly to Liakhov, but he did not get along with his superior officer. And he absolutely loathed Shapshal, whom he considered a self-serving fool more interested in his own interests than those of either Russia or Persia. When Shapshal made a pass at Smirnov's wife, Smirnov tried to have him dismissed, but the shah refused the request. After that, Smirnov did his best to avoid all contact with the "semi-Asiatic, semi-European figure with his ingratiating manner." Unfortunately, Shapshal had made that difficult by positioning himself as the sole liaison between the shah and the Russian mission in Persia. There would be no communication with the throne unless it went through him.

So there Smirnov stood, in the doorway, waiting for Shapshal to stop conferring with Liakhov long enough to acknowledge his presence so that he could deliver his report about the crown prince's progress. Standing behind Smirnov, at the far end of the hallway, was young Ahmed himself, nervously fingering the fringes of his robe. Earlier that morning the young prince had begged Smirnov—just this once, in honor of the sacred holiday—to lie to his father about what a lousy student he was. And he was truly, undeniably, a lousy student. He was lazy and had little patience for studying. He retained almost nothing of what he learned. He could understand Russian but not speak it. His Turkish and Azerbaijani were excellent, his Arabic appalling.

In some ways, Prince Ahmed was like any other ten-year-old boy. He quarreled with his middle brother, Mohammed Hasan, and doted on his younger brother, Mahmoud. He was a handsome boy who carried himself with dignity. But he had the arrogance of a prince, coupled with the lack of concern for the suffering of others that had become the hallmark of the Qajar Dynasty. He was obsessed with all things European—shoes, jewelry, toiletries, whatever he could get his hands on—and dreamed of one day leaving Persia for good and living in Paris.

The problem with Ahmed, as Smirnov would write in his vibrantly detailed memoir of his time in Persia, was that he spent all his time lounging inside the curtained-off harem, surrounded by the women of the court and smothered by his domineering mother, Empress Jahan. Smirnov had warned him that doing so would rob him of his "manliness," and the crown prince did have a habit of throwing fits and wailing at the slightest provocation. But his attempts to pull Ahmed from the harem's grip were constantly thwarted by his mother and by the stern, elderly eunuch who guarded the harem. The only thing that would motivate Ahmed to study was Smirnov's repeated threat to quit. For as much as the prince hated learning, he truly loved his tutor—or, at least, he loved the attention his tutor gave him. And Smirnov had grown to love Ahmed, which is why he had agreed to be less than forthright with the shah about his poor grades. Just for today.

When he was finally allowed into the throne room, Smirnov kneeled before the shah and pressed his forehead to the ground three times in supplication. With Shapshal at his side, the shah tried to greet his son's tutor in Russian. But Smirnov had so much trouble understanding the shah's rudimentary Russian that they were forced to switch to Persian. *What could the shah's Russian tutor have been doing all these years?*

"How does the boy read?" the shah asked.

"Well," Smirnov answered, the report card tucked under his arm.

"How does he write?"

"Little by little he's learning."

After that, the shah asked some general questions about the Turkish army, a subject about which Smirnov knew a thing or two. He inquired as to why Smirnov did not wear his Russian military uniform, the way Liakhov did. Smirnov had retired from the military; he was a civilian now, a teacher, and he thought it best to dress like one. Then the shah suddenly dispensed with all protocols and, to the surprise of everyone in attendance, including Shapshal and Liakhov, ordered his son's tutor to deliver a message to the Russian High Command. His Majesty wanted the tsar to know that his recent troubles with parliament were over. He had made certain arrangements with the delegates. Both parties had decided to put the past behind them and make peace. He wanted to make sure that the tsar knew this. There was no more need for concern. Persia was calm and stable and once again under his control.

"I hope that all past misunderstandings have been removed and that relations of mutual friendship and confidence have been established between myself and the constitutionalists."

With that, the shah announced that he would soon be leaving for his vacation home in eastern Tehran, where he would spend the winter months relaxing with his family. He stood, bid everyone goodbye, and retired to his chambers, leaving Shapshal and Liakhov staring at each other in confusion.

❖

FIVE WEEKS LATER, on the morning of February 28, 1908, Konstantin Smirnov and his wife were in the Russian embassy, patiently waiting in line to renew some necessary forms, when a young British woman standing next to them was told she had a telephone call.

Telephones were an expensive rarity in Persia at the time, so pretty much any phone call was probably an urgent one. All eyes were on the woman as she walked over to the desk and put the candlestick receiver to her ear. The caller was her father, the director of a British-owned bank in Tehran. When she hung up the phone she was pale and breathless. Someone had thrown two bombs at the shah's automobile as it was driving him out of town for his holiday. His Majesty was presumed dead.

Smirnov left his wife at the embassy and ran as fast as he could to the palace. The city resembled a war zone. The shah's bodyguards, thinking him killed, had gone on a rampage, looting homes and businesses, shooting into crowds. Bystanders were stopped on the streets, beaten and robbed.

Smirnov made it safely to the palace grounds, where a mass of horsemen, soldiers, and courtiers were rushing to and fro, unsure what had happened or what to do about it. He pushed through the crowd on his way to the harem, but Prince Ahmed was nowhere to be found. How could they have failed to secure the location of the new shah? Where was the old eunuch who was supposed to guard him?

Frantic and on the verge of tears, Smirnov ran back outside. There, he found the ten-year-old crown prince in the garden, weeping and tearing out his hair. Smirnov went to him and pulled him close. The frightened boy looked up at the face of his tutor and asked if he could hide under his coat.

It turned out the shah had survived the attempt on his life. Having rebuffed Shapshal's repeated pleas not to go on holiday until the matter with parliament could be settled to the court's advantage, Mohammed Ali was heading to his vacation home in eastern Tehran. His family would follow later. The plan was to have the shah's French chauffeur, Monsieur Varné, drive him there in the imperial automobile, while Shapshal and the rest of his entourage followed behind in the royal carriage. When Varné arrived at the palace, however, he was told the plan had changed. The shah would no longer be riding in the car. Instead, he would accompany Shapshal in the carriage.

"If His Majesty does not get in the car, what is the reason for dropping the [privacy] curtains?" Varné asked the shah's guards.

"His Majesty will not ride," the guards repeated. They surrounded the automobile, as they normally would, and ordered Varné to drive.

As the royal convoy was leaving the city, someone flung what looked like a checkered napkin from the roof of a house at the shah's passenger-less automobile. A second later, the napkin exploded. Another bomb followed, killing one of the guards walking next to the car and wounding several bystanders (Varné survived unscathed).

The shah and Shapshal, safe inside the royal carriage, were unharmed. A badly shaken Mohammed Ali was swept from the scene and taken to the carriage driver's home where he waited for calm to descend upon the city. In the early evening, just before the sun went down, he and his entourage made it back to the palace on foot.

Telegrams were sent to the provinces informing the people that the shah had survived the assassination attempt and calling for joyous celebrations to be held in every city in honor of his escape from harm. Candles were burned and fireworks launched into the sky. Prayers rang out from every mosque. Across Persia, homes and streets lit up with illuminations.

"All these expressions of joy and happiness, which came solely from the special love of the nation, with no command from rulers or decree from the municipality, were the best evidence of the nation's warm feelings for His Majesty," the constitutionalist newspapers reported with a healthy dose of sarcasm.

To emphasize the gravity of the situation, and the importance of having every province respond appropriately, the telegram to Tabriz was sent by Ayatollah Behbehani himself. The Tabriz Anjoman sent a telegram back, expressing its sincere regrets over what had transpired, its sympathy for the shah and his family, and its joy over the fact that His Majesty had survived.

That very evening a special session of parliament was called. One by one the delegates took the podium to thank God for the shah's survival and to insist on a full investigation of the crime. The next day, the municipal police began pounding on doors. Anyone suspected of having anything to do with the plot was rounded up and carted away.

At any other point in the history of imperial Persia, what happened next would have been so routine as to be scripted: the police would arrest five or six people who harbored either anti-royalist sentiments or pro-constitutionalist leanings; they would beat a confession out of two or three of them; the guilty would be forced to publicly apologize to the nation for their heinous crimes; and then they would be hanged by their necks in the main square for all to see.

Yet it was precisely this kind of extra-judicial justice that the Persian Constitution had expressly banned. For the first time in the history of Persia, there were actual protections in place to keep the public from facing random arrests and indiscriminate punishments. Never mind that the country was in a state of emergency. What was the point in having a constitution if it did not apply in times of crisis?

So it must have come as something of a surprise when parliament received a formal letter from the Tabriz Anjoman reminding it of its sworn duty to uphold the constitution's guarantee to a fair trial, regardless of the alleged crime. The letter demanded that the delegates take immediate action to uphold the laws that they themselves had written. Feeling cornered by the anjoman and pressed by an increasingly agitated public, parliament had no choice but to comply. It issued warrants for the arrest of both the governor of Tehran and the city's chief of police for violating the constitutional rights of the people in the roundup of all those suspected in the plot against the shah.

It is difficult to exaggerate the historical significance of this unprecedented move. Persia was not the kind of place where the rich and powerful were held to account for their crimes. The protections of the law belonged only to those who could afford them. The notion that officials connected to the crown, much less the governor of the capital city and the chief of police, would actually face consequences for their actions, was just plain laughable. Twelve years before, when Nasir ad-Din Shah had been assassinated, Mohammed Ali had decapitated the assassin's associates and sent their stuffed heads to his father as a coronation gift. That is how justice was served in Persia. To claim that the shah's representatives should be punished for violating a constitution that the shah himself had been desperately trying to annul must have been viewed in Golestan Palace as some kind of joke. It was as though the delegates were daring the shah to try to shut down parliament again.

Yet something unexpected happened when the delegates arrived at the palace to deliver the warrants. Far from flying into a murderous rage, the shah quietly acquiesced to their demands. He ordered all the citizens who had been rounded up and imprisoned to be released at once. He then handed over the governor and the chief of police to be punished for their crimes against the constitution.

"Now that the people do not want me to pursue those who want to kill me," he declared from his throne, "I, too, will forget about it."

The delegates were dumbstruck. Was the shah having a laugh at their expense? Or was he seriously willing to put the attempt on his life behind him and move on in the name of maintaining his hard-fought peace with parliament? Was he now prepared to accept the legitimacy of the constitution? If so, it was truly a new day for the country. This was the constitutional monarchy so many Persians had dreamed of and bled for. The separation of powers. The rule of law. The inalienable rights of the people. It was all, at long last, coming to fruition.

So why not press for more?

A few days later, the emboldened delegates returned to the palace, this time with a petition asking, yet again, for the dismissal of the shah's more problematic ministers, including Shapshal Khan. It was a request that had been made many times before, and it had always been angrily dismissed. Hence, the astonishment of the delegates, when the shah unequivocally accepted the petition. He dismissed Shapshal Khan, expelling him and the other ministers—including the minister of war—from his presence that very day.

When word of the shah's capitulation spread throughout the country, there was dancing in the streets. Outside parliament, a band of euphoric delegates led the people in chants of "Long live the just King of Kings!" Parliament sent a lengthy telegram to the Tabriz Anjoman chastising it for its lack of faith in the shah. This was proof that compromise and cooperation could work. The shah has demonstrated his commitment to the new constitutional order. The people have won. It was time to lay down their arms and give up the fight.

The Tabriz Anjoman, however, remained skeptical. This did not sound like the Mohammed Ali they knew. In fact, the more they learned about the investigation into the assassination attempt, the less sense the whole thing made. The building from which the bombs had been thrown belonged to a goldsmith named Ghulam Reza. He was arrested and interrogated, though nothing came of it. However, one of his neighbors told investigators a curious story. He had seen none other than Shapshal Khan enter the building on more than one occasion. The police who searched the rooftop found bomb equipment and a fake beard. A newspaper published out of Calcutta claimed the bomb makers had been paid in rubles.

Eventually, a revolutionary by the name of Haydar Khan (aka "Haydar the Bomb Maker") was charged and arrested for the crime, but the Tabriz Anjoman continued asking questions about the shah's Russian tutor. None of them could say for certain who he was or how he'd risen to such prominence. He wasn't even Russian! He was a Jew from Crimea, born Seraya ben Mordechai, a revelation that led to a wave of anti-Semitic conspiracy theories about his identity and intentions. All anyone could say for certain was that he'd arrived in Tabriz one day, unannounced, having abruptly left his distinguished post as an interpreter in the Russian Foreign Office. And while he had no qualifications as an educator, and no references save a single letter written by one of his former professors, he was nevertheless given the job of teaching Russian to the crown prince, a position for which he was paid an astounding 16,000 rubles a year. Adjusted for inflation, that would have been about $250,000: a curious salary, considering that, after eight years under Shapshal's tutelage, Mohammed Ali could barely string together two sentences in Russian.

Whatever the truth about Shapshal Khan's involvement, the attempt on the shah's life had disabused Mohammed Ali of the notion that he could maintain peace with parliament. Cowering behind his garden walls, feeling vulnerable and under siege, the shah was now ready to fully embrace Liakhov's plan.

Meanwhile, inside Golestan Palace, Smirnov was doing his best to return to his teaching duties. The children were no longer allowed beyond the palace grounds, and as the room where Smirnov conducted his classes was located across the street, he now spent most of his time strolling through the garden with Ahmed, discussing current events, trying to alleviate his fears. That's where he was on June 3, 1908, when he and Ahmed witnessed the shah abruptly exit the palace along with a huge retinue of guards.

Word was he was leaving for *Bagh-e Shah*, a massive private park situated in the western part of Tehran, which served as a kind of home away from home for Qajar royalty. This, in and of itself, was not unusual. Bagh-e Shah was often used as a summer residence, a place where the Shah could relax, ride horses, and even watch races on his own personal track. What was unusual was the massive contingent of guards accompanying him on the trip. These were not the shah's regular bodyguards; they were hardened members of the

Cossack Brigade. Stranger still, the shah was going to his summer residence alone; his family, including the crown prince, would stay behind in Golestan Palace.

Smirnov went directly to Colonel Liakhov to find out what was going on. How long would the shah be gone? Why wasn't Ahmed going with him? And why had Liakhov sent the Cossack Brigade to accompany the shah on his vacation?

Liakhov, as was his wont, refused to answer any of these questions. Instead, he commanded Smirnov to stay locked inside the palace and to keep careful watch over the crown prince.

On whose authority was Liakhov giving these orders? Smirnov wanted to know.

On no one's authority but his own, Colonel Liakhov answered. The shah had just named him the new governor of Tehran. The city was now his to command.

Konstantin Nikolaevich Smirnov, tutor to Crown Prince Ahmed Qajar.

CHAPTER TEN

We Will Die so Freedom Can Live

FOR HOWARD BASKERVILLE, springtime in Tabriz would have come as a revelation. After a cold, hard winter, the city's gardens were gradually reopened. Everything was in bloom. Families spread out rugs beneath the almond blossoms. The whole of the city was scented in jasmine and rose.

The Persian New Year, known as *Norouz*, falls on the first day of spring, and on that first day of spring in 1908, the festivities in Tabriz were particularly raucous. The winter had been nothing but tension and turmoil. The city was ready for celebration.

For a few days at least, people fired their guns in the air instead of at each other. Children went door to door handing out apples and oranges and brightly colored eggs. Musicians marched through the streets, the *tar* and the *tanbur* kept in time by the rhythm of the *daf*. Bonfires blazed upon the rooftops, where residents gathered to jump over the flames in a New Year's ritual that went back thousands of years. Houses were packed with guests eating sweetmeats and drinking tea.

Now that the snow on the valley floor had melted, it was time to take the horses out again. That meant more time with Agnes. Ever since he'd moved out of the Wilson home, Baskerville had been seeing less of her. He still spent his Friday and Sunday evenings there, reading aloud by the fireplace; they were making their way through Dickens and had just reached *The Old Curiosity Shop*. Next up was *The Pickwick Papers*. During the week he often stopped by to seek help with his French pronunciation. And, of course, he sat with the family every morning at chapel. But the only time he and Agnes could ever be alone together was on horseback: two fresh-faced Americans living in a foreign land, galloping across the open plain, gradually falling in love.

The ripples of their romance are spread across the historical sources. A comprehensive report filed with the US secretary of state after Baskerville's death cites a confidential story told by one of his fellow missionaries: "It appears that Mr. Baskerville, who was very young, about 22, loved the 16 year old daughter of the Reverend Dr. Wilson."

Their romance had been simmering for some time. All those evenings spent reading books together, singing songs at the piano, eating lively Persian meals at the dining table—Howard was practically a part of the Wilson clan. He had, in Annie's words, entered "into all our family and social life."

The riding lessons served as the only opportunity to rekindle the late-night conversations they used to have when they lived under the same roof. But if Baskerville taught Agnes how to ride, Agnes taught him everything else. This was, after all, her land: *Azerbaijan*—"the land of fire." She was born here. She'd lived her whole life in this valley. She knew every ridge and canyon between the plains and the mountains. She could point out which caravansary ruin was once an essential stop along the old Silk Road, where in the village of Basmenj to buy pickled vegetables, who in Maragheh served the best sturgeon and black caviar. This wasn't the story of two Americans falling in love in a foreign land. Agnes was Persian.

Baskerville's riding lessons became so popular that he eventually extended them to his students—girls as well as boys. He began teaching tennis as well, and set up footraces on campus—all part of the school's focus on physical education. When one of the math teachers suddenly became ill, Baskerville volunteered to teach the girls' geometry course (he was always good at math). Little by little his inner circle of devoted students grew. You could see them gathering in the late afternoons, in this garden or that one, sharing a quiet nook, arguing about politics and books.

As each day grew longer and warmer, Baskerville felt more at home in his adopted city. The merchants barely acknowledged his presence in the bazaar, so familiar were they with his face. He could lean over the spice seller's basket and haggle with the best of them. At the same time, he was growing bolder about wading into the political affairs of the country, asking pointed questions of his students about the day-to-day situation in Tabriz. One day, while going over some homework with Sadeq Rezazadeh Shafaq, Baskerville suddenly put the assignment away and asked him his opinion about how the Constitutional Revolution was going. It was the first time the two of them had talked candidly about the topic.

Sadeq's family were committed constitutionalists firmly entrenched in the nationalist camp, and Sadeq himself exhibited a teenager's enthusiasm for the revolution. He told his teacher all he knew about the divisions in the town, the political leanings of its major families, and "the sentimental patriotism which prevailed among the youth." The past few months had been exhilarating: the shah's failed attempt to shut down parliament in December; his public atonement and recommitment to the constitution in January; the attempt on his life in February, and his surprisingly tepid response to it. The fight was far from over, but it was difficult not to feel like the crown was in retreat.

Meanwhile, the pace of progress in Persia was accelerating. The revolution was beginning to fulfill its promises. In March, parliament had finally given formal recognition to the dozens of women's anjomans that had popped up across the country, giving women a voice in government for the first time in Persia's history. There were now female-led unions, health clinics, and schools in almost every province. At the same time, much of the ethnic rivalries and communal loyalties that had riven the country for centuries were being replaced with goodwill and mutual cooperation. Muslims and Christians, Sunnis and Shi'ites, Persians, Turks, and Azeris were working together to build a better, more equitable Persia for all. With each passing day it felt like the Persian Constitution was truly here to stay.

Baskerville's conversation with Sadeq seemed to have unlocked something in him. In class, he began to speak more freely about the American Revolution, drawing direct parallels between the two countries and their respective struggles for freedom from tyranny. Still, these remained mostly private conversations. He was careful never to share his views publicly, lest he be expelled from his post. And the one thing he knew for certain was that he did not want to leave.

When Baskerville had originally accepted his commission to Tabriz, he had broken with protocol and committed only to two years of service, rather than the required three. Now, with his first year at the American Memorial School coming to an end, no one would have faulted him for wanting to go home early. Ever since the battle over the feast of sacrifice, Tabriz had begun to resemble a military camp. What began as occasional skirmishes between lootis loyal either to the nationalists or the royalists—honestly, it was difficult for Baskerville to tell them apart—had devolved into almost daily firefights between well-armed militias. Travel between wards had become difficult, with dozens of surly riflemen positioned at entry points, keeping a careful eye over who came and went.

Back home, Baskerville had likely never seen a dead body; here, they were sometimes sprawled across the sidewalks or slumped over in an alley, waiting for someone to recognize them. This was not what he had signed up for. At no point had anyone at the Presbyterian Board of Foreign Missions mentioned the possibility of civil war.

And yet, there was no denying it had been an intoxicating year. The soapbox preachers standing in the square extolling the masses to rise up against a godless tyrant. Farmers and factory workers willing to die for a constitution none of them knew how to read; the women dressed as men, and ready to die with them. Even the most mundane council debates were weighted with life-or-death consequences. How should tax revenue be spent? What should the powers of parliament encompass? How many seats for Christians and Jews? A republic or a constitutional monarchy? These were not lofty debates made by men wearing powdered wigs and posing in a tableau. They were late-night arguments held in packed teahouses, bodies pressed against each other, the air thick with sweat and smoke and the subtle scent of rose water. There was no way Baskerville was going to miss out on this.

That said, the only way to remain in Tabriz was to keep the revolution out of his classroom—a nearly impossible feat, to be sure, but one he had no choice but to attempt. And so, that spring, as the violence in the city grew worse and his students became increasingly distracted by the politics in the streets, Baskerville made an unusual decision. His English class would put on a play.

Persia, of course, has a long tradition of theatrical performances. The Greek historian Herodotus wrote at length about ancient Persian theater and dance. Yet, by Baskerville's time, Persian theater was largely a religious affair, anchored by the annual passion plays (*Taziyeh*) that reenacted the martyrdom of Husain at Karbala. An entire genre of Persia's dramatic arts was dedicated to "mourning performances," in which the audience would weep and beat their chests while actors took turns recounting stories of righteous suffering and unjust deaths. There were some nonreligious performances: minstrel shows and shadow plays, poetry readings and staged recitations of the *Shahnameh*: Persia's national epic. There was even the occasional musical performance. In fact, once a year, the Wilsons would muster a few instruments—piano, organ, guitar, violin, and a shepherd's flute played by a villager—and put on concerts at their home.

Baskerville, however, insisted on Shakespeare. And the play he

wanted to do was *The Merchant of Venice*, the story of a villainous Jewish moneylender named Shylock—referred to repeatedly throughout
the play simply as "the Jew"—and his foiled attempt to take "a pound
of flesh" from the heroic Antonio (the merchant of the play's title) as
payment for a defaulted loan.

Why Baskerville would have chosen this problematic play, with its
blatantly anti-Semitic themes, is impossible to say. Like most Christians of the time, he probably did not view it as problematic. At the
end of the play, a defeated Shylock's fortune is seized and he is forced to
convert to Christianity. As a missionary, Baskerville may have viewed
Shylock's offscreen conversion as an imitable act, something for his
students to mull over during their summer break.

The play was to be performed at the end of the school year as
part of the commencement ceremonies. Baskerville spent most of the
spring drilling his students in preparation. Rehearsals were excruciat-
ing, with the "actors" sometimes compelled to memorize their lines
one strained syllable at a time. But maybe it was all worth it just to get
to watch a kid like Sadeq, who by his own admission had never heard
of a Jew until he entered the American Memorial School, stand before
his schoolmates in the crowded hall, hand to chest, and say, "I am a
Jew: hath not a Jew eyes? hath not a Jew hands, organs, dimensions,
senses, affections, passions? . . . If you prick us, do we not bleed? . . .
and if you wrong us, shall we not revenge?"

With the end of the school year and the arrival of summer, the
campus grew quiet and the student body thinned out. Most of the
international faculty boarded trains bound for Paris and London, while
wealthy families, like Sadeq's, decamped for their summer homes along
the Caspian Sea. It was common practice for Presbyterian missionaries
to receive at least one furlough during their service so they could return
home for a few months and refresh the spirit. Baskerville could have
used the summer to go back to South Dakota and spend time with his
family or he could have traveled the region a bit, seen some of the sights

he had glimpsed in silhouette in all those brightly colored travel posters. But, then, he would have had to say goodbye to Agnes. Whatever the reason, he chose to stay in Tabriz during the sweltering summer months, which meant he was present on that day in early June when the Telegraph House suddenly went silent.

❖

IT IS IMPOSSIBLE to overstate just how much Persia relied on its telegraph network. The system had originally been built in 1868 by Germany's Siemens brothers, who received a concession from Nasir ad-Din Shah to construct and operate a line stretching from Tehran to Russia via Tabriz, and then onward to London. The telegraph connected Persia to the world. It became the new Silk Road—albeit, made of wires—facilitating trade and commerce with countries throughout Europe and Asia. By the turn of the century, practically the whole of Persia was rutted with telegraph poles, the cables linking one province to the next, like arteries carrying blood to the body, with Tehran its heart.

It was the telegraph that made modern Persia. The network the Siemens brothers built allowed the Qajar Dynasty to lay claim over the entirety of its realm, to centralize authority, and to exert its will upon every citizen, no matter how far-flung. Yet the same network that had rooted the Qajars to the Sun Throne was now being used to strip it away. The telegraph had become the primary tool for coordinating revolutionary activities. It amplified the voice of resistance, making it possible to bypass government censors and communicate directly with the people. Because manning a telegraph station required a high level of education and technical skill, most telegraph operators were primed to be sympathetic to the constitutional cause. The revolutionaries used these friendly operators to create a clandestine communications system that operated right under the government's nose. It's no exaggeration to say that, without the telegraph, there would have been no constitution, no parliament.

From the start, the anjoman in Tabriz understood that whoever controlled the Telegraph House controlled Tabriz. It therefore moved to secure the building in the first days of its fight with the crown. The Tabriz Telegraph House quickly became a kind of central command for the nationalists, a place to meet and discuss their plans for Persia, and then communicate those plans with their comrades in Tehran and elsewhere. Situated in the city's main square, next to the post office and the pockmarked courthouse, where the Bab was executed, the Telegraph House became the symbol of resistance, not just in Tabriz but also throughout the province of Azerbaijan. It was a secular shrine: a place of refuge for constitutionalists. During the darkest days of the struggle, people gathered there at all hours to hear preachers rail against the shah, to be reminded that their cause was just, that God himself was on their side. The Telegraph House is where Hassan Sharifzadeh had made his name. Standing on a crate, his voice booming over the assembled crowd, Hassan would give rousing speeches extolling the virtues of the constitution, patiently explaining the rights and freedoms it guaranteed for all people, in terms that made it easy for the crowd to understand.

"You are the true protectors of the masses!" he would shout. "You are the human empowerment forces of civilization!"

"Long live the revolution!" the crowd would respond.

It was during one of these gatherings that the first shots were fired in what would soon become an all-out war between Tehran and Tabriz. Three gunmen, sent from the capital, snuck into the city, ostensibly with help from royalist sympathizers. They mingled among the crowd in front of the Telegraph House, waiting for the arrival of the anjoman, which often conducted meetings there. As soon as the members arrived, the gunmen pulled out their weapons and began firing. They managed to shoot four members before the crowd turned on them.

After that, the decision was made to fortify the Telegraph House. A trench was dug in front of the entrance and fifty fighters were placed in and around the building to protect it from another attack. It didn't help.

Barely a month later, a militia from one of the royalist wards, spurred by the Islamic Anjoman and armed with weapons provided by the shah, launched a frontal assault on the Telegraph House. This was the summer of 1907, before Howard Baskerville had arrived in Tabriz, before Sattar Khan had taken control over the city's defenses. The constitutionalists guarding the building were taken by surprise: nearly half their force was killed in the first wave of the attack. The rest retreated through the back door. For the first time since the revolution had begun, the royalists were in control of the Telegraph House.

The problem was that the telegraph staff had also fled during the firefight, and none of the royalists had any idea how to use the equipment. They didn't even know how to send a message to Tehran informing the court of their victory. They were still trying to make heads or tails of the situation when the constitutionalists regrouped and returned with a massive force that easily regained control of the building. The Tabriz Telegraph House had remained in the hands of the constitutionalists ever since.

Hence, the concern that immediately flashed across the city on that day in June 1908 when the telegraph sounder, which had been clicking away almost nonstop for months, suddenly stopped, and the Telegraph House fell silent.

The Tabriz Anjoman scrambled to find out what could have happened. It sent out riders to check the lines, but everything seemed in place, at least in the vicinity of Tabriz. If the lines had been cut, it was done in Tehran. But why? What could the shah be planning? Purposely cutting communication between Persia's two largest cities would have been an unprecedented move with devastating consequences for the economy of the country. Could this have something to do with the rumors about the shah having holed himself up in his summer gardens?

What no one in Tabriz could have known—indeed, what the court had gone to great lengths to keep them from knowing—was that while Mohammed Ali was tucked away behind the walls of Bagh-e Shah, Rahim Khan, recently pardoned and released from prison, had left Tehran. He was now speeding toward Tabriz, ripping down telegraph lines along the way.

There was one man in town who had begun to figure out what was going on. Ever since he had been given command over the Constitutional Force, Sattar Khan had emerged as the undisputed leader of the revolution, and not just in Tabriz. His fame had spread beyond the city. Postcards were circulated in every province bearing his image, tall and elegant in his finely pressed suit, a gold chain dangling from his pants pocket, his silk kerchief positioned just so. The photos created a mythic aura around him. He became known as the "Iron Mountain." Persians everywhere were convinced he had magical powers, that he could not be harmed. Rumors were whispered in the shah's court that he was bulletproof. His presence on the battlefield was considered divine protection.

In a short time, Sattar Khan had created a fearsome fighting force composed of hundreds of devoted constitutionalists. Indeed, they called themselves *Feda'i*, "the devoted ones"—their devotion tied as much to the cause of constitutionalism as to the man who most clearly epitomized it. The Feda'i were the embodiment of the egalitarianism and mutual cooperation that Sadeq had boasted about to Baskerville: an army composed of Muslims and Christians, the poor and the powerful, men as well as women. The women, in particular, had become steadfast soldiers. Most no longer bothered cropping their hair and dressing as men. Some fought in veils, a fact that caused quite a scandal in Europe when their photographs were printed abroad. A few came straight from the fields, their babies bundled on their backs, rifles slung over their shoulders.

Sattar knew the devotion his soldiers had for him, and he encouraged it. He had a habit of popping in and out of firefights in multiple locations so that, afterward, fighters scattered across the battlefield would swear he had been at their side the whole time. It goes without saying that Sattar Khan was not bulletproof, yet he went to great lengths to conceal his many battle wounds. Whenever the fighting was at its worst and all seemed lost, he would stand at the front line and shout for his men to charge past him. And they would, without fear of consequence, convinced that nothing could hurt them as long as the People's Commander was there. His very existence on the side of the constitution gave meaning to a revolution whose objectives he himself did not fully understand.

"We are not fighting to put the free in a cage," he would instruct his fighters. "We are fighting to free the caged."

Foreign journalists began to flock to Tabriz in order to write fawning profiles of the brigand turned military commander. "He has the eyes of a leader," read a piece in the London *Times*. "Their tint is the nearest approach to steel-grey that you can find in the Persian coloring, and he shoots a quick convincing glance at you from beneath clearly pencilled brows. . . . The writer has seen him in repose, and also during the stress of engagement that was at the time not progressing well. In both circumstances the magnetism of his personality was very marked."

The Tabriz Anjoman had done an admirable job mobilizing the middle class, turning merchants and artisans, guild members and transportation workers, into amateur revolutionaries ready to strap on a rifle and run headlong into battle. But it was Sattar who attracted the poor and marginalized to the cause. With Baqer always at his side, he would give rousing speeches—not in the flowery language of great orators like Hassan Sharifzadeh or Mirza Ansari, but in the rough colloquial tongue spoken by the vast majority of Persian citizens—urging the people to give up their traditional grievances with each other and focus the fight on the crown. "Our enemies succeed when we become enemies to each other," he liked to say.

Under Sattar's leadership, the Feda'i grew into a well-trained fighting force. He set up target practice in the desert and trained bakers and cheesemongers to become expert marksmen. He drilled theology students in military maneuvers, fully integrated the female fighters with the men, and marched alongside the young and the old. Sitting atop his horse, surveying his troops, he would remind them of what was at stake in this fight. "None of you has the right to deem himself a lord of people, to feel himself superior to those without guns in their hands or, God forbid, bully them," he'd shout. "We will die so freedom can live."

When Sattar found out about the problem with the telegraph lines, he understood at once what it meant: the shah was prepping another attack on parliament. Why else would he have cut off communication? Clearly, he had learned a lesson from the failure of his first attempt to close parliament. The only way to subdue Tehran was to isolate it from Tabriz. The shah knew that if parliament were to call for help, Tabriz would send an army to defend it. But what if parliament couldn't call?

Sattar's hunch was bolstered by an article in the London *Times*, which noted that the shah had been surreptitiously purchasing hundreds of rifles and distributing them among the rural districts on the outskirts of the capital. "The Shah has been continually increasing his force outside the town," the article reported. "Hundreds of tribesmen are joining his camp daily. . . . There are a good many ruffians from the city in the camp. They are supplied with uniforms, provisions, arms, and ammunition."

While the Tabriz Anjoman was deliberating what to do about the cut telegraph lines, Sattar burst into the session and told them exactly what he thought was happening. The shah was planning a coup. The peace agreement had been a ruse, the relative quiet nothing more than preparation for war. He presented the esteemed council members with a proposal. "If the anjoman provides me with fifty horsemen, I will go to Tehran and plant the flag of the Constitution on the roof of the [parliament]."

The Tabriz Anjoman gave him three hundred.

The next day, they left for Tehran, with Sattar and Baqer riding out front. That's when Rahim Khan showed up.

The timing of Rahim's arrival could not have been a coincidence. Considering the decades-long enmity that existed between the two men, Rahim could have expected nothing short of a bullet to the head had he tried to enter Tabriz while Sattar was still around. But with Sattar no longer in the city, Rahim Khan was ready to play his part in Liakhov's plan.

Having ridden all the way from Tehran, he'd stopped short in a village just a few miles from Tabriz. From there, he sent a letter to the Tabriz Anjoman begging to be forgiven for his past crimes. He had turned over a new leaf while in prison, he claimed. He wanted permission to enter Tabriz so that he could "join hands with the people" against the shah. He had come alone; he posed no harm to the city or its inhabitants. All he wanted to do was help. He had heard about the increasingly lawless behavior of the Shahsevan in his absence; he was there to reclaim his position as tribal leader and to bring its members to heel.

The Shahsevan had indeed been causing havoc in the province. Ever since they had ridden down from the mountains at the shah's urging, they'd been rampaging through the region, blocking roads, plundering villages, and inching ever closer to Tabriz. Recently, they had entered Urmia, the closest major city to Tabriz, where they had slaughtered dozens of men, women, and children, tossing corpses beyond the city walls to be eaten by dogs. Sattar had set up fortifications and barricades across the city to prevent a similar attack in Tabriz, but it was only a matter of time before the Shahsevan appeared at the gates. Besides, Sattar was gone; he had taken three hundred fighters with him. What would Tabriz do if the Shahsevan arrived in their absence? Who would defend them?

Despite these concerns, the Tabriz Anjoman hesitated. Rather than allow Rahim to enter Tabriz, it sent representatives to the village where he was staying. There, Rahim was made to swear on the Quran that he would defend the constitution with his life, that he would not raise a hand against the city, that he would do whatever it took to send the Shahsevan back to their settlements in the mountains of Qaradagh. Only then was he escorted back to Tabriz.

Once he was face to face with the Tabriz Anjoman, Rahim formally offered his services to the constitutionalist cause. If Tabriz gave him money and arms, he would ride to Qaradagh and unite the various tribes there under his command. Together, they would go to Urmia and liberate the city from Shahsevan control before returning in triumph to Tabriz to join the fight against the shah.

The members of the Tabriz Anjoman were in a bind. They did not trust Rahim but were genuinely afraid of the Shahsevan. Who knew how long Sattar would be gone or if he would even return? With the telegraph lines cut, there was no way to reach out to the People's Commander for advice on the matter.

In the end, the anjoman gave Rahim Khan eight hundred rifles, two cannons, and 18,000 tomans, and sent him off to Qaradagh to gather a cavalry for the cause. Rahim took the arms and the money and rode directly to Urmia where he promptly delivered them to the Shahsevan—a small price to pay to regain his position at the head of the tribe.

Now armed to the teeth, the riders mounted their horses and turned toward Tabriz.

Sattar Kahn (in white) beside Baqer Khan, posing with members of the Feda'i.

CHAPTER ELEVEN

Today, I Know That I Am a Shah

THIS COULD NOT HAVE been how Vladimir Platonovich Liakhov thought his military career would come to a close: standing in a burned-out garden, on foreign soil, watching the natives scatter blindly before his cannons.

Born to a modest landowning family from the Kuban region on the Black Sea, Liakhov was the picture of the stiff-backed Russian officer: epaulets dangling from his broad shoulders, chest festooned with medals honoring one saint or another, one arm bent formally behind his back, the other resting always on his ceremonial sword. He was blunt, dispassionate, detached, and cold: a man who paid no mind to anyone's thoughts or concerns and who cared about nothing save the greater glory of Mother Russia.

Liakhov was not unaccustomed to dealing with troublesome populations. He had done the same in Tbilisi, where his service on the General Staff coincided with the Russian Revolution of 1905. It was not an easy post. Tbilisi had become a hotbed of anti-imperial activity against the tsar. The city was home to one of the most notorious bank robberies of the twentieth century and was organized by top-level Bolsheviks, including Vladimir Lenin and Joseph Stalin. The robbers, Stalin among them, used homemade bombs to attack a stagecoach transporting money between a local branch of the Russian State Bank and the Tbilisi post office. They got away with 341,000 rubles, about $4 million in today's currency. The money was meant to fund ongoing revolutionary activities against the tsar. But because it was composed mostly of 500-ruble bills, their serial numbers had been marked by the authorities, making it impossible to spend the bills in Russia. After months of trying unsuccessfully to exchange the bills overseas, Lenin ended up setting fire to the loot.

Liakhov had already been reassigned to Persia by the time the great Bolshevik robbery took place, yet he could not help but marvel at the boldness of the act, the sheer valiance and probity of it all. That was the difference between a Russian—even a miscreant like Lenin—and these simple-minded Persians, as far as Liakhov was concerned. A true Russian was motivated by nothing more than love of country. He was a son willing to endure any hardship so that his mother—the person who gave him life—could thrive. The Bolsheviks were misguided, of course; love can make you do foolish things. Liakhov had treated the rebellion in Tbilisi with brutal efficiency. But he had also admired it, in a way he simply could not admire the Persian Constitutional Revolution.

In his brief time in Persia, Liakhov had bribed so many officials and court ministers, coercing them to carry out whatever duty was required, that he now viewed the entire Persian population as little more than a nation of treacherous self-seekers with no sense of nobility. Try as he might, he could not picture a single one of them setting fire to a mountain of money just for the principle of it.

After his success in Tbilisi, Liakhov had received all the requisite honors and accommodations. He should have been a major general stationed in St. Petersburg, serving at the right hand of the tsar. Instead, he was sent to Persia to babysit the shah. No Russian officer wanted command of the Cossack Brigade, least of all Liakhov. The position was short-lived and untenable. The commanders of the Cossack Brigade were all Russians handpicked by St. Petersburg, but they served the shah. They had to constantly balance their allegiance to their homeland with their duty to the Persian government. Russia sought to smooth over the perception of dual loyalties by removing the commanders it sent to Persia from its active-duty list. Liakhov was technically retired from the Russian military. And yet, he still wore his Russian uniform, glittering medals and all. It's just that now his salary was paid by the shah. Sort of.

Liakhov's command of the Cossack Brigade occurred during a particularly difficult time. The brigade was essentially bankrupt. The soldiers were armed with surplus artillery from the Russian military, but the shah's coffers were empty, and the men had gone months without wages. So the shah did what all previous shahs did in times of financial distress: he begged Russia for yet another loan. Nicholas happily advanced him the money he needed, putting Persia even deeper into Russian debt and ensuring that the Cossack Brigade, while still nominally a Persian force, would be beholden to the tsar's largesse.

Liakhov used the money to whip the force into shape. Soon, the Cossack Brigade was, in his humble opinion, "the only force in Persia which can be called a military force, according to the meaning of that term elsewhere in the world." The brigade took on double duty. Not only did it assume all internal security functions on behalf of the shah; it became a kind of independent police force guaranteeing the lives and property of foreign residents throughout the country. Liakhov's men served as guards to the foreign missions and embassies in Tehran and provided protection to most of the foreign-owned banks and businesses. When the Persians began grumbling about paying a toll enacted by a British firm in order to use a particular road, Liakhov sent a detachment of the brigade to enforce payment at the tollgates.

That said, Liakhov's primary mission as head of the Cossack Brigade was as clear as could be: put an end to the Constitutional Revolution. That was the entire reason the tsar had sent him to Persia. It was why he had endured so much during the past year at court—the shah's incessant dawdling, Shapshal's self-serving schemes, Smirnov's sideways glances—all so he could arrive at this moment, when the city would finally be placed in his hands and he could put an end to the crisis once and for all. Maybe then he could finally go home.

The plan was simple enough. Liakhov had detailed every step in a series of back-and-forth memos with his superiors in St. Petersburg. First, he would have the shah lull parliament into a state of complaisance, "pretending that there is a desire to come to terms with it on a basis of mutual concessions, and with that purpose to enter into negotiations." That step had already been achieved, and with little effort, thanks to the sheer gullibility of the elected delegates. They were so desperate to avoid conflict with the shah that they actually believed His Majesty would dismiss and arrest his own ministers—Shapshal even! Any government that foolish deserved to be overthrown.

The next step would be more difficult. Before any military action could be taken, the people had to be disarmed. That was the shah's biggest blunder the first time he tried to shut down parliament. Three years of revolutionary activity had flooded Tehran with thousands of weapons. Any hint of a coup and the people would once again grab their rifles and rush into the streets to defend the constitution. That could not be allowed to happen. If Liakhov's plan had any hope of succeeding, they needed to seize these weapons at once. This is where the tribes came in, the "ruffians from the city in the camp" that the London *Times* article had mentioned.

On the morning of June 4, 1908, at 8:30 a.m., a sudden din arose from the city center as a group of tribesmen, armed by the shah, burst onto the streets, howling and screeching, firing guns into the air. They seized everyone in their path, beating and robbing them in the open. Terrified bystanders rushed for cover, shaken by the noise. The merchants closed their shops. Students ran home from school. No one knew who the culprits were. People assumed a war had broken out.

In the mayhem that ensued, the shah declared martial law. The

Cossack Brigade took to the streets, ostensibly to restore law and order. Whenever they saw a pistol or rifle on someone, they confiscated it. They marched to the homes of known constitutionalists and forcibly removed any weapons stored inside, in the name of security. The arms were collected in a pile and delivered directly to Bagh-e Shah, where Mohammed Ali was holed up, with both Shapshal and his minister of war still at his side.

So far, things were proceeding as planned. Only Tabriz could muck it all up. To avoid that possibility, the shah had taken the extraordinary step of ordering Rahim Khan to cut the telegraph lines, putting a stop to nearly all communications throughout the country. Now, news of what was transpiring in Tehran could not be transmitted to other cities. Liakhov went one step further and cut the wires belonging to the British embassy. During previous disturbances, the embassy had been used as a place of refuge for revolutionaries fleeing the shah's forces. The Russian was determined not to allow that to happen again, even if it meant breaking diplomatic protocols.

Once a measure of calm had been restored in the city, the shah issued a declaration titled "The Way to Salvation and Hope for the Nation." In it, he publicly attacked parliament for the first time since his failed attempt to shut it down the previous December, calling it "a den of thieves" that had "deceived the poor, simpleminded" people.

"What oaths have they taken which they have not broken? What agreements have they made which they have seen through the end?" the shah asked rhetorically. "Do you still doubt that a number of corrupting people had any goal other than to destroy your houses?"

In a brazen attempt at gaslighting the entire Persian nation, the shah declared himself to be the true guardian of constitutionalism and accused the parliament of having undermined democracy. "It is obvious, and one would not be mistaken in saying, that Our Royal Person has taken such steps in advancing the Constitution and the ease and well-being of the kingdom that we have not refrained from any measures," he wrote. "We heard all that they have said. We have done all they requested."

This was as clear a declaration of war as there could be, and it sent parliament into a frenzy. The prime minister took it upon himself to clarify the shah's intentions. Along with his entire cabinet, he appeared before His Majesty at Bagh-e Shah to formally present parliament's concerns regarding his inflammatory rhetoric. The shah listened calmly to the delegation but made no response. He simply heard their words and then bid them farewell before retiring to his chambers. Not knowing what else to do, the delegation turned to leave, only to see their path blocked by Cossack guards, who seized them and put them in chains.

When news of the shah's treachery reached parliament, an emergency session was called. The delegates crowded inside the parliament building, clamoring for their chance to speak. How should they respond to this unexpected act of aggression?

The consensus in the chamber seemed to be that this was all a big misunderstanding. Perhaps another delegation should be sent to the shah to inquire about the fate of the first one? Or they could write a sternly worded letter, reminding His Majesty of his obligations under the constitution. The members were still debating what to do when they heard a rumble coming from the gardens surrounding the building. They pressed against the windows to see what was happening.

What they saw was Colonel Liakhov and his men taking up positions on the perimeter of the parliament building. They had six cannons with them.

Panic gripped the parliament. There could no longer be any doubt as to the shah's intentions. The Ayatollahs Tabatabai and Behbehani, both of whom had been repeatedly urging moderation, wrote an urgent telegram to Tabriz, begging for help. "His Highness suddenly, in a very frightening manner . . . ordered several of the leading chiefs arrested and brought cannons outside the gates [of parliament]. The people are in great turmoil over the current frightful situation."

It did no good, of course. The telegraph lines had been cut.

Realizing that no help would be coming, the anjoman in Tehran took it upon itself to come to the rescue. It managed to gather about a thousand volunteers pulled from members of various councils representing the other cities and provinces in Persia. The volunteers armed themselves with what few guns and rifles they could muster and ran to parliament to place their bodies between the cannons and the building. A standoff ensued.

Days passed as the delegates trapped inside the parliament building repeatedly tried to negotiate with the shah. But Mohammed Ali was hiding out at Bagh-e Shah and not interested in negotiating. Eventually, Liakhov lost patience and sent one of the Cossack colonels, a Persian by the name of Gholam Reza Khan, inside the building to give the delegates an ultimatum. The armed vigilantes outside were only making matters worse, Gholam Reza argued. The shah viewed them as anarchists trying to overthrow his rule. Their presence on parliament grounds was an affront, not just to the court, but to the constitution and the rule of law the delegates claimed to uphold. The shah would not stand for it. If they did not leave at once, His Majesty would be compelled to act with force. "Let them be dispersed so that we might continue our negotiations."

Incredibly, parliament fell for the ruse. Ayatollah Behbehani himself went out and personally ordered the volunteers to disarm and disperse so that the shah could not use them as an excuse to move against parliament. The old cleric was still desperate to avoid bloodshed. He made the men swear not to "kill their brothers" and offered to lead them all in a prayer of blessing for their fallen comrades if only they would put down their weapons and go home. Most of them did. Only a handful refused the order and stayed.

"They had called the people *anarchists*. They want to discredit them among the civilized peoples. Now they can no longer do anything," one delegate foolishly boasted, after the volunteers were made to leave. "The mouth of the enemies who had made [these] shameful accusations, calling [the people] riotous and rebellious, has been shut, and it has become clear to friend and foe that the people do not intend riot and rebellion."

The dispersal of the armed supporters opened the way for the final step in Liakhov's plan. On the morning of June 23, a small group of Cossacks, dressed as civilians, snuck onto parliament grounds and began shooting wildly into the air, "to give an excuse for the bombardment," Liakhov admitted in his secret memos to St. Petersburg.

Accompanied by six Russian officers and a thousand Cossack soldiers, Colonel Liakhov moved swiftly to deal with the "disturbance." He barred the parliament doors so that no one could get out, then surrounded the building with his troops.

Still desperate to come up with a peaceful end to the crisis, Ayatollah Behbehani sent a message to Liakhov, requesting a face-to-face meeting. Liakhov refused. The handful of armed volunteers who had remained inside the building climbed up to the roof and took positions, their rifles aimed at the Cossacks below. They requested permission from parliament to shoot Liakhov. He was mounted on his horse, in the middle of the fray, with no concern for his safety. But the request was denied. No matter what happened, the men were told, they could not shoot any Russian officer—certainly not Liakhov—lest it be used as an excuse for a full-blown Russian invasion.

For a few hours, the two sides exchanged bullets. "Severe fighting this morning in the city between the troops and the political societies [anjomans]," the American legate, John B. Jackson, wrote in an urgent telegram to the State Department. "Artillery was used. State of siege proclaimed by the Shah. . . . Foreigners are in no special danger."

And then, a little after noon, the cannons opened fire. Their roar shook the foundations of the parliament building; the windows shattered at the sound. Liakhov's forces began their slow advance. Every few minutes, the cannons were loaded and fired in unison, followed by the call to move closer. Soon, the Cossacks were mere steps from the building's entrance.

The marksmen on the roof switched tactics and began focusing their shots not on the advancing soldiers, but rather on the those manning the cannons, picking them off one by one. This went on for some time and, for a brief moment, the tide seemed to be turning toward the constitutionalists. Encouraged by their progress, a few of the volunteer fighters made a mad rush to seize the unmanned cannons as trophies. Most of them fell in a hail of bullets, though they did manage to drag two cannons back inside the building. An incensed Liakhov ordered his officers to take command of the remaining cannons, knowing the Russians would not be shot at.

The fuses were lit. The cannons fired. And the parliament building, with most of the delegates still inside, was reduced to rubble.

A few managed to survive the destruction, including the Ayatollahs Behbehani and Tabatabai. They were put in chains and brought before the shah. There, in the presence of their former colleague Ayatollah Nuri, who had been brought to Bagh-e Shah in the royal carriage to witness their humiliation, the two elderly ayatollahs were passed back and forth among the soldiers, beaten, slapped, and punched. Their turbans were removed, their clothes torn off, their beards ripped out by the fistful.

The following day, Cossack soldiers sacked the homes of anyone associated with the constitution. Liakhov pinned up a proclamation around town announcing his takeover of the city: "The regulation of all the affairs and dispositions of the Capital is entrusted to the officers and Cossacks of His Imperial Majesty's Brigade."

The constitutionalists begged the American legate to intervene and put a stop to the arbitrary arrests and mass executions. But John B.

Jackson was unmoved. He had completely fallen for Liakhov's stunt. In a memo to his superiors in Washington, he claimed that Liakhov had personally assured him that "his intention had been to avoid bloodshed, but to arrest certain political leaders. While endeavoring to do this, the Andjumans [*sic*] fired again, and then it was realized that energetic action must be taken."

The constitutionalists turned to Britain, hoping it would support their cause against the Russian-backed shah. But the British had no intention of antagonizing the tsar or violating the Anglo-Russian Convention. Even after Liakhov sent his men to surround the British embassy in order to prevent the fleeing delegates from taking refuge there, the British government still refused to act. It decried the bombardment of parliament in general terms. Yet, like the Americans, it refused to pin responsibility on Russia itself.

"Russia was not responsible for Colonel Liakhoff's [*sic*] actions," the British foreign secretary, Sir Edward Grey, declared. "He had acted without the knowledge and approval of the Russian Government."

This was demonstrably false. Liakhov went to great lengths to pretend that his duty was to the shah. "I am in the service of the Shah," he told a British journalist; "I receive payment from the Persian Government, and therefore in cases of political disorders no other course is open to me but that of active struggle in the interests of the Shah." But the truth was he answered to no one but "the Most Puissant Ruler of Mighty Russia," as he addressed Tsar Nicholas II in his secret memos. In all his communications with St. Petersburg, Liakhov repeatedly cites his "readiness to sacrifice everything for the carrying out of the Monarch's Will"—meaning, of course, the monarch of Russia. Indeed, after the bombardment of parliament, the tsar sent Liakhov a personal letter congratulating him on his great success.

"Well done gallant Cossacks," the tsar wrote. "Thank you brave officers."

The shah, of course, was more than willing to play along with

Liakhov's lie. Now that the coup had succeeded, he assumed full responsibility for it. "My forefathers conquered this country by the sword," he pronounced to his court. "I am the son of these same forefathers and I will reconquer this country by the sword."

Emboldened by his victory, the shah arrested the editors of all the city's liberal newspapers—the ones who had spoken so disrespectfully about him for months. He had them brought before his presence at Bagh-e Shah and watched, stoically, as Shapshal Khan personally strangled each of them in turn.

"Today," Mohammad Ali cried out with satisfaction, "I know that I am a Shah."

Persia's democratic experiment was finished. All that remained now was to tame Tabriz.

CHAPTER TWELVE

Resistance Is Equal to Suicide

THE PLAN WAS TO synchronize the attacks on Tehran and Tabriz—to strike the head and the heart of the revolution at the same time. Despite the downed telegraph lines, the royalists in Tabriz had managed to remain in contact with Tehran; they were fully aware of what was happening there. They had placed their forces at strategic locations along the Mehraneh River, which bisected the city and served as the de facto border between the mostly royalist wards in the north and the nationalist wards in the south. Marksmen were barricaded atop minarets and at other high vantage points, waiting for the signal from Tehran.

On the morning of June 23, 1908, a few hours before Liakhov's cannons began firing upon the parliament building in Tehran, bullets started raining down on the homes of the nationalists who lived on the opposite bank of the river in Tabriz. Few missed their mark. The heaviest casualties came from Khiyaban, Baqer Khan's ward. Baqer, of course, had left Tabriz days ago, along with Sattar Khan and three hundred fighters, en route to Tehran to help protect parliament.

The royalists had been given explicit orders to take the city by force. "We have arrested all the seditious [in Tehran]," read a secret message sent by the shah to the royalist leader Mir Hashem. "Get busy yourself with full force eliminating the seditious [in Tabriz] and ask for any kind of reinforcement. I am ready."

The nationalists managed to repel the royalist advance. The fighting continued for hours, but when the sun finally set, not one inch of Tabriz had changed hands.

Meanwhile, news of the destruction of parliament began spreading to every corner of Persia. Most of the elected delegates were either buried in rubble or dragged in chains to Bagh-e Shah. Their homes had been sacked, their valuables seized as spoils. The Cossack Brigade patrolled the streets of the capital, enforcing martial law. Newspapers were shuttered and all anjomans forced to disband. It was over; the shah had won.

Despair blanketed the country as, one by one, the cities laid down their arms: Isfahan and Shiraz, Ardabil, Mashhad, and Kermanshah. The constitution had been defeated everywhere in Persia.

Everywhere, except Tabriz.

Howard Baskerville was in Urmia, ninety miles west of Tabriz, when the fighting had begun. He was accompanying Samuel Wilson there for a tour of the mission founded by Justin Perkins and Charlotte Bass. This was as close to a summer vacation as Baskerville would get, and he planned to make the most of it. He had spent the previous two weeks in bed with a high fever and severe stomachache. It was thought to be typhoid, but no one knew for sure. Annie stayed at his side day and night, slowly nursing him back to health.

Once the fever broke and he was back on his feet, Samuel suggested a brief jaunt to the mission in Urmia. They could visit the lake region and enjoy the cool breeze, take a hike in the Kurdish mountains, and visit the vibrant Christian community in the nearby village of Seir, where Annie was born. It would be fun to spend some time getting to know the large group of American missionaries stationed in the area.

The Urmia mission was run by the Rev. William Ambrose Shedd, whose parents had served under Justin and Charlotte. Like Annie,

Shedd was born in Seir, though he had moved to the United States in his teens to study at Princeton (where else?). After graduation, Shedd returned to Urmia to take charge of what was now the oldest, largest, and wealthiest mission in all of Persia.

Urmia boasted more than a hundred missionary schools and even had its own teaching hospital. There were twenty-one missionary families residing in the city (compared to about a dozen in Tabriz), along with a number of missionary doctors, nurses, and teachers, nearly two-thirds of whom were women: Charlotte's legacy. And while the air and altitude of mountainous Urmia would have undoubtedly been a welcomed refuge from the dry, dusty valley of Tabriz, there could have been another reason why Samuel Wilson had suggested the trip—one that involved the large number of single Christian women in the city.

Not long before their trip to Urmia, Howard Baskerville had come to Samuel Wilson to ask for his daughter's hand in marriage. This could not have come as a surprise to Wilson, but he nevertheless refused the proposal. It wasn't just Agnes's youth that was at issue; she was seventeen now and past the age of legal consent at the time. It was the plans he had made for her. Agnes had just been accepted to Vassar College in Poughkeepsie, New York. With any luck, she would be leaving for New York in the fall. Howard knew this, of course; it's why he wanted to propose to her before she left. They could spend the next year apart before reuniting in Poughkeepsie. Wilson, however, refused to consider it.

We don't know how Agnes responded to her father's rejection, but it seems to have thrown Baskerville into a fit of depression. William Doty writes about his "strange conduct" during this time. The rejection may have had something to do with his sudden, unexplained bout of illness. But it could have also spurred this sudden trip to Urmia. Awkward as it may have been, this was an opportunity for Howard and Samuel to spend some time together. They could mend their frayed relationship. And if, by chance, the young man happened to connect with one of the many single female missionaries stationed in Urmia, all the better.

It all came to naught, of course. The trip was cut short when rumblings reached Urmia of an attack on parliament. And then the news came from Tabriz.

A distraught Baskerville insisted they go back at once "to help defend the others," and Samuel agreed. The city they returned to was a smoldering wreck. There was debris in the streets. Unfamiliar men squatted in the alleys, rifles at the ready. The anjoman had forbidden all public gatherings after sunset. The bazaar was closed, the mosques boarded up, the garden gates locked.

The American Memorial School was, as usual, untouched by the violence in the city. "None of us at the mission felt any sense of personal danger," Agnes recalled, some years later. The campus was mostly empty, the students gone for summer break. All that remained were the missionaries and staff. They boarded themselves inside the school and waited for calm to descend upon the city. It did not matter which side won the war—whether under the crown or the constitution, the Americans would be safe. This is what Samuel had worked so diligently for; this is why he had remained neutral. As long as he refused to pick a side, he, his family, and the school he built would be protected.

Baskerville, however, had other priorities. He needed to locate his friend, Hassan Sharifzadeh, who was nowhere to be found. His room was vacant; his books and clothes left behind. No one had seen him during the fighting. It was as though he had simply disappeared.

Baskerville could be forgiven for assuming the worst. Hassan had many enemies in the city, and not just among the royalists. Over the past few months, as the revolutionaries in Tabriz had grown more extreme in their response to the shah's actions, Hassan had only amplified his calls for moderation. He condemned both sides for the atrocities committed upon each other and on the city's residents.

But he reserved his scorn for his fellow revolutionaries, from whom he expected so much more. When an angry mob of nationalists tried to burn down the home of a royalist who had been caught in some transgression or other, Hassan physically placed his body between the crowd and the man's house.

"The world is looking at us!" he shouted at his comrades. "Such violence would disgrace our cause."

The intervention had won him few friends in Tabriz. The mullahs hated Hassan for his damning diatribes against them. The royalists wanted him executed for treason. The nationalists wished he would just go away. If, indeed, he had been killed in the chaos that engulfed the city while Baskerville was gone, it would be difficult to know who had pulled the trigger.

As it turned out, Hassan was very much alive. He had taken refuge inside the French consulate in Tabriz as soon as he found out parliament had been destroyed. He knew as well as anyone that he was no longer safe in the city, not even from his fellow constitutionalists. He was anxious and inconsolable, not eating or sleeping. He barely spoke to anyone. He had few visitors. Those who did see him could not recognize the fiery preacher of freedom who had so passionately rallied the masses to revolution. It was as though his confidence in the cause had crumbled along with the parliament building. "I'm seeing an abundance of emotions within myself that I had never seen before," Hassan wrote to a friend from his solitary room in the French consulate. "I sit, then I stand up, I pace up and down the room, sometimes I lie down, but all these movements occur without me instigating them."

It wasn't merely the loss of parliament or the destruction of the constitution that had plunged Hassan into a deep well of depression. Hassan believed what Baskerville believed: that democracy was a divine gift from God bestowed upon all peoples; that those who fought for freedom were acting on God's behalf; that as surely as good conquers evil and light defeats the darkness, the people of Persia would prevail over the blood-thirsty tyrant in Tehran.

But that didn't happen. Evil had triumphed. The tyrant was victorious. Could it be that everything they had bled for was lost? All the marches and speeches, the secret late-night meetings, the sacrifices they had made, the death and destruction—was it all for nothing?

"I struggle to lay back and deceive myself that it's [still] only the beginning," Hassan confessed, "but it is not effective."

Baskerville could not help his friend. He, too, must have felt the same sense of loss and desperation. This was not how he thought the democratic experiment in Persia would end, not according to what Woodrow Wilson had taught him. What about the progress of civilization? What happened to the moral judgment of God?

For the moment, at least, it seemed that God had abandoned Persia. The two friends, who had bonded over their shared commitment to liberty and universal rights, who had spent hours exchanging theories and sharing dreams, could do nothing now but watch the city burn before their eyes.

❖

SATTAR KHAN HAD gotten wind of the attack on parliament before it had even begun and was clever enough to understand what that meant for Tabriz. He was nearly at the capital with his riders when they suddenly turned their horses and raced back home. They arrived around the same time as Baskerville and Wilson, just in time for the fighting in the city to pick up again.

Once more, the royalists tried to advance across the river. Once more, they were thwarted. With Baqer back in charge of Khiyaban and Sattar in control of Amirkhiz—the two largest nationalist wards—the constitutionalists rallied, pushing the shah's allies back to their barricades. If His Majesty thought taking Tabriz would be as easy as taking Tehran, he was sorely mistaken.

For days the two sides exchanged fire at all hours. No one could sleep. Entire neighborhoods were abandoned, houses set ablaze and left to burn. Fear gripped the city. But while little territory was gained on either side, the battle for hearts and minds was already being lost, as the poor in Tabriz began deserting the revolution en masse.

Their loyalties had been shifting for some time. The poor had supported the constitutional cause because they were told it would mean cheaper bread, more jobs, less corruption, a better life. But here they were, three years into the struggle, and prices were higher than ever before, thanks to the ongoing conflict with Tehran. Where were the improvements they'd been promised? Where were the jobs? Now that parliament, the seat of constitutional government, had been destroyed, what incentive was there to continue to suffer? You cannot feed your children with slogans and banners.

The royalists, seeking advantage, stoked these sentiments by appealing to religion. As in Tehran, fatwas were plastered across Tabriz calling for jihad against the constitutionalists. "Muslims! Make an effort! Where is your honor?" the flyers proclaimed. "Islam is on the verge of being lost. Jihad is mandatory for every one of you in order to erase the root of these religionless people from the earth."

The ploy worked. Spurred by threats of damnation from anti-constitutional clerics, the poor in Tabriz began flocking to the ranks of the royalists.

After nearly a week of street battles, with nothing gained or lost, a tenuous calm finally descended upon the city: a chance to put out fires and bury bodies. It was during this brief lull in fighting that the Russian consul in Tabriz, a man by the name of Pokhitonov, took it upon himself to go ward by ward, issuing a general amnesty to all the shah's enemies. The consul claimed to have secured a promise from the crown to forgive anyone who immediately laid down their guns and went back to their homes. The tsar himself would guarantee their safety. All they had to do was to put all this foolishness behind them and return to life as it once was in the land of the Lion and the Sun.

Thousands took him up on the offer: not only battle-weary merchants and farmers who had just learned to shoot, but even some of the most senior members of the Tabriz Anjoman. They took sanctuary in the Russian consulate or flew Russian flags over their homes to signal their surrender. Overnight, the anjoman in Tabriz, which had, from the very beginning, acted as the standard-bearer of the revolution, collapsed.

On Tuesday, June 30, one week after the fighting in Tabriz had begun, Rahim Khan returned, this time with a thousand Shahsevan fighters armed with the very weapons Tabriz had handed over to him. Rahim had been ordered by the shah to personally lead the charge on the city: "act in concert with [the royalists] and punish Tabriz," the shah had commanded. That may have been the plan. But Sattar Khan had beaten him back to the city. He was now fully armed and leading the resistance from inside.

The two men had not seen each other for nearly twenty years, not since their days trapped together inside the Narin Ghaleh prison. But the enmity between them had not cooled. One can only imagine what Sattar Khan must have thought, when he returned to Tabriz to discover that the anjoman had broken open the armory and handed the city's weapons to Rahim Khan. And Rahim, for his part, surely understood he would eventually have to face Sattar in battle, though he'd hoped it would be with their positions reversed: Rahim and his men safely inside the city walls; Sattar outside the gates, trying to enter. It would be foolish to engage the Constitutional Force under the current conditions. So Rahim sent his son, Bayuk, to do it in his stead—the same son on whose life he had loudly and repeatedly sworn, should God free him from prison.

Bayuk took a contingent of the Shahsevan cavalry and launched a reckless, full-scale assault on the Khiyaban ward. In anticipation, Baqer

Khan had constructed a series of barricades around the area, placing a handful of fighters behind each one. As Bayuk's men advanced, Baqer instructed his fighters to fall back to the next barricade, then the next, and the next. Bayuk, believing the nationalists were retreating before his forces, pushed his troops deep into the backstreets and blind alleys of Khiyaban. That's where Baqer was waiting for them. His fighters surrounded the Shahsevan horsemen, pressed them against the alley walls, and opened fire. The cavalry was decimated. Bayuk barely escaped the slaughter, returning to his father's camp in disgrace.

Another bloody week of fighting passed, again with nothing much to show for it. The shah was losing patience. Why hadn't Tabriz surrendered yet? Where was Sattar's head? It should have been stuffed with straw and displayed in his sitting room by now.

The shah sent Rahim a sternly worded message expressing his extreme displeasure at the continuing resistance in Tabriz. "[We hope that] Rahim Khan Sardar Nosrat has not forgotten the oral instructions that we provided him when he left Tehran," the message read. "Now and again, I am instructing you to pull no punches in suppressing the opposition of the government. Treat the opponents of the government in a way that people won't ever forget. Don't hold back on murder, punishment, destroying the houses and looting of the city, as you are not liable to anyone. Follow the example of Colonel Liakhov. The sooner you secure the city, and the more you suppress the opposition, the more you will be mercifully rewarded."

Now Rahim had no choice but to enter the city himself. On July 8, he led the bulk of his Shahsevan horsemen into Tabriz and set up camp inside the Northern Gardens, on the shuttered grounds of the crown prince's palace. Safe behind the gates, Rahim Khan declared himself the de facto governor of the city. He produced a list of ninety people he wanted delivered to him at once so that they could be punished for their treason against the shah; he had brought his own personal executioner along for the purpose. At the top of the list of names was Sattar Khan.

The Feda'i scoffed at the demand. If His Honor "the governor" requested the presence of the People's Commander, he would have to come and get him himself. Or, by all means, he could send his half-wit son again.

Rahim realized there was no path for him to avoid facing Sattar in battle. But if it was going to be war in the streets, then he would take his cue from His Majesty the shah: he would not hold back on murder, on punishment, on looting and destroying. He was not liable to anyone.

On July 14, six days after he had entered Tabriz and declared himself its governor, Rahim Khan let loose the Shahsevan. The men unleashed a vicious campaign of terror upon the people. They plundered the population, tore through the bazaar, looting shops and hanging shop-owners alongside their wives and children. They invaded the public bathhouse on the day it was reserved for women, raping and killing those inside; their screams could be heard across the stretch of the city.

In the midst of the murder and mayhem, William Doty sent a series of increasingly urgent memos to John B. Jackson in Tehran, decrying Rahim's actions and begging for help: "American consulate and mission endangered in line of fire. Urge immediate orders to Government commander to avert injury and consequent responsibility."

Jackson did not respond.

A correspondent for the London *Times* reported the "harrowing accounts of the devastation caused by Rahim Khan's horsemen dispatched there by the Shah to 'establish order,'" noting that his actions had created "a situation of great gravity for the inhabitants."

But Rahim's campaign of terror had only begun. Spurred by the words of the city's anti-constitutionalist clerics, Rahim's men launched a vicious pogrom against Tabriz's religious minorities. The Jews were the first target. Jewish leaders were rounded up, dragged into the open, and beaten in public. Synagogues were looted and set ablaze, entire neighborhoods plundered. Jewish graves were dug up and the bodies desecrated. It was only the intervention of the city's Muslim leaders that kept the pogrom from becoming a holocaust. "Many Jews owe their lives to Mohammedans, who, in some cases, actually stood armed in front of their Jewish friends until they could take them to their own houses," wrote a British diplomat stationed in Tabriz.

By then Rahim had moved on to the Armenian Christians, who overwhelmingly supported the revolution. Then to the city's small but significant Buddhist and Zoroastrian communities. Every enemy of the shah, regardless of religion or political persuasion, was labeled a "Babi": the catch-all term for anyone who supported the constitution. Pro-constitutionalist preachers were called Babis. Merchants who refused to open their shops were called Babis. Jews and Christians, both legally protected minorities in Persia, were called Babis. Pretty much anyone espousing any form of modernism or constitutionalism was accused of being a Babi.

The irony, of course, is that there wasn't really much of a Babi community left in Persia; the Bab had been executed in 1850. When the royalists used the term *Babi*, what they really meant was *Baha'i*. They used the two terms interchangeably. But, either way, the accusation stuck, and not without reason.

The Baha'i, spurred by the Bab's legacy, had been promoting the constitution's goals of economic equity, modernism, democracy, religious and women's rights, for decades—long before most Persians had even heard the word *constitution*. The parallels between the religious goals of the Baha'i and the political ambitions of the revolution were undeniable. That said, the Baha'i community in Persia had been given strict instructions from their spiritual leader, Abdul Baha, to remain detached from the revolution—not because the Baha'i rejected the constitutional cause, but because they had come to renounce violence and political activism as anathema to their spiritual goals of global transformation.

Regardless, the accusation of Babism still packed a punch, especially in this town, where the Bab had been strung up and shot for heresy and treason. Those among the Shahsevan who had no qualms about slaughtering Jews and Christians, but who recoiled at the thought of spilling innocent Muslim blood, were buoyed by the false belief that the residents they'd been ordered to rape and murder were all Babis and Baha'i: *heretics*. Killing them would be a meritorious service, not just to the shah, but to God.

The wanton blood-letting on the streets of Tabriz eventually had its intended effect. After a few days, nearly the entire population had been terrorized into submission. Rahim began distributing little white flags to the residents of every ward in the city, declaring that those who flew the flag over their homes would be spared further violence. Anyone without a flag would be wiped out.

After that, everything fell apart. The resistance in Tabriz all but evaporated. People began making their own white flags and placing them in their windows or over their doors. Some simply hung bedsheets outside their homes, hoping that, if they just gave up the fight, security would be restored and the killing would end. One by one, the nationalist wards fell to the royalists. Even Khiyaban surrendered to Rahim. To everyone's shock and dismay, Baqer Khan, second-in-command of the Constitutional Force, climbed the roof of his house and planted a white flag atop it.

Baqer's surrender surely broke Sattar's heart, but it probably did not come as a great surprise. The two men shared a friendship forged in fire. They had fought for each other: killed, maimed, and bled for each other. But they could not have been more different. Baqer Khan was a successful stonemason; he lived in a large, luxurious home tucked inside the wealthiest ward in the city. He was, for all intents and purposes, a nobleman—and he carried himself like one. He had about him an air of superiority that he could not hide from his comrades-in-arms, not even in the midst of battle. There was certainly no questioning Baqer's strength and courage. He was a shrewd tactician whose clever military arrangements had repeatedly rescued his fighters from overwhelming odds in battle. Nor could his commitment to the constitutional cause be doubted. But, as a nobleman, Baqer's politics were malleable. He was willing to die for the constitution if necessary. But what if it weren't necessary?

Sattar, however, was as far from a nobleman as a former looti could be. He was a thief and a brigand, a horse trader. He came from nothing. His simple home in Amirkhiz made Baqer's house in Khiyaban look like a palace. The Western journalists who visited him were always taken aback by its simplicity and lack of decor. This is how the soldier they called Persia's George Washington lived? For God's sake, the man didn't even own a rug, which, in this country, was as odd as not owning a roof.

Sattar Khan had nothing but the revolution. And now, it seemed, he no longer had that. Barely a month after the attack on parliament, the constitution had been uprooted in every province, city, and neighborhood in Persia. Everywhere the yoke of absolutism had been restored. In the whole of the country, the only place that still resisted the shah—the only place where the constitution remained in effect—was Amirkhiz.

That's where the Russian consul, Pokhitonov, made his final stop: at the simple home of Sattar Khan.

The People's Commander, who at one time led an army of thousands, now had about twenty fighters by his side: this was all that remained of the revolution. Yet, when Pokhitonov arrived at his small courtyard—unarmed and hoping to negotiate—those twenty fighters descended upon him in a flash. They had every reason to be suspicious. A few weeks before, while Sattar was en route to Tehran, the royalists had offered his elderly servant, Abbas Ali, a hefty sum to assassinate his master when he returned. As the story goes, Abbas waited until the two of them were alone in the house. He brought Sattar a steaming glass of tea, and then shot him in the abdomen, before fleeing to safety. Sattar calmly removed the bullet, dressed the wound himself, and instructed his comrades not to tell anyone what had happened.

Those same comrades were now encircling Pokhitonov, wanting nothing more than to cut the Russian into pieces and feed him to the street dogs. But Sattar would not have it. He welcomed the consul into his home.

"I come here to obtain an agreement from you not to initiate fighting so that events might reach a negotiated conclusion," Pokhitonov said. As he had done in every ward he'd visited, the Russian swore an oath to protect Sattar's life and property if only he would surrender to the shah. He had even secured a commitment from the crown to pay him a wage of 300 tomans to abandon the cause and retire quietly to the countryside.

"I am a servant of the people," Sattar replied calmly. "I am the nation's watchdog. Even if they gave me three thousand [tomans], I would not go back from the path I am following. I won't sell my honor for money."

Well then, under what terms would Sattar Khan possibly agree to end the uprising, Pokhitonov wanted to know.

"We did not start the war," Sattar said. "It is the other side that attacked us first, and we're only striking back in defense."

But surely he recognized the cause was lost, Pokhitonov implored. Look around you. The parliament is rubble. The constitution is in shreds. The anjoman has disbanded. Even his second-in-command had surrendered. It was futile to keep fighting. "Resistance is equal to suicide!" he cried out in frustration.

Pokhitonov placed a Russian flag on the table, pressed and folded, and begged Sattar Khan to raise it over his house, "so you will be under Russian government protection."

"I will not go under the flag of a foreigner," Sattar responded. "I swore [an oath] and kissed the Quran when I picked up the flag of freedom, and I am never going to drop it. We will fight till our last breath in order to revive the Constitution."

The negotiations were over. Sattar, like the mountains that birthed him, would not be moved.

After Pokhitonov left, a heavy silence fell like a shroud upon Sattar's home. A shroud is probably what each of those twenty tired and deflated men and women standing at Sattar's side was imagining—the death shroud that enwraps the bodies of the fallen before they're placed in a grave. Throughout the long struggle for democracy in Persia, there were many moments that must have felt like the end. But this was surely it. A revolution that had, at one time, encompassed the whole of the country, had been slowly whittled down to barely two dozen fighters huddled behind the walls of a cramped home, tucked within a single, unprotected neighborhood, deep inside a city that had already surrendered the fight.

Sattar did not speak—not for some time. It's not that he was contemplating Pokhitonov's offer. The revolution could only end in one of two ways for Sattar Khan: with parliament restored and the shah overthrown or with him wrapped in a grave cloth and buried in the ground. Rather, he was thinking: formulating his next move.

The entire democratic experiment in Persia hinged on what Sattar Khan would do now. The movement that had begun with a protest against a tobacco concession and ended with the first constitutional monarchy in the Middle East rested on the shoulders of an exhausted, battle-hardened commander with a bullet wound in his belly and a handful of devoted companions who had nothing more to lose but their lives. Thus, when Sattar finally spoke, he wasn't solely addressing his comrades—the last remnants of a Constitutional Force he had built from the ground up. He was addressing history. He was speaking to us.

"These shameless people have no honor," he said slowly and deliberately, "they are trying to intimidate us and want us to surrender. [But we] have no fear of such nonsensical threats. [We] prefer to wear the white grave-cloths and die for the Constitution, rather than fly a white flag."

An idea began to form in Sattar's head. An impossible idea. A suicidal idea. "Let's get rid of these shameful stains," he said, referring to the white flags that flecked the city. "[Let's] take off the grave-cloth from the body of freedom. [Let's] free Tabriz from the chains of tyranny and injustice."

The next day, before the sun had risen, Sattar and his twenty fighters set out from his home in the early-morning darkness. The streets of Tabriz were never lit; most people carried lanterns made of muslin with a copper top and bottom when they went out at night. Sattar, however, preferred the dark.

At this point, with the war for Persia practically won, the streets were more or less deserted. The lootis hired by the royalists to protect their wards had taken their pay and gone home. The horsemen of the Shahsevan were resting comfortably in the Northern Gardens, dreaming of glory. Rahim had already sent tidings to the shah, informing him of his impending victory over Sattar Khan: "May I be a sacrifice for the most sacred, royal, jewel-like dust of your feet," the message read. "By the invading fortune of your Majesty, of Powerful Imperial Might (may our souls be his sacrifice!), the means to eliminate the rebels and restore order to the city will speedily be prepared."

While Rahim and his men slept, Sattar and his comrades crept through the unpaved streets of Tabriz, ripping down every white flag they saw. They tip-toed through the narrow alleys and back streets, the broad promenades and public squares. Every inch of the city they left in their wake was littered with boot-stained flags: torn, tattered, carried off by the wind.

When the people glimpsed their commander sweeping like a scirocco through their neighborhood, tearing down flags, they began to shake off the fear that had settled upon them and to rise up once more. One by one, cries of "Hail!" rang out over the city—a great outburst of joy and determination, as Sattar's small procession grew from twenty, to a hundred, then a thousand.

When they came to Khiyaban they stopped in front of Baqer's house. "We have come to fight the cavalry and soldiers," they announced, "to kill or be killed."

But Baqer Khan had already received the message. The politics had changed and so, therefore, had he. He was waiting outside, his white flag at his feet, a rifle in his hands.

The Constitutional Force was reborn. Men and women once again picked up their guns and stood behind Sattar and Baqer, ready to take back the city. By the time Rahim figured out what was happening, it was too late. The reconstituted force surrounded the Northern Gardens and opened fire, catching the Shahsevan in the middle of lunch. Rahim, finally face-to-face with Sattar—something he had been avoiding for weeks—flew into a panic. As shots rang out in every direction, he and his commanders hopped on their horses and fled into the desert, leaving everything behind—including the cannons.

This is how the fight for freedom in Persia was renewed.

CHAPTER THIRTEEN

Why Bare Your Chest for a King
Who Does Not Care for You?

HOWARD BASKERVILLE STEPPED out of the American Memorial School gates and into a brand new world. Tabriz had been liberated: the noose removed. There was euphoria in the streets. Strangers embraced each other. Battle-hardened men fell to their knees and wept with joy. Inside the Northern Gardens, a group of barefoot children took turns mimicking Rahim Khan as he flung his cup of tea and ran for his horse when he saw Sattar Khan approaching. Someone brought out drums and an *oud*; there was music and dancing and fires lit.

Baskerville wept and sang and danced along with everyone else, though I can't help but wonder if he found it difficult to find reprieve in the revelry. He knew his life was never really in danger, regardless of how the battle for Tabriz turned out. As long as he remained behind the walls of the American Memorial School, he would be shielded from harm by the place of his birth and the color of his skin. Still, he had reason to celebrate. In the course of a month, much of his worldview had been shattered and put back together again. By some miracle, the Persian Constitution had survived—here in Tabriz, if nowhere else. The fires of revolution had not been fully extinguished. There was still hope.

Woodrow Wilson had been right all along: democracy *was* the moral judgment of God; it would always prevail. He had been foolish to doubt it. He wouldn't do so again. And yes, even now, amidst the celebrations, he had to admit, in the quiet corners of his mind, that he'd had nothing to do with its triumph in Tabriz. One day, people would write about what happened here—Rahim Khan's reign of terror, the white flags waving over the city, the rallying of the people by Sattar Khan—and in all those words there would be no mention of the name, *Baskerville*. It would be as though he weren't there at all.

But he was there! He had witnessed events with his own eyes. And perhaps, at that moment, a small, unspoken intention began to rise in his chest: a promise made to himself and no one else. The next time the city he had come to call his own was threatened by the agents of tyranny and oppression, he would not hide behind the walls of the American Memorial School. He would not use his passport as a shield to protect himself from harm. He would make sure people remembered on which side Howard Conklin Baskerville stood.

The celebrations that night were short-lived; there was too much to do. To begin with, the city wasn't exactly liberated. Nearly half of Tabriz was still in the hands of royalists, including its two largest wards, Davehchi and Sorkhab. The Islamic Anjoman, with Mir Hashem at its head, still boasted thousands of fighters funded and armed by the shah. The morning after Rahim's troops were expelled, the royalists resumed their attack on nationalist neighborhoods.

Some of Sattar's fighters urged a full-scale assault on the royalist wards as a means of freeing the city of the shah's supporters for good. But Sattar refused. "As long as the enemy does not advance, I will not fight," he said. "I do not want the people's blood shed."

Besides, bullets were scarce, and the fighters needed rest. They should be under no illusion: the shah's troops were coming for them. Mohammed Ali would not allow the second most populous city in Persia to remain in the hands of revolutionaries. The garrisons would have to be rebuilt, the barricades patched up. Everyone needed to prepare for the war to come.

The first order of business was to hold elections for a reconstituted anjoman in Tabriz. This new and improved council would be bigger and bolder than the one it replaced. It would hold one hundred seats and be tasked with governing more than mere local affairs. With the destruction of the National Consultative Assembly and the collapse of the Persian Constitution in Tehran, the Tabriz Anjoman would be the de facto seat of popular government: the new Persian Parliament.

The freshly elected representatives set to work rebuilding the war-torn city by levying a series of heavy taxes on its wealthiest residents; those who refused to pay had their property confiscated and sold to the public. The tax revenue was used to repair the homes, schools, and buildings that had been destroyed by Rahim Khan and his men. It also funded the creation of free clinics and public bakeries to keep the population healthy and fed. Teams of uniformed youths were hired to clean out the debris from the bazaar so the shops could reopen. The Telegraph House, which had been badly damaged in the fighting, was repaired and all downed lines restored. Two new government bureaus were established: an education ministry to oversee the reopening of the schools, and a war commission to coordinate the defense of the city. The Tabriz Anjoman even managed to pave the streets!

The sole printing press in Tabriz had been plundered and wrecked by Shahsevan horsemen. The anjoman rebuilt the press and funded the printing and distribution of two newspapers—the only independent press left in all of Persia. These two papers were indispensable, not only in documenting the crimes of the shah to the rest of the country, but also in broadcasting the successes of Tabriz, thus spurring other cities to follow its lead and revolt.

In the midst of all this activity, the Tabriz Anjoman sent a formal notice to all foreign embassies, declaring itself the lone legitimate government in Persia, solely capable of negotiating on behalf of the country. At first, the declaration was greeted with humor and skepticism in European capitals. But when the shah requested a loan from Russia and Britain to help offset the cost of his coup, the Tabriz Anjoman shot telegraphs to London and St. Petersburg reminding them, in no uncertain terms, that the shah was no longer the head of the country. Hence, whatever money was loaned to him would not be repaid when the constitution was restored. "The Iranian nation will in no way consider itself a guarantor of this loan," the telegraphs warned.

The threat worked. The shah's requests were denied.

Meanwhile, news about what had transpired in Tabriz began to spread around the globe. The Tabriz Anjoman released a document it called a "Nationalist Manifesto," written in Persian, Turkish, and French. "To all the lovers of humanity!" the document began. "To all who seek justice in five continents. Though we Persians, in religion and nationality, differ from you . . . in humanity and justice and the seeking of righteousness we are all alike. If we open the heart of a Japanese, who has the love of humanity, will it not be like the heart of a Russian . . . ? Likewise if we open the heart of an Englishman, and of a German, and of a Chinese, and of a Persian. Forget for one moment the bigotry of creeds, the prejudice of nationality, and give us the justice of your unbiased conscience."

This was, at the time, the most successful anti-imperialist struggle in the world. Tabriz became a rallying cry in every country fighting for freedom from oppression. And nowhere was that cry louder than in Russia, where the Bolsheviks took up the Persian cause as their own.

Russia's Social Democrats framed Tabriz's fight against the shah as a natural extension of the Russian Revolution of 1905; and they had a point. The Russian government was fully invested in the shah's survival. The loss of Tabriz was not only an embarrassment to St. Petersburg; it had the potential to rekindle the revolutionary spirit in Russia. At the very least, the ongoing resistance in Tabriz affirmed everything the Bolsheviks had been preaching for years. As Lenin put it: "A revolutionary movement that can offer armed resistance to attempts at restoration, that compels the attempters to call in foreign aid—such a movement cannot be destroyed. In these circumstances, even the fullest triumph of Persian reaction would merely be the prelude to fresh popular rebellion."

Lenin, who was living in exile in Europe at the time, was closely following events in Tabriz. Having met personally with several Persian parliamentarians who had survived the shah's coup and fled to Europe, he was convinced that Tabriz could serve as a model of resistance around the world. And because, in his view, it was a Russian (Liakhov) who had crushed the Persian revolution, it should be Russians who helped restore it.

Relying on his sources back home, Lenin sent an urgent appeal to his fellow Bolsheviks to travel to Tabriz and join the fight. A wave of workers and veterans—some of whom had marched to the tsar's Winter Palace on Bloody Sunday in 1905—answered the call, as did a group of Marxists and socialists from Baku, an oil-rich city on the Caspian Sea. They brought to Tabriz years of experience with urban warfare techniques picked up during their long struggle against the tsar.

In late July 1908, one hundred seasoned Georgian soldiers from the capital, Tbilisi, secretly crossed the Aras River and entered Tabriz via the Jolfa Road. The Georgians carried with them a mobile bomb-making factory that would end up shifting the balance of power in the war with Tehran. Not long after, a group of Armenian Christians, skilled in tactical training, also joined the fight. The Armenians were put in charge of transforming Sattar's ragtag band of fighters into a well-trained military, drilling them in maneuvers and hand-to-hand combat.

Rahim's brutal pogrom in Tabriz had provoked the city's religious minorities to "get off the fence," as it were, and fully join the ranks of the nationalists. Two young Jewish revolutionaries, David Abraham, a tailor by trade, and Aziz Asher, a photographer, became commanders in the revolutionary army. A number of prominent Zoroastrian residents took up arms, too, as did more than a few Baha'i, defying the direct orders of their spiritual leader not to engage directly in the fight.

All of these different religious communities mixed together as a single fighting force: a multiethnic military composed of about four thousand workers, students, merchants, clerics, and professional soldiers that cut across all religious, ethnic, and social divides. The fighters came from different countries, spoke different languages, worshipped different gods. But none of that mattered. They were all united in the fight against tyranny.

This was the closest the revolution had ever come to creating a professional army. The soldiers were paid a salary and provided with matching uniforms. They were separated into different squads, each with its own commander, and with a strict chain of command to maintain order. Fighting units were given regular shifts of duty. Special task forces were created to focus specific talents on specific targets. A field hospital with twenty-five beds was constructed to patch up the wounded. A camp kitchen was built so soldiers could share meals together.

Everyone who joined the army, regardless of race, religion, or class, was now called Feda'i—or "Fids," as the young diarist, Sarah Wright, had taken to calling them.

Meanwhile, Sattar Khan had reached god-like status in Tabriz. Persians showed up at the city gates at all hours, claiming to have been called by him in their dreams. His name and image were passed around like currency. People literally fell at his feet when he patrolled the city. If he happened to pass through a neighborhood, the residents would bring out a sheep and slaughter it in his honor. Sarah Wright's diary contains an amusing passage in which she and a friend were standing in front of a small shop when the cry of "Sattar Khan! Sattar Khan!" suddenly pierced the air. The People's Commander was riding past on a big white horse, a rifle slung across his saddle.

"I looked around, but only in time to see the side view of the great hero," Sarah swoons. "It was the best sight of the whole day."

Sattar Khan maintained strict discipline over the Feda'i. Fighters were forbidden from looting or stealing from merchants. "If you've come to pillage, leave," he told new recruits. "I only want people who are fighting for freedom and justice."

No soldier under his command was allowed to accept any contributions from the citizenry, financial or otherwise. Nor were they allowed to harass the population in any way. Anyone who defied these prohibitions was forcefully punished. "The strength of a fighter doesn't come from his gun but from the people's support," Sattar would say. "I have reached the rank of commander from the power of the powerless and the strength of the weak."

Although Sattar and Baqer put the past behind them and again cooperated as brothers-in-arms, their relationship had strained after the affair of the white flags. In some quarters, Baqer Khan was still being called "that traitor." Whereas Sattar and Baqer had once been considered more or less equals in the struggle against the shah, there was now no question which of the two was the Father of the Nation. Once, when Baqer and his men made a show of refusing to dine at the same table as the Christian soldiers in the camp kitchen, Sattar dressed him down in front of the entire army.

Sattar's success in Tabriz began earning him grudging respect in Europe. E. G. Browne gave speeches in the British Parliament extolling his leadership and demanding that Persia's revolution be taken seriously now that it had proven itself capable of resisting the shah. Yet even Browne knew his efforts were fruitless. Although the Labour Party and Britain's socialists vocally supported Tabriz, the government itself was genuinely panicked about what was happening in Persia, convinced that the revolution's success would embolden its subjects in India and Egypt to ask for the same rights Tabriz was demanding from the shah. "England shews that the Persian Question, as such, does not interest her, and that in the Anglo-Russian Convention she is primarily interested in the question of the defense of her Indian Empire," a frustrated Browne confessed.

Nevertheless, money and weapons continued to pour into Tabriz from all over Europe. The greatest support came from Constantinople, where the Young Turks, inspired by the Persian Constitutional Revolution, had just overthrown their own tyrant, Sultan Abdul Hamid II— the kaiser's friend. The very week that Tabriz was liberated, Turkey officially transitioned from an absolute monarchy to a constitutional government; Turkish nationalists were now eager to support their brothers and sisters in Persia.

By the middle of August 1908, a little more than a month after expelling Rahim Khan, Tabriz had all the soldiers, arms, and ammunition it needed to successfully defend itself from an outside attack. And just in time for the shah's troops finally to show up.

❖

IT WAS PRECISELY as Sattar Khan had predicted: a massive force of cavalry and infantry fortified with bands of tribesmen and ruffians, lootis and riflemen, and a couple of hundred hapless villagers who had been seized, dressed, and armed for the occasion. At the head of the force was a man Sattar had not seen in years: Abdol Majid Mirza Ayn od-Dowleh, known to his enemies as "the Prince."

Ayn od-Dowleh was Mohammed Ali Shah's cousin and the grandson of Fath Ali Shah. Proud, hot-tempered, stubborn, and ostentatious, he was a true Qajar, a man of culture and refinement. He had spent decades in and out of government service, even acting as "Head of Court" in Tabriz under Muzaffar ad-Din, back when Muzaffar was crown prince and Mohammed Ali just a petulant child. He had known Sattar then as just another of Muzaffar's many hired thugs: the kind he liked to employ as his personal bodyguards. Now that same thug was in possession of Persia's second city, and the Prince had come to take it back.

The Prince's force encamped in a village a few miles east of the city, on the side of a small knoll, surrounded by ill-kept orchards. Rahim Khan joined him there, falling under his command by order of the shah. A journalist from the London *Times* who visited the camp described it as bringing to mind "the bridal processions of some broken-down Indian princelet, who clings to the tarnished relics of a dead magnificence, in the empty hope that the present state of decay may be confused in the wraith of past pretensions." Be that as it may, there was no denying that this was a formidable force, its size and strength meant to scare Sattar Khan into submission.

It had the opposite effect.

Sattar took great pleasure in the Prince's presence on the battlefield. He sent the shah's cousin a cheeky letter, boasting that his arrival in Tabriz had assured the nationalists' victory. "If God forbid, and that will not happen, Your Highness wins, it is no shame for me because it is not astonishing that a prince with such power and majesty should win over Sattar Qarahdaghi," the letter read. "If, however, God willing, I win, and of course I will win, then for the rest of your life Your Highness will be ridiculed. Everyone will say that Prince Ayn od-Dowleh, with a ferocious force of thirty thousand men, lost to Sattar Qarahdaghi."

The Prince got the message. Rather than launch a direct attack, he sent three emissaries to negotiate with Sattar Khan on his behalf. The three were distinguished governors of nearby provinces—learned men of aristocratic stock dressed in fine clothes and dripping with eloquence. The ploy was obvious: the Prince wanted Sattar to look like the ruffian that he was. But Sattar refused to play the game. Instead of meeting with the emissaries himself, he decided to send his own eloquent negotiator: Hassan Sharifzadeh.

After Rahim's defeat, Hassan had come out of hiding in the French consulate and quickly resumed his role as one of the most articulate voices of the revolution. He once again began making public speeches in defense of the constitution and helped organize the Persian teachers and staff at the American Memorial School. He took it upon himself to act as the unofficial spokesperson of the bazaar, making sure merchants were properly compensated for damages to their property and helping them navigate the bureaucracy of the new anjoman in Tabriz. He was also one of a handful of orators sent by Sattar Khan to the edge of the royalist wards, often in the middle of firefights, to plead with the peasants and the pious poor to abandon the shah and cross over to the nationalist side.

"Why bare your chest for a king who does not care for you?" Hassan would shout over the sound of bullets exchanged across the Mehraneh River. "Why die for those who have no idea what it means to work the fields from dawn to dusk and get nothing in return?"

Like his friend Howard Baskerville, Hassan understood that he'd been given a second chance. His life had been saved by the city he loved, even after he'd abandoned it for the protection of a foreign government. He was no longer afraid or forlorn. He had learned his lesson; never again would he doubt the revolution. He would give his life to it, if that's what was asked of him. Thus, when Sattar Khan asked him to be his chief negotiator with the Prince, Hassan threw himself into the role.

Not everyone was happy with Sattar's choice. There were many who viewed Hassan as too accommodating to be trusted with handling such delicate negotiations. This was a man who was still advocating moderation, even after all that had happened! Why not send someone the Prince would fear?

But Sattar would not budge. Hassan was capable and tactful. He came from a respected family of religious clerics. His father was a sayyid. He was well admired by the other side and could speak their language. The Prince's emissaries would have no choice but to take him seriously.

Hassan met the dignitaries out in the wilderness, far beyond the city gates (Sattar had wisely refused to let the men enter Tabriz). There, the emissaries laid out the Prince's proposal in stark terms: The nationalists were to turn their weapons over and beg forgiveness of the shah. In return, the shah would give them amnesty and allow for a new constitution to be written, eventually.

"A Constitution was [already] obtained two years ago, and no one is fit to abolish it," Hassan's team countered. "Since Mohammad Ali Mirza [Shah] has disobeyed the Fundamental Law and has smashed [Parliament], we shall stand firm until he has no choice but to reopen it." In any case, Hassan continued, if the Prince truly wanted to negotiate in good faith, he should begin by arresting Rahim Khan for rape and murder and sending him back to Tabriz for punishment.

That was obviously out of the question, as Rahim and his men were already dispersed among the Prince's army. Nevertheless, the emissaries agreed to convey Tabriz's demands to the shah. The important thing was to maintain dialogue and diplomacy. The shah was a reasonable man; he did not want any more bloodshed. In fact, the emissaries continued, His Majesty was prepared to publicly commit to reopening parliament in three months' time. That timetable could even be accelerated, if only Tabriz would surrender.

Surrender was not an option; the people would die first. But Hassan was heartened by the shah's promise to reopen parliament in three months; he would take that news to Tabriz. In the meantime, he agreed that negotiations between the two sides should continue: talking was always better than fighting.

Hassan returned to Tabriz in high spirits. He had failed to secure Rahim's capture, but he eagerly conveyed the shah's promise to reopen parliament. That was surely a good sign. At the very least, they now had an open line of communication with the court. Given enough time and incentive, Hassan was certain he could extract even more concessions from the shah.

To his surprise, however, the people flew into a rage. They were not interested in the shah's promises. They could not care less about open lines of communication. They wanted revenge. If the Prince wasn't going to punish the rapists and murderers who had terrorized their town, they would do it themselves. They would begin by ridding the city of all royalists, wiping them out once and for all.

On August 25, thousands of angry Tabrizis took to the streets. They grabbed their rifles and marched to the headquarters of the Tabriz Anjoman, demanding action. "We must fight!" they cried. "We must attack the enemy!"

Sattar tried to calm the crowd, reminding them once again that they needed to conserve their ammunition. The intermittent fusillade and small incursions from the royalist wards was nothing more than a nuisance. They could not squander their bullets shooting across the river at their neighbors. They had to focus their efforts on the invading army outside the gates. But the people's thirst for vengeance would not be sated, not even by the People's Commander.

That was when Hassan Sharifzadeh decided to intervene. He may have been sent by Sattar Khan. It may have been his own idea. Either way, in the midst of the frenzy, as the crowd was clamoring for blood, he made his way to the front of the mob and stood upon a crate. He begged the people to put aside their violent thoughts and think of the future. What would the world say about them if they slaughtered their neighbors? The revolution would not succeed with such "radical acts." If Tabriz was to be the seat of Persia's popular government, it had to act like it. It had to obey the very laws it was fighting for, or else what was the point? The struggle for democracy was far from over.

"Do not say, 'we have fought battles; we have succeeded,'" he warned the crowd. "We are still at the beginning of our battles."

The speech did not have its intended effect. The crowd found Hassan's words to be confusing and cruel. Was he blaming them for the violence that had occurred in the city? Some in the crowd thought Hassan was being patronizing in his tone and his choice of words. People hurled insults, called for him to shut his mouth. "What is this atheist saying?" someone shouted. Wasn't this the same man currently negotiating with the enemy? Why should anyone listen to him?

The crowd grew louder and more incensed until Hassan had to be pulled down from the crate and scurried away to safety. Another speaker stood up and tried to calm the situation, begging the crowd to forgive Hassan for his unintended slight. He meant no offense to the fighters; he was a hero of the revolution. The people must remember that.

Eventually, the crowd dispersed; Hassan had gotten his way. But the anger and distrust that had been building against him for months had reached a boiling point. Whoever he once was—whatever he had accomplished for the cause—the revolution had passed Hassan by; there was no appetite left in Tabriz for patience and restraint.

On his way back to the French consulate, Hassan was stopped by three men. They were drunk and angry. They had heard his speech advising them to forgo revenge, to live in peace with the royalists. They did not care who he was or what he'd done in the past; in their eyes he was a coward and a traitor. Hassan tried to ignore the men and continue on his way, but they would not let him pass. They continued flinging insults at him. And then, one of the men pulled out a pistol and shot Hassan in the chest.

At the sound of the bullet a crowd rushed over. The three men, suddenly aware of their actions, quickly sobered up and fled the scene. Hassan was badly injured but still breathing. He was lifted onto his feet and dragged inside the French consulate.

When word got out that his friend had been shot, Baskerville wanted to rush to his side. But he couldn't get far. Just at that moment, the entire city was suddenly echoing with gunfire. The royalists were attacking, and, this time, they were being backed by the Prince's recently arrived troops. It turned out the negotiations were nothing but a ploy to buy time to coordinate with the Islamic Anjoman and take the city by force. Bullets rang out from behind the royalist barricades. Cannonballs crashed into the homes of nationalists.

This was precisely what the Feda'i had been training for these past few weeks. They took positions along the city walls and responded with their own heavy cannon fire. The Georgian bomb makers went to work, flinging homemade mortars down upon the invading army, splattering the desert floor with body parts. The Prince was unprepared for the assault from above; his men were forced to retreat. At the same time, the royalist advance into nationalist wards was successfully thwarted by Sattar's squads.

The fighting lasted no more than an hour before the enemy was repelled. Yet that brief encounter with the combined forces of the Prince and the royalists had sent a chill up Sattar's spine. No longer could he afford to ignore the enemy residing within the city walls. The people were right: he had to deal with the problem now.

"We resisted so far," he reluctantly admitted to his commanders. "From now on, we attack to take back the neighborhoods."

Sattar and Baqer led the charge on the royalist wards themselves. Only Tabrizis were allowed to participate in the assault. This was a family affair; there could be no foreigners or outsiders involved.

They crossed the Mehraneh River in full force and made short work of the royalist opposition. Davehchi and Sorkhab fell in a few hours. Sattar's squad fought its way to the headquarters of the Islamic Anjoman, destroying the building in which it was housed and arresting its members, though Mir Hashem managed to flee to Tehran. The rest were ordered to lay down their weapons and surrender. Those who refused were shot; everyone else was pardoned right there on the battlefield.

When the fighting was over, Sattar Khan issued a general amnesty, warning his soldiers that if any of them were caught looting, they'd be shot on the spot. It was his intention to spare every home in the royalist ward—every home, but one. The house of Mir Hashem and everything inside it (including a certain stuffed camel's head) was burned to the ground. All of Tabriz was now under Sattar's command.

Miraculously, the nationalists had managed to avoid the bloodbath that Hassan had so feared, though he would not know it. For while the last of the shah's supporters was being chased out of town, Hassan Sharifzadeh lay in his bed in the French consulate, taking his final breath.

Hassan died before Baskerville could reach him. He was his first and closest friend in Persia, the man who had opened his eyes to what was truly happening here and what it meant, not just for the country, but for the world. Now he was gone, and he never had the chance to say goodbye.

That night, Hassan's murderers secretly made their way to Sattar Khan's home where they formally asked the People's Commander for sanctuary. Sattar, however, was not in a forgiving mood. He may have wanted nothing more than to put a bullet in each man's head, but that was no way to honor the legacy of Hassan Sharifzadeh. Instead, he did what he knew Hassan would do: he followed the law. He had the accused arrested and sent to the Tabriz Anjoman for judgment. The men were questioned, found guilty, and sentenced to death. They were taken to the city's main square and shot by firing squad, their corpses tied with ropes and hung from posts.

The following day, four thousand people came out for Hassan's funeral. His body was washed, wrapped in a white cloth, and carried to the cemetery with solemn ceremony. The faculty and staff of the American Memorial School were all there: Samuel and Annie Wilson; their children Agnes, Rose, Annie Rhea, and Robert; the Jessups, the Pittmans, and the Wrights. Hassan had been one of their own, after all: a surrogate son to Wilson. He was a shy, awkward teenager when he arrived at the gates of the school, begging to be taught English in secret; he was being buried a hero and martyr to a cause that would forever bear his name.

Sattar said a few words. William Doty conveyed the condolences of the US government. But, as far as we know, Howard Baskerville did not speak; there's no record of it, anyway. He may have merely stood there, silently with everyone else, and watched as his friend was lowered into the ground.

When the service was finished, the mourners returned to their duties. There were declarations to sign, announcements to be made.

Most of the captured royalist fighters had switched their allegiance, thanks in no small part to Hassan's eloquent arguments; they needed to be prepped, uniformed, and fully conscripted into the Constitutional Force. After so many months of struggle and sacrifice, there was a real sense of optimism among the people. Tabriz had changed.

So had Howard Baskerville.

PART THREE

Hear this! My one and only Cause is true.
The words I speak mean victory to you.

Off with rags of law and pious fashion!
Swim naked in the sea of compassion!

How long will you drift through this world of war,
far from the safety of your native shore?

Sing, Be! Our Cause stands strong, both clean and plain:
What comes from God returns to God again.

—Tahirih

CHAPTER FOURTEEN

Either You or Constitutionalism

THEY SAY IT WAS WHEN the crows came that Mohammed Ali Shah knew he might lose the war. They appeared in the skies above Tehran in a whirling black cloud that blotted out the sun. The noise was deafening: like a scraping inside the skull. At first, the crows were a mere oddity, an amusing distraction from the disquiet that had settled upon the capital over the past few months, as the conflict with Tabriz raged on with no end in sight. People came out of their homes to see the strange spectacle. They tilted their heads to the sky, mouths agape. One or two pulled out rifles and began shooting in the air, hoping to make the crows scatter. But they would not be intimidated. What were they looking for? Rats and snakes? There were plenty of those in Tehran.

It wasn't until evening that their target came into focus. Just before the sun fell, the crows made their way to Golestan Palace—to roost, everyone assumed. For a few moments, they clustered above the palace roof, on the east side of the compound, where the red royal flags of the Qajar Dynasty flew three abreast. The shah's courtiers were drawn outside by the noise. They stood in the rose garden and watched as, all at once, the crows set upon the Qajar flags in a frenzy, ripping them to shreds with their claws and their beaks.

Mohammed Ali Shah wasn't at the palace when this happened; he was still holed up at Bagh-e Shah, where he'd been since before the attack on parliament. It was now his permanent residence. Both his family and the entirety of the state apparatus had been transferred there from Golestan. It was too risky to go back to the palace, his advisers kept telling him. It wasn't yet safe, and it wouldn't be until Tabriz surrendered and the war was finally over.

But when would it be over? It was now nearly February 1909. Seven months had passed since Rahim Khan was expelled from Tabriz. It still did not seem possible. That uncouth brigand had a thousand horsemen! He was given all the arms and ammunition he needed. He had unlimited funds and *carte blanche* to do whatever he wished with the population. And yet he was chased out of Tabriz like a stray. At least he had the good sense not to show his face in Tehran again. He and what remained of his Shahsevan fighters were now encamped on the outskirts of Tabriz, still trying to penetrate the town's defenses. Still failing.

The shah blamed himself—not publicly, of course. But he must have known it was a mistake to place the task of taking Tabriz in the hands of an illiterate horseman. If a weasel gets into the hen house, you don't send another weasel to root it out. You send in a fox.

Ayn od-Dowleh was supposed to be his fox. If anyone could take Tabriz, he thought, surely it would be "the Prince." That was why Mohammed Ali had plucked his cousin out of a comfortable retirement lazing in his country estate, named him the new governor-general of Azerbaijan, and sent him off to Tabriz to do what Rahim Khan could not. It had been a risky proposition. The Prince was a pretentious, calculating man. He was older and wiser than Mohammed Ali Shah— more experienced; certainly more respected. He had served four shahs, all of them more beloved than the present occupant of the Sun Throne. There was no doubt in Mohammed Ali's mind that the Prince had ambitions of his own. Sending him to take Tabriz could very well lead him to keep Tabriz. That was the price one paid for employing the fox: you may lose the hen house for good. But the shah no longer cared. Better to bury every man, woman, and child in Tabriz than to leave the city of his birth in the hands of Sattar Khan.

When the Prince arrived at the edge of Tabriz six months ago, he had sent daily reports detailing how close he was to taking the city, how much damage his cannons had caused the perimeter walls, how many dead revolutionaries were piling up in the city's cramped cemeteries. Yet Tabriz still had not surrendered. On the contrary, it was more powerful now than when the Prince's campaign began. The city had become a beacon of the Constitutional Revolution, its light shining all the way to Europe and the United States. What started as a few smoldering embers of revolutionary fervor had sparked into a raging fire, and it was now spreading to other cities. Isfahan and Mashhad had rebelled. Shiraz, too. The southern port of Bandar Abbas had just declared its independence. In Rasht, the largest city on the Caspian Sea, the shah's hand-picked governor had been assassinated. Nationalists had overrun the city of Qazvin; that was barely a hundred miles north of Tehran!

Mohammed Ali Shah did not have the manpower to deal with all these uprisings. He had sent the bulk of his fighting force to the province of Azerbaijan, confident that if Tabriz fell, the rest would follow. Sever the head and the body will die—isn't that what they say?

But where was the head he'd been promised? With each day that Sattar survived, the shah lost more of the people. The Qaradaghi horse trader had become something of a saint to the gullible masses. People across the country reported seeing him in their dreams, beckoning them to Tabriz. Two friends would share the same dream; one of them would disappear in the middle of the night.

The shah's loyal mullahs in Tehran had done their best to combat Sattar's mystical influence. Every once in a while they would roll out an elaborately carved wax figure of the People's Commander, display it in the city square, and make a big show of praying for his defeat at the hands of the shah. They would hang the effigy from a tree, pull out a sword and cut it in half. They would burn the remains in a great bonfire that could be seen for miles. It was all fantastic theater. But it was just that. Try as they might, they could not touch the man himself.

And now this business with the crows and the flags. Mohammed Ali Shah was an extremely superstitious man. He knew what the people would say about the crows: that they were a portent; that they signaled the end was near. Already some infuriating verses had been written about the incident in one of Tabriz's independent papers.

> *Have you not seen what happened to the Qajar flag?*
> *The [crows] tore it up with their beaks*
> *And ate it all, corpse and carrion.*
> *Indeed, in this is an admonition to he who perceives.*

A few months ago, no one would have dared to write such a thing. In the immediate aftermath of his successful coup against parliament, the shah had shut down all the country's newspapers. Those were heady days for him, filled with promise and excitement. His decision to bombard parliament had been bold and decisive. He had restored honor to the Qajar Dynasty. Every revolutionary who fell on his face and begged for mercy—every naked, shivering body dying slowly in his dungeons—was a reminder of what it was supposed to be like to rule Persia on behalf of God. After years of turmoil, the country had been calm and orderly once more. Everyone knew their place again.

Now the shah tromped through the empty halls of Bagh-e Shah in a huff, the slap of his silk slippers on the marble a warning bell to his advisers to steer clear. Not that there were many advisers left. Shapshal Khan was gone. The shah's tutor and closest companion had been finally exposed as a Russian agent, but that isn't why he was expelled from court. The people—the ones who mattered—objected to the perverse enjoyment Shapshal had taken in the torture and execution of the shah's prisoners, the relish with which he would spit on each corpse and declare, "one dog less."

It wasn't just Shapshal's actions that offended these people; it was the fact that he was a Jew abusing Muslims. That felt, somehow, unseemly. Shapshal had tried to ward off the criticism by converting to Islam, but it was clear to all that his conversion wasn't genuine. In the end, and despite the shah's wishes, Shapshal was forced to flee Persia. He was now back in St. Petersburg working at the Russian Foreign Office, teaching Turkish and Azeri at St. Petersburg University.

Colonel Liakhov, too, was nowhere to be found. He was still in Persia, of course, but he somehow always managed to avoid spending time with the shah. He was a busy man: the governor-general of Tehran. The city was still technically under martial law, and it was the chief duty of the Cossack Brigade to maintain order on the streets. The shah understood why Liakhov rarely left the barracks unless specifically summoned. But that didn't keep him from suspecting the colonel's motives for making himself scarce.

At least the shah knew Liakhov, unlike Shapshal, had nowhere else to go. The liberal papers in Russia were demanding he be recalled and punished for his role in the attack on parliament. Apparently, the reports of Persia's elected government being buried in rubble had given Russia a black eye in the foreign press.

"Russia's assistance in strangling the Persian revolution . . . had given rise to a feeling of hostility against Russian subjects in Persia," argued one prominent Russian politician, "and was therefore, prejudicial to Russian international relations."

With Shapshal and Liakhov no longer around, the shah was forced to rely increasingly on his son's tutor, Konstantin Nikólaevich Smirnov, to keep him apprised of the temperature in St. Petersburg. The shah had sent representatives to the Russian court to appeal for assistance in dealing with the revolutionaries in Tabriz. He was hoping for a clear declaration of support from Tsar Nicholas II himself. But no support was forthcoming. Smirnov patiently explained to His Majesty that the Russian government was pursuing a policy of noninterference in Persia's political affairs, as mandated by the Anglo-Russian Convention of 1907.

The shah was skeptical. Was not Tabriz in the zone of influence ceded to Russia under the agreement with London? Had not the tsar read the reports describing waves of Russian and Georgian fighters sneaking across the border to join the revolution? Did he not realize these were the very same Marxists and Bolsheviks who had led the uprising against the tsar himself? That meant the shah and the tsar shared a single enemy. They were in this together. So then why, with everything at stake, was Nicholas still pledging neutrality, even as his cousin, Kaiser Wilhelm II, was brandishing his self-ascribed role as "the Western protector of Muslims against the infidels" by offering to send whatever military help the shah needed to defend Persia against the godless rebels who threatened her?

Should the shah take the kaiser up on the offer?

That would be a grave mistake, Smirnov advised. Germany and Russia were already at odds in the Balkans; the conflict there had the potential of erupting into an all-out war between the two countries and their allies over control of Europe. Inviting the kaiser to Persia would be seen by the Russians and British alike as a declaration of support for Germany. It could lead to a full-scale invasion and occupation of the country by Russia in the north and Britain in the south. Instead, Smirnov counseled Mohammed Ali to pledge publicly to reopen parliament. Doing so would, at the very least, placate the European powers and give cover to the tsar to throw his support behind the shah.

At first, the shah had taken Smirnov's advice. In fact, he had sent the Prince to Tabriz with the promise to establish a new parliament within three months. But three months had passed and nothing happened. The shah then announced he needed two more months to properly prepare the country for elections. When those two months passed, the shah claimed he couldn't possibly hold national elections without the participation of Persia's second most populous city. But this was just an excuse. The truth was he couldn't reopen parliament, even if he wanted to. As usual, his decisions were being made by others—in this case, by Fazlullah Nuri.

With the collapse of the constitutional order, Nuri had become the most powerful man in Persia—more powerful, even, than the shah. While Ayatollah Behbehani was exiled to Kermanshah and Ayatollah Tabatabai was living under house arrest, Ayatollah Nuri sat at the right hand of the Shadow of God, advising him on all matters great and small. He traveled back and forth to court in the shah's own royal carriage, the same one the shah was riding in with Shapshal when someone threw two bombs at his empty motor car. The carriage was now, for all intents and purposes, the private transport of Nuri and his ever-expanding entourage.

Everywhere he went, the old cleric was showered with money and gifts. At court, Nuri was given a place of extreme prominence, with all the respect and splendor befitting his elevated station as the country's top religious authority. Smirnov would often come into the shah's presence, only to find the ayatollah whispering defiance into his ear, the gray whiskers of his unwashed beard rubbing against the royal cheek. Under no circumstance could the shah compromise with the rebels, Nuri advised. He could not even consider reopening parliament. He must declare once and for all that representative government is contrary to the laws of Islam and give up entirely the idea of democracy. He must not even mention the word *constitution* ever again. And he must punish Tabriz without mercy for daring to challenge his God-given authority.

With no hope for compromise, Mohammed Ali knew that the conflict with Tabriz could end only in absolute victory or absolute defeat. But what else could he do? He was more afraid of Fazlullah

Nuri than he was of Sattar Khan. So until the Prince brought him the severed and stuffed head of the People's Commander, he was stuck in Bagh-e Shah, taking orders from Nuri.

His retainers tried to soothe his nerves by holding a series of horse races on the property. That is, after all, what Bagh-e Shah had been built for: the two-story residence curved along a wide, dirt track in the shape of a crescent. The shah could relax in the shade of a veranda on the upper floor and watch the races below. But it was no use; nothing would ease his anxiety.

There were reports of him roaming the grounds alone in the evenings, after the official business of court was complete and Nuri and his entourage had left in the royal carriage. He would remove the Kiani Crown from his head, exchange his silk slippers for leather boots, and walk out into the sweet-smelling garden. There are four hundred fountains scattered across Bagh-e Shah, and a small zoo. In the center of the oasis is a bronze statue of Mohammed Ali's larger-than-life grandfather, Nasir ad-Din, resplendent atop a muscular horse, the tips of his mustache so sharp you could impale a prisoner on them.

When the statue was first unveiled, dignitaries from around the world came to Bagh-e Shah to celebrate. As the cover was pulled, a few foolish foreigners, oblivious to proper etiquette, had bowed before the bronze image. Word got out and the people rose up in protest. "Idolatry!" they cried, as the ignorant so often do when confronted by something they do not understand. The statue remained but, ever since that time, no other shah had dared cast his own image in bronze.

This is what Mohammed Ali was dealing with: a population so simple-minded and crude that they feared statues and saw omens in the behavior of birds. Even so, the shah knew he had to win the people back. There was only one way left to end this mess. Because the residents of Tabriz continued to resist his troops, he had no choice but to starve them into submission. Already, he had ordered the Prince to blockade most of the roads leading into the city. But to completely encircle the town, to besiege it from all sides and cut off access to food and water, required more troops. Not bandits and horsemen, but actual soldiers. What he needed was the Cossack Brigade. It had come to his rescue before; it would do so again. Perhaps it wouldn't be the dramatic victory he had envisioned a few months ago. Back then he had dreamt of Sattar splayed between two trees in Bagh-e Shah and sliced cleanly down the middle: a fitting sacrifice. Now, he would settle for the image of the People's Commander curled into a ball: all skin and bones and fighting with dogs for the last scraps of food left in the city.

Colonel Liakhov was ordered to select four hundred of his best men and provide them with whatever they needed to get the job done—rifles, cannons, horses, as well as a new kind of British-made weapon the shah had recently purchased from France: the Maxim machine gun, a violent weapon of war capable of firing sixty rounds without pause. Liakhov, himself, would stay behind. The shah needed him close in case the rebels in nearby Qazvin got it in their heads to march on Tehran. Instead, the Cossacks were led by Liakhov's second-in-command, Captain Ushakov, an artillery commander who had played a vital role in the attack on parliament and, thus, earned the shah's trust.

On the eve of their departure for Tabriz, as the shah watched from his second-floor balcony, Liakhov gathered the troops at Bagh-e Shah for final instructions. Before him stood two hundred cavalry, one hundred and fifty infantry, fifty gunners, and four gleaming Maxim machine guns.

"You should know that conquering Tabriz is a matter of life and death for you," Liakhov shouted at his men. "If you win, the Constitution will be lost, but if the victory is with the supporters of the Constitution, our Brigade will disintegrate; you, your women, and children will be left hungry. Do not forget this point. Fight like lions. Either you or Constitutionalism!"

❖

PICTURE IN YOUR mind those four hundred well-armed, well-trained men standing at attention before Colonel Liakhov, being roused to duty by his ominous exhortation. Now focus your attention on the front of the line. There, standing behind one of the four Maxim guns is a thirty-year-old soldier named Reza Khan Savadkuhi. His friends call him *Reza Shast-Tir*—"Sixty-Bullet Reza"—a nickname he'd earned for his proficiency with the new British-made machine guns.

Reza was born in an isolated village in the highlands of Mazandaran, not far from the Caspian Sea. He is, like Sattar Khan, a child of the mountains. His mother immigrated to Persia from the Caucasus after the region was lost to the Russians. He is poor, uneducated, barely literate, but also tall, handsome, and remarkably muscular. Orphaned at a young age, and with few prospects before him, he entered the Cossack Brigade at fifteen and quickly advanced up the military hierarchy. On the day he was sent by Liakhov to take Tabriz, he had earned the rank of commander.

Reza Khan Savadkuhi hates Mohammed Ali Shah and the entire Qajar Dynasty. He isn't all too fond of Colonel Liakhov, either. He resents the Russians and the British equally for their interference in Persian affairs. And he's barely given a thought to Sattar Khan, though he cannot abide by the anarchy his followers have caused. Nevertheless, he will follow his orders and march to Tabriz. He will unleash the full fury of his Maxim machine gun upon every rebel in the city without a shred of mercy. He will do these things, not so he can deliver Tabriz to the shah. He will do them because it is his duty—because he believes with all his might that the only force truly capable of saving Persia is the military.

A few years from now, Mohammed Ali Shah will be flung from his throne and exiled to Russia. Vladimir Liakhov will be recalled by the tsar to fight and lose his own country's popular revolution. Sattar

Khan will fall from his lofty perch as the People's Commander and live out the rest of his life drowning in alcohol and regret. And Howard Baskerville, who was, at that very moment, about to abandon his teaching post to join the revolution, will be buried next to an overgrown apricot tree.

After the last shot of the Constitutional Revolution has been fired and the entire affair reduced to little more than a chapter in a history book, Tabriz, Tehran, the throne, and the country—*all of it*—will fall into the hands of the poor, uneducated, barely literate Cossack from the mountains of Mazandaran you see there, lifting his gun in the air and shouting with the rest: "Down with Constitutionalism!"

The Ayatollah Fazlullah Nuri.

CHAPTER FIFTEEN

This Is My Own, My Native Land!

A LIGHT SNOW fell on Tabriz that February morning in 1909: the tenth day in the month of Muharram, according to the Islamic calendar. It was *Ashura*, the most important holiday in Shi'ah Islam—the day that commemorates the martyrdom of the Prophet Muhammad's grandson, Husain. A small, curtainless stage had been constructed in the center of the city's main square for the *Taziyeh*, the annual passion play reenacting Husain's death.

Despite the cold, it seemed like the entire city had shown up for the performance. It was, according to Sarah Wright, the largest crowd Tabriz had ever seen for the Taziyeh. The fighting had ceased for a few days in honor of the sacred holiday, and people felt safer gathering outdoors. There were Russians, Georgians, Turks, and Armenians among the audience: Christians, Jews, and Baha'i. They sat around the stage on the bare pavement, forming an open-air theater-in-the-round. The Americans came, too: the Wilsons, the Wrights, the Jessups, the Pittmans. Howard Baskerville was almost certainly there, along with an Irishman named Arthur Moore. Moore was a journalist sent to Persia on behalf of a consortium of British newspapers to report on the Constitutional Revolution. He had arrived in Tabriz earlier that winter, "half dead with cold and half blind with snow," just before the siege had begun. He was supposed to pass straight through to Tehran, but with the roads now blocked by the Prince's men, he was stuck in Tabriz for the time being.

Baskerville could not have fully understood the flowery Persian spoken by the actors on stage, but he didn't need to. The Taziyeh is a morality play; it's about the ancient conflict between good and evil. It did not require exposition. Besides, he was familiar with the story; everyone in Persia was.

It is AD 680. Husain is en route to Kufa, in modern-day Iraq, with his family and a small band of followers in order to raise an army to unseat the Syrian caliph, Yazid. He has no hope of success. The caliph commands a force of thousands; Husain has seventy-two fighters. But he cannot ignore the suffering of his people at the hands of an illegitimate ruler. So he musters what he can and marches toward certain death. He doesn't get far. In the city of Karbala, he is besieged by the caliph's soldiers, who surround his camp and slowly starve them to death. Days pass. The women and children die horribly of thirst and hunger. The men are picked off one by one. In the end, Husain has no choice but to try and break the siege. Sword in hand, he hops on his horse and rides headlong into a wall of Syrian soldiers.

It was easy to tell the characters apart by the color of their costumes and the way they delivered their lines. There's Husain, resplendent in green (the color of paradise), a stark, white shawl draped over his shoulders to symbolize the sacrifice he's about to make. And there, riding up on his horse, is the Syrian general Shimr, dressed in red (the color of violence), two long, crimson feathers jutting out of his helmet.

The Taziyeh script is written in verse. Husain and his companions sing their lines in lilting voices, in tune with the traditional melody being played by the accompanying musicians. The villains, in contrast, shriek their lines. Their voices are sharp and discordant, their movements heavy and off-beat, as though they are in conflict, not just with the music and rhythm, but with the very nature of things.

The Tabriz production was a simple affair—nothing like the sumptuous performance being staged in Tehran's Royal Theater at that same moment. There were no set decorations: just a bowl of water on one edge of the stage and a bowl of fruit on the other. The Syrian soldiers carried bronze swords and shields, dulled and dented by years of performance. Young boys dressed in veils played the female roles. It was common practice to portray the heroes and villains of the Taziyeh as contemporary figures. Baskerville may have noticed that the actor portraying Husain bore an unmistakable resemblance to Sattar Khan; he had the same greased-back hair and elegantly waxed mustache as the People's Commander. The actor playing the villainous caliph was short and fat and looked for all intents and purposes like a farcical Mohammed Ali Shah.

At the end of the play, Husain's companions are scattered across the stage, prostrate and still. The bowl of water has been knocked over, symbolizing the cutting off of water to the camp. The bowl of fruit is stomped by a Syrian's boot. Husain is alone. His white shawl is splattered with fake blood. He circles the stage slowly, staring into the face of every spectator. He has a message for those with the wisdom to hear it: you can live under oppression or you can die with dignity. Husain's choice is clear. What is yours?

"We are for God," he intones. "And to God we shall return!"

The audience wails and beats their chests, crying out, "Husain! Husain!"

Afterward, when the stage had been cleared and the crowd dispersed, Baskerville could still see audience members huddled together here and there: their eyes bleary; their chests heaving. They held each other and wept for Husain, as though they had all been there with him at Karbala—as though he had just died. It was not an unfamiliar feeling.

Howard Baskerville had sat through many passion plays depicting the death of Jesus Christ. He may have even starred in some as a child. He knew why the audience wept with such ferocity. He did not need to stretch his mind to consider Husain's final question. It is the question all Christians must ask themselves.

Had he been there, at Gethsemane, when they came to take his Lord—had he been forced to watch as Jesus was tortured and nailed to a cross—what would he have done? Would he have run away and hidden himself? Or would he have been that disciple in Gethsemane: the one who drew his sword; the one who was ready to defend the Lord with his life? What was it Jesus had said, just before they dragged him away? "Greater love has no one than this: that he lay down his life for his friends" (John 15:13).

He must have read those words more times than he could remember. He had based his life on them. One can argue that the entirety of the Christian religion rests upon that one verse, and the absurd challenge it poses to believers: that they should be ready to forfeit their lives—not for gold or silver or any riches of this world; not suddenly or in response to some unexpected danger, but deliberately and with forethought, as an act of faith, so that others may live. Isn't that what he'd been taught ever since he was a boy, fidgeting in a pew, in one of those old, box churches where his father preached: that the highest reach of love is the sacrifice of the self?

❖

ONE CAN FORGIVE Howard Baskerville for being lost in such thoughts. The past six months had been a whirlwind of highs and lows. The fall felt like a dream. The city was, for the first time, fully under nationalist control, united in a way no one here could recall. These were Tabriz's happiest days: security was restored, the bazaar fully reopened, and all barricades inside the city removed. The residents of Davehchi, Sorkhab, and the other royalist wards had been pardoned for their role in the civil war and most had simply switched sides and begun fighting for Sattar Khan instead. Rahim's cannons were redistributed across the city. One was even placed atop the Citadel, and with William Doty's permission. Like most everyone in Tabriz, the American consul general had become enamored with the People's Commander and the nationalist cause, to the annoyance of his superiors in Tehran.

"Mr. Doty has been drawn into official relations with the Andjumans [*sic*] and other revolutionary bodies," John B. Jackson wrote, in yet another complaint about Doty's behavior to the State Department. "My impression is that he has allowed his natural personal sympathies with those who appear to be in favor of some form of popular government to carry him too far, and that he has more or less compromised himself as a partisan."

Meanwhile, support continued to trickle in from all corners of the country. Fighters had begun arriving from Isfahan, Mashhad, and elsewhere in Persia. The grand ayatollahs of Najaf in modern-day Iraq had issued a series of fatwas explicitly comparing the constitutionalists in Tabriz to Husain and his comrades in Karbala. "Cooperation with the opponents of the Constitution and obedience to their commands against [its] supporters is [akin to] obedience to [the Caliph] Yazid," one fatwa read. Another fatwa declared that paying taxes to the state while the shah remained on the throne would be counted as "one of the greatest sins."

These declarations helped neutralize the campaign of the shah's mullahs, who were still trying to paint every revolutionary as a "Babi" or an "atheist." They also brought the pious poor back to the side of the constitutionalists, boosting the ranks of the Feda'i. Armed with the fatwas, Sattar dispatched his soldiers across Azerbaijan to recruit those living in nearby towns and villages to the cause, training and arming their impoverished populations for combat. The hope was to turn these villages into something like an advance defense system, to create a ring of support around Tabriz that would slow the enemy's progress. By mid-November 1908, a considerable portion of the province was, at least nominally, under the authority of Tabriz.

Inside the city, there was a seemingly endless stream of parties, parades, and celebrations. A spate of weddings broke out in the fall—sometimes three or four a day. A great many of the foreign fighters took Persian wives, cementing their bond with the city and its people. It was as if a new country was being born, one united not by religion or race—and certainly not by language or culture—but by a common belief: that people should be masters of their own fate; that they should be free to act and think without coercion; that they should have a say in the decisions that ruled their lives.

A new country needed a new flag, so Tabriz created one. The Persian Constitution had already mandated the design of a new national flag. It would be tricolored with horizontal stripes of green, white, and red—a saber-wielding lion emblazoned in the center, a golden sun rising from its haunches. Tabriz maintained the new national colors, but it replaced the Lion and the Sun—the ancient symbols of Persian royalty—with an inscription penned in Kufic calligraphy: *Long Live the Constitution*.

The new flags were carried from ward to ward with great pomp and ceremony. One flew high over Khiyaban, another over Amirkhiz. A third was unfurled in the main square, over the headquarters of the Tabriz Anjoman.

With the start of the fall semester of 1908, the American Memorial School was once again bursting with activity. The fact that wealthy parents, such as those of Sadeq Rezazadeh Shafaq, felt safe enough to return to Tabriz from their summer residences and reenroll their children in school was viewed by all as a hopeful sign. Perhaps the worst was truly behind them. Nearly the entire faculty had returned as well—foreigners as well as well as Persians. There was, of course, an unfillable hole where Hassan Sharifzadeh should have been. His friends and former pupils mourned his death, but the Union of Students, which Hassan had established at the school, continued his legacy by meeting regularly to discuss ways to promote the revolution across the country.

There was one other missing faculty member that fall. Mirza Ansari, the school's popular international law instructor, had failed to return from his summer home in Maragheh, just south of Tabriz. The town was one of the first seized by the Prince's troops when they arrived back in August. They terrorized the residents, arresting and killing anyone deemed even remotely supportive of the constitution. As one of the most strident voices of the Persian Constitutional Revolution, Mirza Ansari was singled out for special treatment. He was arrested, beaten, flogged, stripped naked, and flung into a frozen pool until he died of hypothermia. His body was then dragged out and hung by the ankle from an elm tree in front of his wife and children.

Mirza Ansari's murder shocked the student body at the American Memorial School. Samuel Wilson was apoplectic. In the course of a few months he had lost two cherished faculty members. Mirza Ansari had been at the school for years; Hassan, he had known since he was an awkward English student. These were not just two of the most popular teachers at the school; they were his dear friends. Nevertheless, he now had before him the urgent task of filling their positions.

It wasn't too difficult to procure an Arabic instructor; there were many qualified candidates in Tabriz. But finding someone to teach Ansari's international law course proved more challenging. In the end, and on the advice of the students, Wilson chose someone who was already a member of the faculty: Howard Baskerville.

Baskerville plunged himself into the work. The extra course offered him the opportunity to keep his mind busy and focused on something other than his fallen friend, Hassan. He was familiar with international law, having taken two courses that covered the subject at Princeton, both of them taught by a man who would one day redefine the field with the founding of the League of Nations. He had been well briefed in its sources and guiding principles: the right to govern one's affairs free from outside interference; the rules necessary for civilized conduct in war; the authority of individuals in a given territory to make their own governing decisions. These legal pillars of the modern world were as familiar to him as the ancient scriptures.

The question was not: Would he be qualified to teach the class? The question was: How could he do so with a straight face? After all, he was lecturing his students on theoretical concepts for which they and their families were literally dying on the streets of Tabriz. Their previous instructor had been slowly tortured to death for teaching these very ideas.

Baskerville needn't worry about that, of course. He was American; no one would dare touch him. He could say whatever he wanted. He could stand in front of his class and argue forcefully for the rights of the individual over the state, as long as he was willing to ignore those rights once class was over. That is, more or less, what he'd been doing for much of the previous year. He had been forced, under threat of expulsion and deportation, to keep his thoughts about the revolution to himself, at least in front of his students.

Yet his new teaching responsibilities made silence impossible. There was simply no way to teach a course on international law without delving into the current political situation in Persia. And so, little by little, that is what he did.

He no longer refrained from bringing the action on the streets into his classroom. In his lectures, he made direct parallels between Persia's fight for freedom and the American Revolution. He made known his bitterness toward the British and Russians and the role they had played in keeping the shah on his throne for their own benefit. And he expressed his deep dissatisfaction with the lack of interest from the United States in supporting Persian democracy.

Under the guise of prepping for lesson plans, Baskerville started studying Persian history and politics. He familiarized himself with the tobacco protests, the history of the Qajars, and the early days of the Constitutional Revolution. He interviewed high-ranking members of the Tabriz Anjoman, asking their opinions on what was taking place in Persia, and what would happen next. In the evenings he took food to the soldiers serving on the front lines, then sat with them as they ate, listening to their exaggerated tales of glory. And, unbeknownst to nearly everyone in Tabriz, he began to meet with Sattar Khan. It would be months before the nature and purpose of these secret meetings would be revealed; and, by then, it was too late to do anything about it.

As the fall semester was coming to an end, Samuel Wilson asked Baskerville to give that year's annual Thanksgiving Day sermon. It wasn't the first time he had preached in chapel; preaching was part of his regular duties. It's why he had brought that one "first-class outfit." All the male missionaries took turns giving sermons, with Frederick Jessup delivering the lion's share. But this was a special service. After Christmas and Easter, it was the largest worship gathering of the year. The chapel would be filled with nearly the entire student body. Their families and special guests would be in attendance. Whatever Baskerville said from the pulpit would ripple across the city.

Unfortunately, the text of Baskerville's sermon has been lost to history. But those in attendance that Thanksgiving morning—Americans and Persians alike, whether Christian or Muslim—were deeply affected by it. Annie Wilson swore she would never forget the sermon. Sarah Wright wrote about it in her diary that night. It was, by all accounts, a passionate defense of patriotism, and a thinly veiled call to action to those in the room. He closed the sermon not with scripture, but with a poem by the Scottish poet, Sir Walter Scott.

> *Breathes there the man, with soul so dead,*
> *Who never to himself hath said,*
> *This is my own, my native land!*
> *Whose heart hath ne'er within him burn'd,*
> *As home his footsteps he hath turn'd,*
> *From wandering on a foreign strand!*

Walter Scott was a fervent Scottish nationalist, and the poem was his paean to his native home. Written a century after union with England, it reflects the bitterness of the Scots in losing their independence and national culture. The message of the poem is unmissable: He who does not love his "native land"—who is not willing to fight for it, to die for it—will, as Scott warns at the end of the first stanza, die twice. He will die physically, and he will die in the memories of those he leaves behind. Both he and his name will be forgotten forever.

> *The wretch, concentred all in self,*
> *Living, shall forfeit fair renown,*
> *And, doubly dying, shall go down*
> *To the vile dust, from whence he sprung,*
> *Unwept, unhonour'd, and unsung.*

Baskerville could have been merely speaking to the Americans in the chapel, preaching predictable, anodyne exhortations about "love of country" on Thanksgiving Day. But it wasn't just Americans in the audience. There were Russians and Armenians, Georgians and Turks, and, most numerous of all, Persians—all of them currently engaged in a fight for their respective homelands; all of them willing to die for it. They got Baskerville's message loud and clear. So, it would appear, did Samuel Wilson and William Doty, both of whom appeared to be genuinely disturbed by Baskerville's words and the passion with which he delivered them.

After chapel, the Americans gathered at the Wright home to share Thanksgiving dinner. Sarah Wright, who admits in her diary that she was unsure why Baskerville's sermon had caused such a stir—"Mr. Baskerville gave an elegant and highly patriotic talk, no doubt, but since I am Persian it didn't inspire me at all," she writes with charming naïveté—sat at the table between Baskerville and Doty, with the Wilsons directly across from them. One can feel the night's awkwardness in Sarah's account. When dinner was over and the dishes cleared, Agnes—the woman Baskerville had been forbidden to marry—played some "Sattar Khan songs" at the piano, while her father—the man who had forbidden the marriage—stood silently at the fireplace, a drink undrunk in his hand.

It could have been a coincidence, but soon after that Thanksgiving sermon, Baskerville was forced to move again—this time off campus. He vacated his tiny dorm room on the school grounds and moved into a spare bedroom in the home of the Wrights for much of that second winter in Tabriz. He was heading there now, on that cold February evening, as the last of the Taziyeh mourners were leaving the main square and the curtainless stage was torn down and placed in storage for next year's performance.

❖

WITH THE ASHURA celebrations of February 1909 complete, the Prince resumed his attack on Tabriz. The Cossack Brigade sent from Tehran had finally arrived, and the Prince now boasted a fighting force of nearly twelve thousand men. He divided his troops into squads and had them encircle the city. The ring of support that Sattar Khan had attempted to build around Tabriz, by arming and training the neighboring towns and villages, did not hold. The villages were easily overrun, their populations massacred. Those who had pledged Sattar support were bound to the mouths of cannons and pointed in the direction of Tabriz: their flesh and bones splattered across the white valley floor.

The Prince made the village of Basmenj, a few miles east of Tabriz, his command center. The four hundred Cossacks under the command of Captain Ushakov were distributed at strategic locations along the perimeter wall of Tabriz, some of them positioned just a few hundred yards away, Maxim guns at the ready. The squad under the command of Reza Khan Savadkuhi was sent to Qaramalik, which used to be its own independent village just west of Tabriz but, with the slow expansion of the city at the end of the nineteenth century, was now just a suburb of sorts, separated from the city proper by nothing but a few fields and an orchard.

The Prince's most devastating move was to send Rahim Khan and his Shahsevan horsemen to close the Jolfa Road. This was the life-blood of the city—the shortest trade route between Tabriz and Europe. It supplied Tabriz with a steady stream of goods and staples—not to mention arms and volunteers—ferried across the Aras River (the Jolfa Road is what Baskerville had taken to Tabriz).

With the city encircled, the Prince sent a final ultimatum to Sattar Khan. Tabriz had forty-eight hours to lay down its guns and surrender, otherwise his troops would "do what had to be done."

Sattar Khan laughed when he received the message. "What is this ultimatum about?" he wrote in reply. "What is this 48-hour reprieve about? Have you been joking until today, and now you want to fight?"

But the Prince had no intention of fighting. He had a different plan in mind. He had formed a ring around Tabriz, cutting off all access to food and water, and ordered his men to shoot anyone trying to leave or enter the city. He was done trying to defeat Tabriz. He was going to starve it instead.

Still, Sattar Khan was unworried. There was plenty to eat in Tabriz. He had ordered the farmers to stockpile basic goods such as wheat, barley, and rice in case of a prolonged siege. They could melt and drink the snow. With the closing of the Jolfa Road, there would soon be no more sugar or oil in the city, and very little coal or firewood. But the people could cut down their fruit trees for warmth. Future generations may mourn the gardens of Tabriz. But the city would survive.

The 48-hour reprieve lasted a lifetime. With the pause in fighting, the city grew eerily quiet. No one seriously considered surrendering, but there was a palpable sense of unease among the population. There was too much time to think about the Prince's threat. They had food now, but for how long? Tabriz had seen its share of victories and defeats over the past few months. The people had gotten used to the erratic cannon fire and mortar attacks. But siege and starvation? Would the children have enough to eat, if it came to that?

It was time for the People's Commander to spring into action, to add one more chapter to his already lengthy legend as the hero of the revolution. He gathered a small band of mostly Armenian and Georgian soldiers—those with urban warfare experience—and crept quietly out of town before first light. They made their way north to try to force open the Jolfa Road, hoping to take Rahim Khan by surprise.

The sound of gunfire beyond the wall awakened Tabriz. *Sattar was gone! He had left to break the siege! Our very own Husain!*

A roar of excitement swept through the city as residents flocked to the northern edge of town to see if they could catch a glimpse of what was happening. They were keen to watch their leader smash through the enemy and return victorious. For who could defeat the People's Commander?

The Shahsevan were not fooled by the surprise attack. They quickly rallied and pinned Sattar and his soldiers behind a makeshift barricade. Rahim himself joined the fight. The two sides were mere yards apart—close enough to curse each other by name. Sattar was stuck, unable to advance or retreat. One by one his soldiers fell around him, until there were only two or three fighters left. At any point during the early hours of the fight, he could have retreated safely back to Tabriz. But he would not leave his fallen comrades behind.

The hours ticked by slowly as the Shahsevan slowly advanced from all sides onto his position. Sattar could keep Rahim's men at a safe distance, but he was only delaying the inevitable. As the sun set, he made the decision to kill himself rather than fall into the hands of the enemy. Those who were with him that day say he laid his gun against the barricade, leaned back casually, and called to one of his soldiers to pass him a final smoke.

It was several hours after midnight, when the Feda'i suddenly burst out of the city gates in a blaze of gunfire. They shot their way to where Sattar was holed up, placed him and their dead comrades in a carriage, and raced back to the city under cover of darkness.

The sight of the People's Commander returning to Tabriz, bruised and bloodied, and with only a fraction of the force he had taken out with him, filled the people with fear. As usual, Sattar had shown courage and honor in battle. Once again, he had faced overwhelming odds and survived. But he had also *lost*, and that was something the residents of Tabriz were not accustomed to. It shook the city in a way no cannon or mortar attack could.

With the rising of the sun the following morning, the 48-hour reprieve came to an end. The siege of the city had begun. No matter what happened now, the fate of Tabriz rested in God's hands.

CHAPTER SIXTEEN

I Must Go. I Am Gone.

THE SOUND OF THE BLAST shattered windows across Tabriz. It was 5:00 a.m. Baskerville jumped out of bed, half-clothed and disoriented, and peeked out the window. The sky outside was bright but the sun had not yet risen. Streaks of red, orange, purple, and black fanned out from the horizon. The black signaled smoke.

He had been boarding with the Wrights for the past few months: a small room on the second floor. He went up to the roof for a better view and found Sarah Wright already there; the noise had awakened the entire neighborhood.

A great battle was taking place on the western edge of the city. The gunfire sounded strange. It was rapid, percussive: a sharp, loud, unreceding, *takka takka takka takka*. No one in Tabriz had ever heard anything like it. From where Baskerville stood, he could see explosions flashing all along the length of the orchard that separated the city from the village of Qaramalik, where some of the Cossack Brigade were stationed. The trees were on fire.

He left Sarah shivering on the roof and raced down to see what was happening. It wasn't a long distance, but Baskerville's course was slowed by having to crawl through a honeycomb of house and garden walls: a necessary precaution. The surrounding hills were stippled with the Prince's marksmen. They lay in wait morning, noon, and night, sites focused on the town below, taking potshots at unsuspecting citizens. One moment you'd be standing in line at the public bakery, waiting to receive your daily ration. The next moment, the head in front of you would splatter against the wall.

Sattar Khan had ordered the population to cut holes in their walls to allow for safe passage from neighborhood to neighborhood. Residents could travel through most of the city simply by passing through each other's homes, as Baskerville was doing now.

As he drew closer to the noise, he came upon several wounded men being ushered inside the city. They were nude, their feet bloody and torn, their bodies blue from the cold. They had walked all the way from Maragheh. Rather than continue feeding and housing their prisoners, the royalist force occupying that city thought it would be amusing to strip them naked and have them walk the eighty miles or so across the snow-covered desert back to Tabriz. Dozens had been released. Three had arrived.

Baskerville was about to help with the prisoners when a sudden commotion caught his eye. A group of Sattar's soldiers were running across the cemetery, yelling and waving their arms in a panic. Beyond them, Baskerville could hear the sound of bugles being blown. The Prince had chosen this day, Friday, March 5, 1909, to try to breach the city.

The Feda'i were caught completely by surprise. Although sporadic fighting between the two sides had been unabating throughout the now nearly month-long siege and blockade of the city, it had been some time since the Prince had attempted an incursion. Partly, this had to do with the city's improved defenses. The Georgians had planted bombs across the hills and valley so that whenever the Prince's men approached, they were blown to bits; the cannon atop the Citadel made short work of survivors. But it was also due to the Prince's shift in strategy. Having cut off all access to food and water, he seemed content to let the city die on its own. Why risk his life and those of his men only to speed things along?

Yet, that is exactly what Mohammed Ali Shah kept demanding of him. "Why have you not finished with the city?" His Majesty would ask again and again. Like a child wailing to be fed, the shah wanted satisfaction; and he wanted it now. He had begun to lose faith in his esteemed cousin. Rumors circulated in court that the Prince was deliberately taking his time with Tabriz, all the better to seize power himself. He must have known that the longer the rebels remained in control, the more cities would take their cue from Tabriz and revolt. There were bands of Persians, Armenians, Georgians, Jews, and Baha'i, all across the country, fighting together under the same revolutionary flag. The situation was intolerable.

Tabriz had become an international *cause célèbre*, with governments as far away as America pressuring the shah to end the conflict before it spread beyond the borders. The so-called Nationalist Manifesto, which the Tabriz Anjoman had sent to foreign capitals, was starting to cause a headache at court, with near-daily telegrams sent from dignitaries around the world demanding to know what exactly was taking place in Tabriz. Are they to believe that the people there were being starved? What about their foreign nationals, their banks and their businesses? How could the government have lost control of its second city?

The shah was running out of time. What he wanted was blood. "I shall not give up until the rebels have been chastised and their fathers have been burned," he had telegrammed the Prince, "even if a million [soldiers] are spent."

The Prince had no choice but to oblige.

An hour before sunrise on March 5, his troops entered the orchard that served as the western entrance to the city. The Feda'i had cut a series of deep trenches to keep the Prince's men at bay. But the trenches were easily demolished by an early-morning volley of cannonballs, and the fighters stationed there were forced to retreat. They were pursued into the orchard by a barrage of bullets fired from the Maxim guns: *takka takka takka*. The bullets tore through the trees and ripped apart most of the retreating fighters as they abandoned the barricades and ran for their lives.

These were the men Baskerville had seen yelling and running through the cemetery. They looked lost and confused. They would stop occasionally and ask each other, "Where shall we go? Where will we hide the women and children?"

In previous battles, this would be the moment when Baskerville would withdraw behind the gates of the American Memorial School. He would huddle inside the chapel along with the rest of the Americans until the city grew quiet again, then return gingerly to the streets to find out what had happened, who had died. But that was before Hassan had been murdered; before Mirza Ansari was tortured to death; before he had been compelled by his teaching duties to no longer ignore the suffering he saw on the streets. He still taught at the school, but he no longer lived there. No one need know where he was at this moment, what he was doing out here in the middle of the firefight, why he was running toward the battle, instead of away from it. For the first time since arriving in Persia, he was following his conscience. And perhaps that conscience was eased somewhat knowing that, while he was running across the cemetery, in the direction of the blaring bugles, Agnes would be lying flat on her stomach beneath a wooden pew in the chapel, hands clasped over her head, waiting with her family for the noise to stop.

Not even ten minutes had passed since Baskerville had climbed down the roof of the Wright home and began running toward the commotion. That's how long it took for the first of the Prince's men to exit the flaming orchard and make his way inside the city. They came one-by-one, in single file, creeping slowly along the alley walls, taking two or three steps, then stopping to shoot their rifles, before continuing their advance. In this way, they moved slowly but with ease.

The first ward in the city the soldiers reached was called Hokma-var. The residents here were mostly farmers; there were a large number of cows, sheep, and donkeys tethered to the exterior walls. The Prince's men executed the animals. They beat on people's doors and, if they weren't immediately opened, broke them down and entered the homes. The residents were unmolested, so long as they did not resist. The soldiers were not there to capture farmers and their families; they had a different target in mind. They pushed past the frightened women and children until they reached the granaries, where the town's wheat and barley were stored. This was all that separated the residents from abject starvation. The men loaded up whatever they could on stolen horses and carried it off, along with any valuables they happened to come across.

Meanwhile, more of the Prince's men were emerging from the burning orchard, some on horseback, dragging cannons. The truth hit Baskerville all at once: this wasn't an incursion; it was a full-scale invasion. He could not have known it then, but there were battles taking place in all four corners of the city. Khiyaban was under attack from the north, while another squad of soldiers was advancing on the city from the south. The Prince himself was commanding the force on the eastern edge of the city. Rahim Khan and his horsemen had left their base on the Jolfa Road to join the fight, though they had yet to enter the orchard. Cannonballs dropped on the city from six separate locations. But the fiercest battle was being fought right here, in Hokmavar.

The shah's troops pushed their way to the cemetery and closer to the city center. With each advance, the Feda'i were forced to abandon their positions and fall back, leaving their weapons behind. It appeared that nothing could slow the enemy's progress. At this rate they could take the city in a couple of hours.

When the attack on the city had begun, Sattar Khan was on his rooftop, using a telescope to survey the field. It did not take long for him to realize what was happening. "Quick bring the horse!" he shouted down to his attendant. "They are killing the boys!"

He jumped from the roof of his house onto his horse and charged past the retreating forces. As he drew close to the cemetery, he pulled out his sword in one hand and his pistol in the other and jumped from his saddle directly into the fray. He was an army unto himself, cutting down one man after another, oblivious to the danger around him.

When the Feda'i saw their commander take the field, everything changed. A zealous cry erupted across the city as the people came out of hiding. Even the city's mullahs grabbed their rifles and headed to battle. They rallied the population to come out and join them in defending the city. Bit by bit, they emerged, flocking to Hokmavar, some without weapons.

In Khiyaban, Baqer Khan quickly got the upper hand over the invading troops, using the same tried-and-true tactic of luring the soldiers deeper and deeper into the neighborhood and then trapping them in the twists and turns of the alleyways. With victory there in sight, some of his men broke off and went to join the fight in Hokmavar, where Sattar Khan and a group of fighters were holed up on the balcony of a private home, firing down on the Prince's men.

The enemy copied Sattar's tactic, climbing up on other balconies. As the two sides shot at each other from three dimensions, someone near Sattar pointed out that one of the cannons the fleeing fighters had left behind was sitting idle, on the far side of the cemetery. They then watched in astonishment as an old man—a merchant from Hokmavar—came out of his home and walked calmly across the cemetery, as though out for a stroll. When the old man reached the cannon he grabbed hold and dragged it—by himself, in the middle of a firefight—behind a wall where some of Sattar's fighters were hiding. The fighters swung the cannon toward the balcony where a mass of the Prince's men had assembled and fired. A roar of thunder and the entire building came crumbling to the ground.

The cannon was reloaded and fired again, as Sattar and his comrades continued shooting from above. The invaders had advanced too far into the city and were now caught in a cage of bullets and cannon fire. They had no choice but to retreat back into the orchard. The Feda'i gave chase, dropping the fleeing soldiers one by one. They pursued them nearly back to Qaramalik, but were stopped by the Cossacks and the Maxim guns. It didn't matter. The battle was over. The day had been won.

Afterward, when it had grown quiet again, Sattar climbed down from the balcony and exited the private home. He sent his fighters door to door looking for enemy stragglers. He ordered his attendant to gather all the loot the fleeing soldiers had left scattered in the streets and take it to a mosque so the owners could collect what was theirs. That's when he saw Howard Baskerville, standing on the edge of the cemetery.

He called out to him by name.

If anyone from the American mission had been there to watch the two men come together and clasp hands, to see the People's Commander speak warmly and with evident familiarity with the young Christian missionary from the Black Hills of South Dakota, they would have been utterly baffled. Did these two know each other?

Baskerville congratulated Sattar Khan on the great victory. The two men spoke privately for a moment, neither well-versed in the other's language. Then Sattar got on his horse. He was about to leave, but he hesitated. He was waiting for Baskerville to join him.

Sattar's attendant brought out a horse. The American grabbed the saddle, swung his leg over, and followed the Father of the Nation back to the barracks.

❖

WORD TRAVELS FAST in a town like Tabriz. Soon, everyone was talking about the young American who had joined up with Sattar Khan. The missionaries at the American Memorial School were stunned. It's not that they were unsympathetic to the cause; quite the contrary. They knew better than most what Tabriz was fighting for. "This is not really a revolution but a stand for the rights of the people to the Constitution which was granted by the late Shah [Muzaffar ad-Din] and which this king [Mohammed Ali] has many times solemnly sworn to uphold," Frederick Jessup wrote in a dispatch explaining the situation in the city to the Presbyterian Board of Foreign Missions in New York.

The Americans in Tabriz were deeply pained by the people's suffering. These weren't faceless revolutionaries. They were friends and neighbors, students and parishioners. There were young men and women dying on the streets who had been born in missionary hospitals and delivered by missionary doctors. Samuel Wilson, in particular, was absolutely nerve-wracked by the blockade, and he could not hide it. He had aged significantly in the past few months. Shuffling through the bazaar in his wide-brimmed hat and black cassock, clerical collar loose and dangling at his neck, he would often stop one resident or another and ask, "What will happen to Tabriz?" The question was rhetorical. It was, more than anything else, an invitation to stop for a moment and grieve together—to shake their heads and sigh together.

In the face of such pain and misery, it was preposterous to think the West Persia Mission could remain "neutral." Yet, that is precisely what it was expected to do. The Presbyterian Board of Foreign Missions forbid the men and women it sent out into the world from intervening in what it deemed "temporal matters." Missionaries were encouraged to put aside their concerns for the civil conditions in which they found their flocks and focus instead on the work of evangelization. Under no circumstances were they to impose upon foreign lands the social and political liberties they enjoyed as Americans back home. They should, instead, heed the words of Jesus Christ, who counseled them to, "Render unto Caesar that which is Caesar's, and unto God that which is God's" (Mark 12:17).

That was, of course, easier said than done in a place like Persia, in the midst of a revolution, with children dying at your feet. In the face of such injustice and oppression, wasn't the West Persia Mission morally required to engage in "temporal matters?" After all, this wasn't exactly a "foreign land." Most of the American missionaries had lived here so long they were practically Tabrizis. Samuel was the only member of the Wilson clan *not* born in Persia. His children, Agnes especially, referred to themselves as Persians. And they were. This was their "native land." They knew no other. Their lives were bound to the fate of the city. How could they not interfere in its "civil conditions?" Indeed, as William Shedd, who ran the mission in Urmia, argued, they already interfered in every aspect of the people's lives.

"We have interfered when a daughter or a donkey has been stolen," Shedd wrote in a report to the missions board. "We have interfered when a church or a fence had to be built. We have interfered when a man was to be buried or married. We have interfered in the behalf of the oppressions of the rich & the poor. We have interfered in time of war & in time of peace. In fact, there is no time or occasion in which we have not had our say in the administration of this people."

It would be fair to say that the majority of American missionaries stationed in Tabriz agreed with Shedd in this matter. They sympathized with the plight of the Persians under their care. They felt great pity over the dreadful famine that was just beginning to grip the city. They excoriated the shah for his persecution of the people. And they fully identified with the cause of constitutionalism. "All the sympathy of liberty-loving and of thinking people must be on the side of the nationalists," Jessup wrote in his dispatch.

That said, the notion that any one of them would pick up arms and actually fight alongside those they served was beyond the pale. It was as great a violation of a missionary's code of conduct as there could be. When John Wright found out what Baskerville had done, he rebuked him severely for his conduct and asked him to find other lodgings in town.

Samuel Wilson was more sympathetic. He understood what Baskerville had been going through. Hassan's death had hit him hard. The murder of Mirza Ansari was dreadful. The suffering on the streets could not be ignored. Still, if the rumors were true and Baskerville had joined up with Sattar Khan, it could undermine everything he and Annie had built in Tabriz. Worse, it could put the lives of his fellow missionaries at risk. Wilson had witnessed for himself the revolutionary fires slowly brewing in the young man's chest. The Thanksgiving Day sermon was a wake-up call of sorts; it prompted Wilson to keep better tabs on his actions and whereabouts, though, admittedly, that had become more difficult now that he was living off campus. He had hoped Arthur Moore's unexpected presence in the city would serve to temper Baskerville's passions. The two young men had hit it off immediately. Moore was only five years older than Baskerville and also a minister's son. He, too, had spurned the pulpit for a life of adventure. Perhaps Moore would be able to draw Baskerville away from his growing involvement in Persian affairs.

But Moore had had the opposite effect on Baskerville. The Irishman had made a name for himself as a globetrotting adventurer with an affinity for revolutionary causes. After graduating from Oxford in 1904, he had traveled to the Balkans to write about the plight of the Christian population in the Ottoman Empire. From there he had gone to Macedonia to report on the Young Turk revolution. He had only been in Tabriz a short time, but he'd already written numerous articles about the successes of the rebellion, the heroics of the Feda'i, and the villainy of the shah. Far from dousing the revolutionary fires in Baskerville, Moore had given it oxygen. In fact, if what Wilson was hearing was accurate, Moore had also thrown in his lot with the revolutionaries and placed himself under Sattar Khan's command.

Very well, that was Moore's prerogative. Wilson had no authority over him. But Baskerville was employed by the school. He was in Persia by the grace of the Presbyterian Church. If he would not abide by the rules of the mission, then surely he would obey the laws of his country. It was time to call upon William Doty: to inform him of Baskerville's actions and encourage the American consul general to bring the full weight of the US government to bear in deterring the young man from his present course.

What no one in the West Persia Mission knew at the time was that Doty had been aware of Howard Baskerville's growing relationship with Sattar Khan for months. At the beginning of the year, Baskerville had begun spending nearly all of his free time in the consulate library, bent over its collection of *Encyclopaedia Britannica*, taking reams of notes. Doty assumed he was doing research for class. The truth was, he never asked. He welcomed Baskerville's presence and truly enjoyed the company. It was January, and the nights were long.

It wasn't until a few weeks later that Doty discovered Baskerville had been sent to the library by none other than Sattar Khan. Apparently, the two had been meeting in secret for some time. Sattar had asked Baskerville to use the library to secure some much-needed information pulled directly from the *Encyclopaedia Britannica* about explosives, how to improve infantry charges, and where to more effectively employ field artillery.

The information regarding explosives was particularly vital. The Georgian bomb-makers had turned the tide of the war with Tehran. They had arrived in Tabriz as experts at making grenades and other small, hand-thrown devices. Over the course of the fighting, those simple bombs had evolved into long-range projectiles and sophisticated booby traps. Their greatest achievement—"one of the masterpieces of the history of the constitutional revolution," in the words of the historian Ahmed Kasravi—was the development of the package bomb. The Georgians had devised a clever incendiary disguised as a parcel and sent through the post to the Prince's generals stationed in neighboring villages. As soon as the package was opened it would explode, leaving a crater the size of a horse carriage in the ground.

If the rebels were to win this war, they needed to expand their bombing techniques, and that is what Sattar had sent Baskerville to the consulate library to research.

When Doty discovered the truth he was aghast. Heartsore and bitter at being so easily duped, he had locked up the *Encyclopaedia Britannica* and barred Baskerville from using the library again for any reason. He also made him swear to stop associating with Sattar Khan. "Our government is strictly neutral in the struggle and it would give great offense at Washington and at Tehran were an American to give any aid whatsoever to either side in this conflict," Doty warned. "I believe that you would not only compromise our government but also the interests of the American Presbyterian Mission. . . . I earnestly beg of you not to be drawn into this contest at all."

Baskerville promised he would abide by Doty's command and, to his credit, Doty kept his actions a secret. He reported Baskerville's activities to his superiors in Tehran—"I am very glad to inform you that Mr. Baskerville has been careful to abide by my caution to him to refrain from giving advice to Sattar Khan on the question of explosives," he wrote—but there's no evidence that he told anyone else what he had caught Baskerville doing. He did, however, send a memo to the entire West Persia Mission, reminding everyone associated with it—the doctors, the teachers, the ministers, the spouses, and children—that "insurrection against an oriental government (where our government exercises extraterritorial rights)" would be considered a form of treason against the United States and, therefore, a "capital crime."

Treason! Every missionary got the message. But it was meant for one missionary in particular.

Doty was out of town during the March 5 invasion. He had been working with the Russian and British consuls to negotiate the delivery of wheat and other badly needed supplies through the blockade, with the promise that it would be used solely for the needs of the foreign residents and not the local population. When he returned to Tabriz and was informed that Howard Baskerville had followed Sattar Khan to the barracks—that he was, at that moment, performing military drills in the parade grounds—Doty nearly wept. Reading his account of what happened, one can tell that he was genuinely bruised by Baskerville's betrayal. He confessed to his superiors in Tehran that he had done all he could "to dissuade Mr. Baskerville from joining the Nationalists." But he had obviously failed.

Nevertheless, he decided to make one final attempt at convincing Baskerville to abandon his present course of action. He rode directly to where the Feda'i were training. There, he saw Sattar Khan, clad in white and wearing his ever-present felt hat, his face sunburnt and expressionless. The People's Commander was hunched over a table, discussing strategy with his inner circle of advisers. There were thousands of fighters all over the parade grounds, shouting and shooting into the air, galloping about on horses or drilling in groups. After the failed invasion of the city, Sattar had plastered posters all over Tabriz asking for volunteers. Anyone of any age—male or female—who wished to become a soldier was told to come to the parade grounds for training. They would be armed, given a uniform, and put through a series of drills to get them up to speed and ready to fight.

Among the volunteers, Doty spied two familiar faces: Howard Baskerville and Arthur Moore. Baskerville wore the same felt hat as the other fighters. He carried his rifle well—upright and tight against his chest. His movements were crisp and under control. Doty could see how the other volunteers deferred to him. They mimicked his maneuvers: rifle switching from one shoulder to the other; the butt of the weapon slowly lowered to the ground, the muzzle vertical.

Doty alighted from his horse, pale and nervous, and walked right up to Sattar Khan. The two men saluted one another, and Doty congratulated him on his recent defense of the city. Through an interpreter, Sattar thanked Doty and welcomed him to the parade grounds. "I am sure the American nation has full sympathy with us in our struggle," he said with a grin, his eyes small and fiery.

Doty smiled and made small talk. He thanked Sattar Khan for all he had done to protect Tabriz. He greatly admired the sacrifices his fighters had made on behalf of the Persian nation. But he had come for a different reason. He wanted to speak to Howard Baskerville.

"We are very proud to have Mr. Baskerville take active part in our national striving against despotism and foreign infiltration," Sattar said. "But, on the other hand, this is a dangerous undertaking which may lead to fatal consequences. We would regret this very much. I would rather advise that this young American continue with his teaching, which we need badly and leave the fighting to us. If, however, he insists, he is very welcome, although we cannot take any responsibility for what may happen."

Baskerville spied Doty standing with Sattar Khan across the parade grounds. He knew why he was there. He shouldered his rifle, excused himself, and walked over.

Doty patiently explained to Baskerville that Washington would consider his intervention in the political affairs of Persia to be a grave violation of American law. He warned him, yet again, that he could be opening himself up to prosecution—perhaps to charges of treason. "As an official representative of the United States of America I am compelled to remind you that you as an American citizen have no right to interfere with the internal politics of this country and you are here to act as a teacher and not as a revolutionary."

Baskerville could see how pained Doty was by the circumstances in which they found themselves. He had lied and concealed his intentions for months: promised one thing and done another. He had kept his activities a secret from those he cared about most. He had broken his word. And, now, for the first time, he was being asked to explain himself. Why risk everything—his job, his freedom, perhaps his life— for another nation's revolution? What did he think his presence on the battlefield would accomplish? Why not give up this foolish idea and return to his friends and family?

Standing in the middle of the dusty parade grounds, rifle in hand, Baskerville was finally ready to give his answer.

"I thank you for your kindness," he began, his voice tinged with emotion, "but I cannot remain calm and watch indifferently the sufferings of people fighting for their rights. I am an American citizen and I'm proud of it, but I'm also a human being and cannot help feeling deep sympathy with the people of the city. I am not able to go on teaching calmly and quietly while tragic events happen daily around me. I assure you I am not afraid of any fatal consequence and I am determined to serve the national cause of Persia."

Doty grew agitated. The national cause of Persia? Baskerville was American. His duty was to the United States, not to a foreign country. He had no choice but to desist these activities at once and return to his teaching duties. This was not his fight.

Baskerville's gaze swept the parade grounds. He gestured to the mass of volunteers who had come to Tabriz from all over the world, ready to give their lives for the cause of freedom. "The only difference between me and these people is the place of my birth," he said, "and that is not a big difference."

Doty kept trying to change his mind, but it was no use. Baskerville was firm and implacable. He knew what he was doing, and he accepted the consequences.

The American consul put his hand out and reluctantly asked Baskerville to relinquish his passport. If he would not obey the laws of his country, then he could no longer be "regarded as under its protection." From here on out he was on his own—"cut off from all appeal to the American government." He bid Baskerville a sad farewell, and rode back home alone.

Baskerville's ties to his country had been severed, but there was still the matter of his position in the American Memorial School. Considering how hard he had worked to keep the conflict out of the classroom, he owed his students an explanation. In Sadeq Rezazadeh Shafaq's telling, Baskerville's decision had been some months in the making. But even he must have been taken aback by Baskerville's appearance in class, dressed in the uniform of a Fida'i.

Standing in front of his students, Baskerville confessed that he could no longer bear to watch from a classroom window the starving inhabitants of the city who were dying for the same rights that he took for granted as an American. He could no longer speak his conscience in the classroom and then ignore that conscience when he stepped off campus. The best way he knew to serve his students was to leave school and go fight for them.

The class was speechless. Incredibly, after Baskerville bid them goodbye and turned to leave, a number of his students, Sadeq included, rose from their seats and walked out with him. "We left the class pledging to follow our teacher who was ready to give his life for our country," Sadeq recalled.

The last time the students had tried to join the fight, Sattar Khan sent them back to school with a stern admonition. This time, when they arrived at the barracks, Sattar had them dressed, armed, and prepped for combat.

This was all too much for Samuel Wilson. It was one thing for Baskerville to risk his own life, but he was now risking the lives of his students. Baskerville had been brought to Tabriz to teach these kids English and history. But, like some sort of demented pied piper, he was now leading them out of the classroom and onto the battlefield. What would their parents say? Who would they blame if, God forbid, something were to happen to their children?

Wilson appreciated Baskerville's motives and his willingness to sacrifice his life for a cause. But he was certain the young man was making a grave error. He sat him down in his office and tried desperately to get him to rethink his decision. What he was doing was unwise, rash, impractical, suicidal even. What about his duty to the church his father and grandfather served? What about the missionaries in Persia whose lives he was jeopardizing? What about Agnes?

Whatever Wilson said must have struck a chord with Baskerville, for he suddenly wavered in his decision. The truth was, he did not want to fight. He would have loved nothing more than to stay out of the whole mess. Indeed, that is what he had been trying to do ever since he arrived in Tabriz. He had kept his head down, just as he'd been asked to do. He did everything expected of him. But no matter how hard he tried, he could find no relief from the weight pressing down on his shoulders. He felt overwhelmed by it. He was like a man drowning in the sea; the only way to save himself was to stop struggling, to swim further out into the depths, to let the waves take him where they will.

And yet, he could not bear to disappoint this man he had grown to love like a father. Perhaps he was acting rashly. He began to question his decision, to doubt his course of action. He was Saint Peter, having heard the cock crow once, twice. He could not bear the third crow.

"All right," he replied, at last. "I will go and tell them I will not come."

Imagine the relief on Samuel Wilson's face at that moment, knowing he had managed to sway the young man—that somehow, by the grace of God and the sheer force of his argument, he had skirted disaster.

Now imagine Wilson's face the following morning, as he walks into his office and sees a typewritten letter on his desk: three short sentences that buckle him at the knees.

I must go. I have gone. Please forgive me for not taking your advice.

CHAPTER SEVENTEEN

The Army of Salvation

ALL HEADS TURNED as Howard Baskerville entered the rear of the chapel. It was April 4, 1909: the first Sunday morning service since he had officially resigned from the school. There were some among the faculty and staff who assumed they would never see him again, certainly not on campus. Not only had he quit teaching in order to fight another country's civil war, but he had also taken many of his students with him! Word on the street was that he had converted to Islam—that in abandoning the mission, he had also abandoned Christ. He now served the same "false prophet" as those he fought alongside. Yet, here he was, walking into chapel as if nothing had happened, heading for the same seat he'd sat in every Sunday morning for a year and a half—second seat, front row—right beside his former foster family, the Wilsons.

He had come to church dressed in leather riding chaps—the kind the Feda'i wore in battle—as though he were leaving directly from the service to the front lines. The chaps weren't his; nowhere in the meticulously packed steamer trunk he'd dragged all the way from South Dakota had he thought to bring clothes appropriate for war. He had borrowed them from the school's French instructor, Monsieur Vauthier, who, alone among the school's faculty, had lauded his decision to join the fight. Everyone else had been strictly warned by the American legate in Tehran to "disassociate with Baskerville."

Can you see all those suddenly stiffened backs that Sunday morning as Baskerville strode down the center aisle and took his seat? There's Samuel Wilson, sitting right beside him, sweating beneath his cassock, eyes focused squarely to the front. Next, Annie, her heart beating out of her chest, her hand squeezed hard by her husband to keep her from jumping from her seat and clutching the young man she had come to love as her own son. Then, Agnes. My God, Agnes.

Six months ago she would have married Howard Baskerville, had her father approved. What could she be feeling now, as the man she loved sat a few seats away? Was it regret that she had obeyed her father? Anger, that he had joined the fight without consulting her? Fear, that he was being reckless with all of their lives? Pride, that he was doing what she knew she never could? Whatever it was, Baskerville's decision had sealed their fate. No matter what happened next, there would be no second chance for them.

At the pulpit, Frederick Jessup preached a perfectly fine sermon about charity and love— "and though I have all faith, so that I remove mountains, but have not love, I am nothing"—his gaze falling everywhere but on the front row. His wife, Helen Grove, sat a couple of rows back, along with the Pittmans and the Wrights. In her diary entry for the day, sixteen-year-old Sarah Wright can barely conceal the thrill of seeing her friend and former riding instructor dressed as a soldier in church. She hadn't spoken to him in days, not since he was forced to move out of their house after joining the Feda'i. "I don't know where he will stay," she writes with genuine concern.

Somewhere, in the back of the chapel, sat William Doty, pretending to pay attention to the sermon. Doty still hadn't fully given up trying to convince Baskerville to reconsider his present course. Even after their confrontation at the parade grounds, he had spent hours meticulously laying out the consequences of what he called Baskerville's "morally reprehensible" decision: he was "embarrassing the American Government in its treaty relations with the Government of Persia . . . he was jeopardizing the lives of other American citizens . . . he had compromised the American Presbyterian Mission with which he had been associated nearly two years . . . he had broken his contract with the American Mission School," all of which would be held against him were he to "seek appointment under the Presbyterian Mission anywhere later."

Yet nothing Doty said would change Baskerville's mind. He had tried asking his colleagues at the British consulate in Tabriz for advice. They told him that if Baskerville were a British citizen, he would have been locked up already. That seemed a bit extreme. Where would Doty even keep him? In the consulate basement? In the city prisons? The Feda'i controlled all of those.

Not knowing what else to do, Doty sent a telegram to his boss, John B. Jackson, in Tehran, begging him, as the highest American authority in Persia, to take Baskerville's case off his hands. "I recommend a telegraphic order from yourself expelling him from Persia," he suggested.

For Jackson, the telegram was the last straw. The American legate had been complaining about William Doty ever since Doty had arrived in Persia two years earlier. His inappropriate proselytizing, his penchant for drama and exaggeration, his lack of balance and judgment, his need to insert himself in matters beyond his concern—all of these had caused Jackson no end in trouble. And now this business with Baskerville! A missionary taking up arms against a foreign government? Who ever heard of such a thing?

Doty had asked Jackson to find some way to expel the young man from Persia. But how was Jackson supposed to do that when the consul had already demanded Baskerville's passport when confronting him at the parade grounds? By his own admission, Doty had made it clear to Baskerville that he should henceforth consider himself "a man without a country," and Baskerville had agreed. So then, how could he be expelled by a country that was no longer his? If he'd been refused the protection of the United States, how could he be expected to accept its laws?

Jackson was incensed with Doty for dumping the problem on his lap. Still, he had no choice but to try to clean up the mess. All he could think to do at this point was to appeal to the Presbyterian Board of Foreign Missions. They were the ones who had sent the young man to Tabriz; only they had the authority to recall him.

Jackson sent a lengthy memo to the State Department, explaining the situation in Tabriz to the newly appointed secretary of state, Philander C. Knox. Actually, Jackson sent two memos to Knox. One was an appeal to reach out to Robert E. Speer, head of the Presbyterian Board of Foreign Missions, and ask him to intercede in the Baskerville affair on behalf of the US government. The other was a formal request to transfer William Doty to "a quieter post," somewhere his duties could be confined to "the certification of invoices and similar work" rather than "work of a political character." Jackson didn't care where Doty was posted, so long as it was not Persia.

Knox was a US senator from Pennsylvania who had been recruited to the State Department by the newly elected president, William Howard Taft. He hailed from the same area of Pittsburgh as Samuel Wilson. Although an Episcopalian, he had close ties to the Presbyterian Church and understood immediately how Baskerville's actions could compromise not only American interests in the region, but also the interests of the Presbyterian mission. He instructed his office to send an urgent telegram to New York, addressed directly to Speer, asking him to intervene. "Cannot your Board recall or disavow [Baskerville] at once, since there appears to be no other way to counteract the harm he has done?"

Inside the missions board building, on that busy corner of Fifth Avenue and Twentieth Street, where Howard Baskerville had begun his 10,000-mile journey to Tabriz, Speer read Knox's letter in a panic. This was, to put it mildly, an unprecedented situation for the Presbyterian Church. In the eighty or so years in which it had been formally sending its missionaries to every corner of the globe, it had never dealt with such a scenario. The notion that one of its missionaries would take up arms and fight in a foreign country's civil war was so preposterous, so beyond anyone's imagining, that the missions board had never thought to plan for such a contingency.

Speer recognized at once the existential threat Baskerville's actions posed to the Presbyterian Church. His decision not only threatened the success of the West Persia Mission, but it also had the potential to destroy the entire missionary enterprise. Would the Chinese emperor allow the church's missionaries into his country, knowing that one of them may take up arms against him? Would the Russians? The Presbyterian Church had been called to bring Christ to all nations, but what nation would welcome them after this? Who would believe their missionaries had been sent solely to conduct spiritual matters?

The State Department had acknowledged this very threat in a series of ever-more urgent memos, warning Speer that Baskerville's conduct could serve to "prejudice the work of the Board in that part of the world." One follow-up letter, written by Huntington Wilson, the assistant secretary of state, urged the Presbyterian Board of Foreign Missions not only to "disavow Baskerville's acts and to recall him" but also to "sever their relations with him" because of the fact he was harming "the missionary reputation." The chief clerk to the State Department wrote his own separate memo to Speer, expressing the department's view that the missions board should "fully understand the circumstances" that Baskerville's actions in Persia had created for the Church, and take "any practicable measure to prevent a recurrence" in other Presbyterian missions around the world.

This was a worst-case scenario for the Presbyterian Church. It had to act fast, not only for the sake of its West Persia Mission, but to secure its future missionary endeavors. It wasn't enough simply to deal with the Baskerville situation; it had to come up with a way to "prevent a recurrence," whatever the cost.

On April 6, 1909, Speer sent a succinct, four-sentence response to the State Department. "Mr. Baskerville is not one of our missionaries," the statement read. "He is a teacher employed by our Tabriz Boys' School for two years. His term expires this summer. We disavow the actions reported and have cabled our missionaries that Baskerville must desist from interference in politics or return to America immediately."

The memo took everyone by surprise. What did Speer mean, Baskerville was not one of their missionaries? His missionary application, in which he had detailed his desire to enter "the foreign mission field" in order to "advance the Kingdom of Christ," had been signed, stamped, and received by Speer himself. Baskerville's acceptance letter, while reiterating his desire to be sent to China, nevertheless acknowledges Speer's preference to post him in Persia, specifically to pursue "the Mohammedan work."

It may be true that his job at the American Memorial School was to teach English and history. But his mission was to preach the Gospel. On this point, there is no ambiguity. Asked in his missionary application if he would commit to making the leading of souls to Christ the chief duty of his work in Persia, "no matter what other duties may be assigned to you," Baskerville replied: "I do."

That application, it should be mentioned, included glowing recommendations from both the president (Woodrow Wilson) and the dean (Henry B. Fine) of Princeton University, Speer's alma mater. Speer's colleague and friend, the Rev. S. W. Beach, pastor of the First Presbyterian Church of Princeton, was one of Baskerville's primary references. So then, what was Speer suggesting? That Baskerville's application to become a missionary had been rejected, despite his qualifications, but that he was sent to Persia anyway—not as a missionary, but as a teacher in a missionary school? What was the difference anyway?

The State Department did not know how to respond to Speer's memo. "They disavowed his action, and said that he was not one of their missionaries but only a teacher who had been sent out by them," Huntington Wilson reported to Knox, adding in parentheses, "I don't quite see the importance of the distinction!"

Back in Tehran, John B. Jackson was equally confused. "It seems like splitting hairs to make a point at saying that Baskerville was not a missionary, although this may be correct technically (as his contract was with an individual missionary [Samuel Wilson] and not with the New York Board itself)," he wrote Knox, "but as he lived at the mission and was employed by one of its members, his identity with it was practically complete."

Jackson was right. Perhaps it was the case that Baskerville's meager salary as a teacher was paid by the American Memorial School and not the Presbyterian Board of Foreign Missions, but it was the missions board that had paid for his passage to and from Tabriz. Why would it have done so if he wasn't one of theirs?

In any case, the American Memorial School where Baskerville taught was, without question, a missionary enterprise. Its function, purpose, and priorities were indistinguishable from those of the West Persia Mission. That is certainly how the missionaries themselves saw it, which explains why they viewed Baskerville as one of their own. Indeed, Frederick Jessup, in a letter to one of his Princeton friends, explicitly acknowledges Baskerville as a missionary assigned to the school. "We have a force of five male missionaries, four of them married," he writes. And then he lists them: Samuel Wilson, John Wright, Charles Pittman, Jessup himself, and Howard Baskerville.

Whatever the truth of Baskerville's employment in Tabriz, it is not difficult to understand why both the State Department and the Presbyterian Board of Foreign Missions were so desperate to distance themselves from the entire affair. There is, in all the anxious handwringing in these memos, a clear anticipation of the century of theorizing to come about

Baskerville's actions and motivations. What the young man had done defied simple categorization. His decision to join the Persian Constitutional Revolution transgressed the acceptable boundaries of his identity as an American, as a Christian, and as a missionary.

To the State Department, Baskerville's actions were, by definition, un-American. US law forbids an American citizen from being recruited into a foreign army. Written inside every American passport is an explicit warning that one could lose citizenship by serving "in the armed forces of a foreign state." That is why Doty threatened Baskerville with treason: by volunteering to fight in another country's civil war —one in which the United States had pledged neutrality— Baskerville was, in effect, taking up arms against US interests. That made him a traitor to America.

Yet Baskerville had specifically addressed this charge in a letter he wrote to Doty laying out in detail why he believed his actions were lawful. "I am not engaging in revolution," he wrote, "but merely acting in self-defense and in the defense of American lives and property, as well as the lives and property of innocent Persian friends." As to the threat of treason for violating American neutrality in Persia, Baskerville had a response to that charge as well. "I am not resisting any lawful government, but merely helping the 'de facto' government to maintain order and defend innocent citizens from lawless pillage, rape, and murder."

To the West Persia Mission, Baskerville's actions were deemed un-Christian, so much so that some assumed he must have abandoned his faith. Yet the Presbyterian Church had never doubted the notion that war could be a valid expression of faith. On the contrary; the image of the zealous Christian, "Marching as to war / With the cross of Jesus / Going on before"—to quote the popular martial hymn *Onward, Christian Soldier*—was deeply baked into the psyche of the church. The consensus of the great Christian patriarchs was that war is inherently neither bad nor good. "It depends on the reasons for which men undertake war and by which they do it," argued St. Augustine.

Martin Luther said it best: "We must discriminate between a war begun voluntarily and gladly and a war into which one is driven by need and compulsion. The former may be called a war of pleasure; the latter a war of necessity. The first belongs to the devil—may God not prosper it! The other is man's misfortune—God grant his help!"

There can be no question that Baskerville understood his actions to be "driven by need and compulsion." In his letter to William Doty, he explicitly casts his decision to fight as having been thrust upon him by the dire circumstances faced by the residents of Tabriz. "They cannot surrender to these brigands," he writes, "for surrender means robbing, rape, and murder." It may be a misfortune, but, as far as Howard Baskerville was concerned, there was no other choice but to pick up his rifle and do whatever he could to "help a distressed people defend themselves"—God grant his help!

To the Presbyterian Board of Foreign Missions, Baskerville's actions were a gross violation of his missionary duties. As the missions board had repeatedly reminded him, he was not to concern himself with material matters. His sole mission was "to implant the life of Christ in the hearts of men." It may be difficult for the missionary to ignore the suffering and injustice taking place before him. But, as Robert Speer himself wrote: "I had rather plant one seed of the life of Christ under the crust of heathen life than cover the whole crust over with the veneer of our social habits or the vesture of Western civilization."

The Presbyterian Church had sent Baskerville to Persia to save souls, not lives. But in Baskerville's mind, those two goals were one and the same, especially in a country like Persia, where piety was indistinguishable from sacrifice, and faith was empty without action. Even Samuel Wilson admitted as much in a personal letter to Robert Speer, meant to clear up any false notions he may have had about Baskerville's motive and intentions. "I think he entered into the work from purely unselfish motives, and if you hear anything to the contrary you can discount it," Wilson told Speer. "His act seems in the eyes of the Persians and Armenians as one of ideal self-sacrifice for the good of others."

It is understandable why the US government, the Persian mission, and the Presbyterian Church would all want to wash their hands of Howard Baskerville. If he were no longer American, no longer a Christian, no longer a missionary, then no one—not William Doty, not Samuel Wilson, not Robert Speer—could be held responsible for his actions.

But Baskerville had not abandoned his American identity. On the contrary, this was him exerting it. He had not renounced his faith; this was him putting it into practice. And he most definitely had not withdrawn from "the Mohammedan work"; he had merely taken it from the chapel to the streets.

When the Sunday service was over and the final prayers made, Samuel Wilson stood from his seat in the front row, briefly shook hands with Baskerville, and ushered his family out of the chapel as quickly as he could. Frederick Jessup did the same, as did the rest of the Americans. Among the faculty, only Monsieur Vauthier lingered. The Frenchman put his arms around Baskerville, pulled him in close, and called him "old man."

The rest of the congregation, freed by the absence of the Americans, flocked to Baskerville, pushing each other to get to him, to shake his hand or pat him on the back. "The Moslems [sic] in the church nearly ate him up," Sarah Wright gushes in her diary.

Later that day, Baskerville stopped by the Wilson home, surely unaware that they had been ordered not to associate with him. He may have been trying to see Agnes, but only Annie would speak to him. Defying her husband's wishes, she pulled him aside for a moment alone. Here was the boy she had considered a second son for a year and a half. She had brought him into her home, fed him and clothed him, nursed him back to health when he was sick. Unlike Samuel, she could not conceal her sympathy for his decision to risk his life for the city and its residents. Annie was Persian; this was her country. She understood.

But she nevertheless begged him to reconsider his decision—for her sake and for the sake of his mother back home.

"You are not your own," she reminded him.

"No," Baskerville replied. "I am Persia's."

❖

SATTAR KHAN NAMED Baskerville his new second-in-command—effectively replacing Baqer Kahn's position—and moved him into his own small home. They now spent almost all their time together, whether out in the field surveying troops and reinforcing barricades—Sadeq always there to translate—or huddling at night by the fire in his courtyard, ears tuned to the sound of bullets echoing beyond the wall. On one or two occasions, Baskerville and Arthur Moore went on moonlight excursions, crawling close to the enemy lines in order to map their positions. At least twice he was sent out on sorties accompanied by a squad of Georgian and Armenian fighters. Perhaps Sattar Khan thought Baskerville would feel more comfortable surrounded by fellow Christians. The Armenians, especially, had grown quite fond of the young man. They even threw a little party in his honor, during which Baskerville led everyone through a rousing rendition of "My Country 'Tis of Thee." In fact, everywhere Baskerville went in the city he was feted by the Feda'i. After so many years of begging America for help in their fight for freedom, they simply could not believe that one of them had actually answered the call.

However, Baskerville's chief duty as Sattar's second-in-command was to oversee the organization and drilling of the new volunteers. These were mostly youths: many of them students, a few the sons of merchants and mullahs, all of them untrained and eager to prove their mettle. Together with Arthur Moore, he would call the new recruits to the parade grounds every morning and evening to undergo a series of drills and exercises meant to hasten their preparation for war. There were approximately one hundred fifty young fighters under

Baskerville's command. They called themselves the "Army of Salvation." Every member took a vow to always be brave, to never retreat, to approach the enemy without fear, to attack without hesitation, to kill or be killed.

As the days passed and Sattar became more comfortable with Baskerville, he began to give him even greater responsibilities. For some time now, Rahim Khan, ensconced on the Jolfa Road, had been confiscating most of the mail coming in and out of Tabriz. "We miss the mail very much," Samuel Wilson complained in April. "We have had two or three mails since the last of January. Some has [arrived] destroyed." The mission and the consulate had managed to maintain communication with the outside world by relying on the generosity of the Russian consulate, which would occasionally include American letters in its outgoing mail (it was surely not a coincidence that only the Russian post remained unmolested). However, personal correspondences had ceased almost completely, even for the Americans. There are a handful of heartbreaking passages in Sarah Wright's diary in which she waits for the mail carrier to arrive at her door, only to be told that there was, yet again, nothing for her.

Without mail, the people of Tabriz were feeling forgotten, isolated from the rest of the country, desperate to hear from family and friends. The Georgians, Turks, and Russians, in particular, had lost all contact with their homes. Some of them had been in Tabriz for nearly a year now. Did their families even know if they were still alive?

William Doty had already tried to convince Rahim Khan to release the mail he'd seized, but the Shahsevan leader claimed not to know what Doty was talking about. So Sattar sent Howard Baskerville.

Baskerville obeyed the order of the People's Commander but he did not like it. He was absolutely repulsed by Rahim Khan, whom he called a lawless brigand, a rapist, and a murderer. Reading Baskerville's letters, it is clear that he viewed Rahim Khan as the chief villain in the drama in which he was now engaged. The shah, "the Prince," the tsar—these were faceless adversaries. They were distant and obscure, their visage familiar only in portraits or sketches. But Rahim's face he knew well. He was in Tabriz the previous summer, when the Shahsevan had plundered the city. He saw the bodies of the merchants hanged in the bazaar. He heard the screams of the women being attacked in the bathhouse.

Nevertheless, he followed his orders and dutifully met Rahim on the Jolfa Road, alone and unarmed (not even Rahim Khan would be so foolish as to abuse an American). Baskerville may have known his face, but it's likely Rahim had never set eyes upon the rosy-cheeked young man riding toward his barricades. And yet, he must have heard about the American missionary who had joined the fight against the shah. Was this him: the slight, bespectacled youth climbing down from his horse and walking toward his camp, arms raised in the air?

Baskerville had been in Persia long enough to understand the complicated cultural rules of deference that would have been expected of him in such a situation. He knew he would need to shower the Shahsevan leader with respect if he had any hope of succeeding, even if the thought of bowing to this man turned his stomach. When he came into Rahim's presence, he lowered himself and pled with the "merciful Khan," in well-practiced Persian, to please release the mail in his possession.

In the end, the groveling did no good. Rahim simply shrugged his shoulders and walked away, leaving Baskerville standing alone in the tent. He rode back to Tabriz empty-handed.

It may seem somewhat absurd for Sattar Khan to have entrusted Howard Baskerville with such command and authority, given the fact that the young man had joined the Feda'i only a few weeks earlier. There seems to be some confusion in the sources over whether Baskerville himself had had military training in the United States or whether he'd learned his drilling tactics from the same *Encyclopaedia Britannica* that had taught him how to make grenades. But regardless of his previous training (or lack thereof), Baskerville was by no means a military expert.

I suppose one could say the same of practically every one of Sattar's fighters, including the People's Commander himself. Yet most of them had been actively engaged in the fight for years; Baskerville had been involved for barely a month. His combat experience was limited to a couple of sorties. Nothing in his background would have warranted a command position, certainly not second-in-command to the Father of the Nation.

It's obvious why Sattar Khan had so enthusiastically welcomed Baskerville into his ranks. If the people of Persia knew that an American had joined the cause, it would provide a huge boost of morale, precisely at a time in which the revolutionaries needed it most. If the rest of the world learned of Baskerville's engagement in the revolution, it could bring both international recognition and legitimacy to the fight against the shah. Indeed, it did not take long for the global press to pick up the story.

"AMERICAN DEFENDS TABRIZ," screamed a headline in the *New York Times*, dated April 5, 1909.

But why make him second-in-command?

It's possible that Baskerville's elevated status was a ploy on Sattar's part to keep him safe from harm by giving him the shield of command. He could send him into battle with the knowledge that he would likely be barking orders to his troops from a safe distance. But there is also the opposite possibility to consider—that Baskerville's command was meant not to keep him alive, but to ensure his death.

That seems to be what the American diplomats assumed. William Doty, who in his memos repeatedly notes that Baskerville's decision to join the fight was made voluntarily and under his own volition, nevertheless began to suspect Sattar Khan's motives for entrusting the American with command. Doty had recently been spending a lot of time with the British and Russian consuls in Tabriz, organizing the distribution of supplies to their respective citizens, and he had begun to hear a different story about Sattar Khan—one that was being widely spread in London and St. Petersburg. Doty now spoke of the revolutionaries in biting terms, accusing them of "seeking their own aggrandizement at the expense of the common wealth." As to Sattar Khan, Doty claimed the People's Commander was now interested only in "power and loot."

This was quite the about-face for the American consul, who had, at one point, aligned himself so deeply with the nationalist cause that he had allowed a cannon to be placed on the roof of the consulate. Even John B. Jackson, who never had anything positive to say about the Persian Constitutional Revolution, was surprised by the sudden shift in Doty's rhetoric. "After being violently nationalistic," Jackson wrote to Knox in June, "Mr. Doty has become entirely Russian in his sympathies and now speaks of Sattar Khan, Baghir [sic] Khan and the revolutionary leaders as 'degenerating into a set of malcontents.'"

Doty knew that Sattar Khan was not forcing Baskerville to fight. But he could think of no legitimate reason for Baskerville's elevation to command, unless there was some nefarious purpose to it. And he may not have been wrong.

The truth of the matter is that the fight was not going well for Sattar Khan. The Feda'i were still winning battles, but the war was all but lost. For months, they had fought the forces of the shah to a virtual stalemate. But that was no longer sustainable, as stalemate now meant starvation. That breathless *New York Times* article, which reported on Baskerville's participation in the defense of Tabriz, also went on to predict the worst for the city. "The sufferings of the town are increasing daily, and it is not doubted that a great tragedy is approaching," the article read. "If Tabriz holds out, thousands must die of starvation, while if it falls probably tens of thousands will be massacred."

The situation was growing dire. Bread and rice were scarce. There was very little wheat or grain left in the city. The merchant's stores were as empty as their stomachs. The foreign residents still had access to basic goods such as flour, as long as they did not share it with the locals, per the agreement struck by Doty and his fellow consuls. But even the Americans were starting to grow thin and ragged.

There was almost constant fighting in the city-run bread shops; people quarreled for their turn at the window. One day, a mother clamoring for bread for her child pulled out a revolver and shot another mother doing the same. "The sight of the bake-shops surrounded by throngs of hungry women stretching out their arms and begging for bread, the knowledge that many stand till the early morning outside the bakeries trying to get their turns to secure a few pieces of bread, and then perhaps having to return empty-handed, makes one very sad," wrote Frederick Jessup, in a dispatch to the Presbyterian Board of Foreign Missions.

The poor began to descend upon the orchards and meadows. They crawled on their hands and knees, chewing grass and weeds. They picked clover and alfalfa by the handful and stuffed them into the mouths of their starving children.

Still, the people refused to surrender. In the midst of the suffering and starvation, a group of women sent a defiant letter to Ayn od-Dowleh, "the Prince," damning him for his crimes against Tabriz. "It is amazing that you think that, with all your cruelty, the nation will abandon Constitutionalism and will give in to your depriving us of food. But, Honorable Sir! You are wrong and your assumption is incorrect," they wrote. "We will eat fruit, plants, and the leaves of the trees. We will even eat the flesh of cats and other animals and finally die. But we will not be subservient to the whims of Mohamed Ali Mirza [sic]."

At the beginning of April, Sattar Khan received word that there was wheat to be had at a nearby village, if only they could reach it. With no other choice but to try, he sent three fighters under cover of night to investigate. They returned unharmed and carrying a load of wheat each. Encouraged by their success, Sattar sent out a group of forty men the following night, in hopes of securing a large enough load to distribute to the entire city. This time, only three of the forty returned. The rest had been captured. The entire thing had been a setup. The Prince had deliberately allowed the first trip to succeed, in the hopes that Sattar would then send a larger force. The fox was finally learning how the weasel thinks.

The People's Commander was no longer himself. It was obvious to everyone. Rumors circulated around town that he was drinking at night, despite the fact that he himself had prohibited alcohol among the troops. His fraught relationship with Baqer Khan had begun to split the Feda'i into competing factions. The two men openly quarreled with each other (one can only guess what Baqer Khan thought of Howard Baskerville assuming his previous position).

One night, some of Baqer's men were stopped by the night watch and asked to provide the evening password. The men could not remember and so tried to make a run for it. The night watch opened fire on them as they fled. No one was hurt, but the next day an incensed Baqer Khan went to the night watchman and beat him nearly to death. Sattar had to personally intervene and put Baqer back in his place. The incident only further fueled the growing animosity between the two men.

Meanwhile, Sattar's fighting force was dwindling by the day due to disease, death, and desertion. There were now almost daily executions in the city's main square. An Armenian woman was shot for plying some fighters with alcohol and sex, and then extracting their secrets and relaying them to the Prince. Three men were discovered with maps on them showing entrances into the city; all three were shot. A bread baker was shot because he took the wheat given to him to bake for the people and instead sold it privately at a high price.

The weight of the war had grown heavy on Sattar's shoulders. He hardly resembled the man profiled by all those fawning European journalists. He had lost his magic. He could see it in the eyes of the blank-faced mothers staring at him when he patrolled the streets. He could feel it in the blue cheeks and sunken eyes of his men as they rode, sometimes two to a horse, into battle. The people thought he was semi-divine, that he was bulletproof, that he could not possibly lose. Maybe he had begun to think so, too. But now he knew that wasn't true. The city still fell at his feet. The children still went door to door like carolers singing hymns about his glory. But it was clear to all that the endgame was near. The *New York Times* article was right: either thousands will die, or tens of thousands will die. That is what the future held for Tabriz.

So perhaps there was something to the accusations being flung by the Americans that Sattar had some nefarious plan in place for Baskerville. After all, one American fighter would not save the cause. But one *dead* American fighter—that could change the course of the revolution.

Who knows how Baskerville felt about all this or if he even knew what was being said about him? I can't imagine it would have mattered. He had pledged his blood to the revolution. He had no qualms about laying down his life for the city and its people. Howard Baskerville was Christian. He had been raised to believe that this world is but a shadow of the real world. Death had no power over him. And if, by chance, he had lost sight of that fundamental truth, he would have received a timely reminder in chapel the following week.

It was Sunday, April 11. Easter Sunday. This is the day that Christians proclaim the Good News at the heart of their faith: that Jesus Christ—beaten, killed, and buried in a tomb—has risen from the dead. In this city of myriad faiths, Easter is the bookend to Ashura: one is the remembrance of a redeeming death; the other, a celebration of death's defeat.

For Presbyterians, the resurrection of Jesus Christ is believed to have inaugurated a brand new age. The church teaches that when Christ rose from the dead, a whole new world arose with him. It wasn't just Jesus who was transformed, but all of humanity.

"Because I live, you, too, shall live," Jesus told his disciples.

The message of Easter Sunday has always been this: that those who accept Jesus as their savior—who fear the Lord and pursue His righteousness—shall never die, but have eternal life. They may be beaten, crucified, and buried in a tomb. They may be shot in the back, the bullet ripping through the rib cage and exiting the chest in a plume of blood and bone. But if they love the Lord, and if they serve Him with all their might, then though they die, yet they shall live.

CHAPTER EIGHTEEN

So Costly a Sacrifice Upon the Altar of Freedom

NOTHING LEFT TO DO NOW but try and break the siege.

The plan was to focus the full force of the Feda'i on the Prince's western flank, to push forward in wave after wave of coordinated attacks until it gave, no matter the cost. They would fire their cannons and lob homemade grenades. They would climb over the bodies of their fallen comrades if necessary. But they would not stop. They would keep moving, inch by inch, until they finally burst through the siege and liberated Tabriz.

Sattar Khan had tried something like this once before. About a month ago, on March 24, 1909, he had gathered every fighter under his command, Baskerville included, and launched a surprise attack on the Prince's forces. Unfortunately, the Prince had gotten wind of Sattar's plans—there was treachery everywhere in the city these days—and his soldiers were ready. It was the bloodiest battle either side had fought in the nearly four years of the Constitutional Revolution. The death toll was immense. "In one barricade alone, I saw seventeen corpses next to each other," one eyewitness reported.

The Feda'i had brought to the battle a wagon loaded with bread and water to replenish the fighters, but after a few hours of fighting, the bread was soaked in blood and could not be eaten. Sattar did manage to push the shah's troops further back from the city perimeter, and that, in itself, was a kind of victory. But when night fell and the fighting ceased, the roads remained closed.

This time, the decision had been made to push forward without pause for as long as it took to break the siege, regardless of how much blood was spilt. What choice did they have? There was no more wheat or grain left anywhere in the city. The grass and alfalfa fields had been picked clean. A few enterprising residents had begun disassembling old shoes and unused saddles and boiling the leather in a pot until it was soft enough to chew. Others had been reduced to eating dung.

Arthur Moore had been tireless in chronicling the suffering in the city, sending occasional dispatches to the London *Times* and other newspapers in Europe, describing in detail the "fearsome figures, all but naked, scarcely recognizable as human beings," who were dying of starvation on the streets of Tabriz. Embarrassed by the international attention the siege was receiving abroad, the Russian and British representatives had gone to Bagh-e Shah to try to mediate between Tabriz and Tehran. The hope was that the growing desperation in Tabriz would make surrender a more palatable option. It had not. Sattar Khan had drawn a line in the sand: there would be no surrender until the shah reopened parliament. That was not going to happen—not with Ayatollah Nuri calling the shots in Tehran.

The British and Russians had proposed a temporary ceasefire so that, at the very least, some food and assistance could reach Tabriz. But the shah refused. After months of frustration and futility, he finally had the upper hand. Even from Tehran, he could feel the press of his boot on Sattar's neck; he had no intention of pulling it back now.

For Tabrizis, there were only two options left: die waiting for the siege to be lifted or die trying to break it themselves.

Everyone would take part in the attack: Persians, Turks, Russians, Azeris, Armenians, Georgians, Jews, Baha'i—those trained for combat, and those who had never fired a gun. The force would be divided into a dozen or so individual squads, each with its own commander, each tasked with attacking one part of the western barricades from a different direction, like ants swarming an elephant. Baqer Khan would coordinate the forces on the ground, while Sattar Khan stayed on the roof of his house, monitoring the fight through a telescope, a chain of swift-heeled messengers at his side, ready to pass his orders from squad to squad.

There was one great obstacle to the plan, and that was the Cossack Brigade stationed at Qaramalik, on the opposite side of the orchard from Hokmavar. They were not a large force; only a few dozen of the four hundred men sent from Tehran had been posted on the western edge of the city. But they were rooted to the spot, and they had with them at least two of the four Maxim guns, one of which was manned by "Sixty-Bullet Reza" himself. Those guns would rip the Feda'i to pieces before they even had a chance to exit the orchard. They had to be dealt with if there was any chance of success. A small squad—no more than forty or fifty fighters—would have to sneak through the orchard in the early-morning darkness, before the main attack began, and try to take the Cossacks by surprise.

That squad would be the Army of Salvation.

This is what Howard Baskerville had been drilling his students for these past few weeks. He had told the one hundred fifty youths under his command that they should expect to form the vanguard of the fight to come. This was now that fight.

Baskerville's students responded to their teacher and commander with zealous devotion. Forty of them volunteered for the mission, including his favorite student, Sadeq. Each took an "Oath of Steadfastness," vowing to fight until the mission was complete. They would creep up to the Cossack camp before dawn, take their positions at the edge of the orchard, and use their rifles to take out as many soldiers as they could before they had the chance to regroup and react. The students would drag a cannon behind them so that, once the Maxim guns began firing, they could respond with a volley of cannon fire. With luck, they would clear out the Cossack camp by first light, then circle back and join the main attack.

At first, Sattar Khan balked at the notion of allowing Baskerville and his band of privileged youths to form the front line of the battle. And he absolutely refused to hand over one of the precious cannons to them. When Sadeq came to him to relay Baskerville's plan, Sattar turned him down on the spot. "You will go have the American killed and then flee, leaving the cannon with the enemy," he said.

But Baskerville had been living with the People's Commander for some time now, and he knew how to get his way. He was no longer the wide-eyed missionary who had arrived by carriage a year and a half ago. When you picture him now, do not picture the rosy-cheeked kid in a white waistcoat and striped tie you first saw on that street corner in New York City. Picture him sunburnt and chiseled, a pistol tucked into his belt, his chest crisscrossed with bullets, the stiff bowler hat replaced with a black felt fez. He had even grown a mustache—a fuzzy, red, bristly thing that drooped across his upper lip like a lounging caterpillar.

He was twenty-four years old; his birthday passed just a few days ago, on April 13. Sarah Wright mentions Baskerville's birthday but says nothing about any sort of celebration. That would make sense; his American friends had been expressly warned not to associate with him. A birthday party would have violated William Doty's direct orders.

Twenty-four years old and a new man. He had traveled halfway across the world, made friends and lost friends, fallen in love and broken his heart. He had seen things he'd only read about in books, witnessed pain and suffering he didn't know was possible. He had surrendered his citizenship, abandoned his mission, and cast off the expectations of his church. He was, like Jesus bursting forth from the tomb, a brand new being: born not of water and blood, but of fire and spirit.

Baskerville would not take Sattar's "no" for an answer. Over the past few weeks, he had grown more confident in questioning the People's Commander. Perhaps it's because he had a front-row seat for Sattar's slow deterioration. He could see for himself the way Sattar fidgeted in his sleep, how he constantly looked over his shoulder, as though he thought someone might be sneaking up on him. He was seeing enemies everywhere—only some of them imagined. And he had taken to drinking in the open, no longer concerned with pretenses. There is no reason to think that Baskerville ever wavered in his devotion to the constitutional cause. But he may have begun to doubt the man leading it. All the more reason to put everything he had into this final battle.

In the end, Sattar Khan relented. Baskerville's Army of Salvation would lead the charge. Perhaps this was the only way to win the war: Baskerville would either be the hero who saved Tabriz with his bravery or the sacrificial lamb who saved it with his death. Either way, the survival of the city and its population, perhaps the very future of the Constitutional Revolution, was now in the hands of a 24-year-old missionary from South Dakota and his band of teenaged soldiers.

❖

THE ATTACK WAS to begin just before dawn on Monday, April 19. The day before, Baskerville went to the American Memorial School to see his friends one last time. He found Frederick Jessup on campus and pulled him aside to give him what he called "the inner track of things." The Feda'i were about to launch what everyone assumed would be the final battle, he told Jessup. One way or another, the war for Persia would come to an end. Baskerville felt confident in their victory, but he nevertheless wanted Jessup to gather all the Americans and take shelter at the British consulate. No matter who won, they would be safe there.

Jessup hesitated. Weeks ago, William Doty had begged the Americans to close the school and send all the missionaries north to the Russian border until the conflict in Tabriz could be resolved. The missionaries had refused. They would not abandon the city and its inhabitants, not in its greatest hour of need. Baskerville understood; he shared the sentiment. But he wasn't asking Jessup to withdraw from the city, only to lay low for a day or two, just until the battle was won and the roads reopened.

Jessup accepted Baskerville's counsel. He promised to go door to door that very evening to inform his fellow Americans of the plan. He would make sure everyone was ready to leave for the British consulate at first light. Baskerville, however, insisted on delivering the message to the Wilsons himself.

As evening fell on April 18, Howard Baskerville returned to the home where he had lived those first few months in Persia. The entire Wilson clan was there: little Robert Graham, now six years old and rambunctious; Annie Rhea, growing into a prim and proper lady; fifteen year-old Rose; and resplendent Agnes, already packed for Vassar. Annie Wilson gave him a great hug and sat him down at the dining table. She began mothering him, just as she did when he lived under her roof. She could not believe how thin the young man looked. Baskerville confessed to being famished; he had eaten nothing but his soldier's ration of flatbread and water for going on a month. Annie brought out some fresh baked bread and butter and placed it before him. She poured him a cold glass of milk, and he laughed at the sight: a child's drink for a soldier.

In Annie's telling, Baskerville appeared confident, or at least pretended to be. He explained in detail their desperate plan to open the roads and get food into the starving city. Annie thought it was a foolhardy mission, and Baskerville did not disagree. But it had to be done, and he had to lead it. His students were relying on him. The whole city was. He could not let them down.

He did, however, make one request. Should anything happen to him, he wanted Annie to write his mother and explain that he knew what he was he doing. "Tell her I never regretted coming to Persia," he said, "and in this matter I felt it was my duty."

The family stood in a circle, hands clasped, and prayed together one final time. Samuel begged God for His protection and for victory over the enemy. But Baskerville prayed only for his students, for the city to be relieved, for the dear ones of the mission to be kept in safety, and for peace to be obtained.

"Not a word for himself," Annie wrote.

Afterward, he reminded them once again to go to straight to the British consulate first thing in the morning. If the attack failed and the Feda'i were defeated, he would join them there. He hugged everyone goodbye, lingering just a bit longer with Agnes, and went off to gather his squad.

They camped at a small mosque at the edge of the city in Hokmavar, but no one could sleep. The youths were nervous and jittery, eager for the fight to begin. Baskerville got everyone up and had them perform drills in the mosque to keep their minds occupied.

At 10:00 p.m. a messenger appeared with word about a plot among the shah's troops to assassinate the Russian and British consuls in Tabriz as a means of turning their governments against the revolutionaries in the midst of negotiations with the shah. Baskerville was mortified. He wrote an urgent note to Samuel Wilson, telling him not to go to the British consulate as he had suggested, but to stay home until the attack was over. He gave the note to a soldier, who gave it to a gatekeeper, who slipped it under the Wilson's door.

Baskerville had another letter with him. It was addressed to his family back home. He had written it a week before, right after the Easter Sunday service. But with no way to mail it, he had decided to fold it and keep it in his shirt pocket until he had killed that beast, Rahim Khan, and opened the Jolfa Road.

"Before this you have heard, probably, that I am engaged in helping those who are defending the city," the letter read. "We are now drilling troops and making plans, and we hope that inside of a week or two the siege will be raised. Possibly we have peace in a few days without fighting. However, if these barbarians will not leave by order of the Shah, we are ready to fight them, and they may be sure that they will get the worst of it."

"Please do not worry about me," the letter concluded, "I am all right. Hoping to see you all now very soon, I remain as always, Your affectionate son and brother, Howard C. Baskerville."

A little after midnight, the Army of Salvation took their positions at the entrance to the orchard, rifles loaded and ready. All they needed was for Sattar Khan to arrive with the cannon they'd been promised. Hours passed, with no sign of the People's Commander. Just before dawn, Baskerville sent a messenger to find out what was going on, and the messenger returned with a simple reply: "We are coming."

But no one came. They waited another hour at the orchard entrance until the sun rose and it was too late to move forward with the plan. Baskerville sent his squad home.

When Sattar Khan finally arrived at Hokmavar he was visibly drunk. Apparently he had spent the entire night fighting with Baqer over the battle plans. Unable to agree on the strategy, the two commanders had made the decision not to move forward with the operation.

Baskerville was furious. There was a heated argument between the two, with Sadeq caught in the middle. We do not know what he said to Sattar, but Arthur Moore, who had joined him on the mission solely as a "war correspondent" and not as a soldier, claims that Baskerville resigned his commission on the spot.

Eventually, the Tabriz Anjoman intervened and begged Baskerville to stay. It was decided they would try again the following morning. Sattar agreed, but he also made clear that there would be no cannon forthcoming. The Feda'i couldn't spare it. Baskerville and his boys would have to find some other way to get through the Cossack Brigade.

That night, the Army of Salvation gathered once more at the mosque. This time, however, only eleven out of the original forty volunteers showed up. The rest were either too frightened or too disheartened to join the operation; some had been kept home by their parents when they discovered what had happened the night before. Sadeq came, of course. He had vowed long ago not to leave his teacher's side, even if that meant dying beside him in battle.

After everyone had fallen asleep, Baskerville rose and walked out of the mosque. He retired to the shadow of a wall, where he sat and spent the night in prayer, the darkness covering him like a blanket.

A few hours later, they were up and dressed for battle. As they exited the mosque they took turns passing beneath a Quran hung by a rope from a tree, while an elderly cleric prayed for God to keep them safe.

It was pitch black when they entered the orchard. They advanced through the trees slowly, quietly, in single file. After about an hour, they came upon the trenches the Feda'i had dug on the far side of the orchard, the ones they had been forced to abandon during the March 5 invasion of the city. Beyond the trenches was a wide-open field. Beyond the field was the Cossack Brigade. Baskerville could see the soldiers relaxing in their camp. Some slept, a handful were on patrol. One of them was twirling a charcoal brazier in preparation for lighting the water pipe. The Maxim guns were unmanned. Clearly, they were not expecting an attack.

Baskerville split his squad in two so as to flank the brigade from opposite sides. The two groups barricaded themselves behind some trees and waited for the signal to attack.

About an hour before the sun rose on that April 20, Baskerville gave the order. They aimed their rifles at the Cossack camp and fired.

It did not take long for the brigade to react. They jumped to their positions and immediately returned fire. Bullets rang out from all directions. The squad was pinned behind the trees, with nowhere to go but forward. Baskerville gave the order to charge and the two groups advanced from opposite ends at the Cossack camp. They would aim, fire their rifles, run to the next tree, reload, and fire again. This went on for some time until the squad came upon a large mound of dirt a few hundred feet from the Maxim guns.

"Lie down!" Baskerville yelled at his students. They fell to the floor and crawled their way up to the mound. Bullets whizzed past their heads. They were stuck in place, unable to move from their position. Someone needed to engage the Cossacks from an adjacent position, to draw their fire so the others could continue the advance. The entire attack depended upon their success.

As his students watched in disbelief, Baskerville began crawling away from the dirt mound and toward the bed of a small waterway that led into a private garden. There was a hole in the garden wall; Baskerville crept through it. Once on the other side, he rose and began firing at the Cossacks, trying to divert their attention. He shot once, twice, then turned to his students to give them the call to charge.

Suddenly, his body convulsed, as though it had been zapped by a bolt of electricity. From where he lay behind the mound, Sadeq could see a dark stain start to spread across Baskerville's chest, just above his heart.

"The American is hit!" someone shouted.

Baskerville swayed for a moment, then buckled at the knees. He slowly dropped to his stomach, legs splayed, blood soaking into the soil.

It was 5:30 a.m.

Sadeq and the rest of the students managed to crawl through the hole in the garden wall until they reached their teacher's body. They turned him over on his back. He was still alive, but gushing blood. Sadeq pulled him to his breast, while another student tried to stem the bleeding. Baskerville looked up at Sadeq's face and smiled.

"I am shot," he said, with a little laugh. Those were his final words.

Just then, the Cossacks began to advance. While Sadeq held on to Baskerville, the rest of the squad emptied their guns in vain. They were caught in a terrible position. They managed to drop two of the advancing Cossacks, but it made no difference. They were trapped, taking fire from all sides.

That's when the Armenians arrived. They engaged the Cossacks from their right flank, unleashing a barrage of bullets that forced them to retreat to their positions. It was all the cover the students needed to drag Baskerville's body out of the ruined garden and back through the orchard. It took another half an hour, but they managed to exit at Hokmavar and rush Baskerville to the field hospital.

Elsewhere, the fighting continued. The other squads had no idea whether the Army of Salvation had been successful in clearing out the Cossack Brigade, but they each had their own part to play and they could do nothing but assume the best. The battle continued well into the night, with waves of Feda'i flinging themselves at the western barricade from three directions. "After a little over thirty years, it is as if the sound of that day's rain of bullets, which from afar was like a furious downpour of hail, is still in my ears," wrote the historian Ahmed Kasravi.

Later, one of the Prince's commanders gave a newspaper interview in which he admitted that, had the battle gone on for another half an hour, the siege would have broken and he and his men would have begged the Tabrizis for quarter. But the fight did not last.

Unbeknownst to everyone in Tabriz, the Russian and British delegations at Bagh-e Shah had finally made a breakthrough in their negotiations. They were horrified at the reports being sent from Tabriz and fed up with the shah's resistance to their demands. They threatened a full-scale invasion of Persia if His Majesty did not call for an immediate ceasefire in Tabriz and allow food and supplies to be sent to the population. The shah had no choice but to agree.

The telegram arrived in Tabriz just before nightfall. After hours of fighting, and more than a thousand deaths, the Feda'i got what they wanted. The Jolfa Road would be opened. The siege was over.

❖

ANNIE WAS HOME when she saw a young boy running down the street, tears streaming down his face. He held in his hands a pair of leather riding chaps. They belonged to Monsieur Vauthier. They were covered in blood.

William Doty sent a servant in his carriage to the field hospital to pick up Baskerville's body and bring it to the Wilson home so it could be washed and prepared for burial. The carriage returned with Baskerville wrapped in a white shroud. He was carried into his old room and placed on the bed. His face was bruised a little on one side from where he had fallen when shot. But otherwise, he looked beautiful and noble, his mouth set in a look of resolution, his whole face calm in repose, as though he were merely taking a little nap. Annie removed the white shroud and gently took off his blood-stained clothes. There was a tiny hole in the front and back of his shirt: "so small, so fatal," she wrote.

The bullet had entered through his back and come out just above his heart, cutting through a large artery. Inside his shirt pocket, just below the bullet hole, she found a folded letter. It was addressed to his family. She would make sure to send it.

Annie washed the blood from his body and dressed him in his first-class outfit. She gave him a kiss on his cold forehead, "for his mother's sake." Agnes brought a white carnation and placed it in his buttonhole. The other Wilson children made a cross and crown out of almond blossoms and placed it on his chest.

His students came in, still dressed in their uniforms, still caked in blood and dirt. They walked upstairs to the room where he lay and gathered around the bed. They wept and beat their chests, crying out that his name would be written in their hearts forever. Annie gently calmed them. "May each of you be as ready as he was, when your hour comes," she said, before leading the boys in prayer.

The town mortician volunteered a beautiful coffin, covered with a fine black cloth and lined with soft white muslin. When Samuel Wilson tried to pay the man, he refused. Baskerville was our guest, the mortician said. He was our responsibility. We failed him.

The funeral took place the following day, April 21, at 9:00

a.m. Thousands of Tabrizis lined both sides of the road leading to the cemetery. The Feda'i stood at attention, rifles pointed down, as Baskerville's coffin—accompanied by sixteen of his students—was carried through the city. Behind it rode soldiers on horses, swords drawn, some carrying the red, white, and green flag of Tabriz. A band of Persian musicians played a funeral march. Two carriages with members of the Tabriz Anjoman brought up the rear. "Never did a foreigner or Christian have such a funeral before," Annie recalled.

At the grave site, speeches were made. "I now have no doubt that the constitution will succeed," declared the head of the Tabriz Anjoman, "for the pure blood of this guiltless youth has been shed for its sake."

Frederick Jessup gave a prayer in English; Charles Pittman did the same in Turkish. Samuel Wilson spoke of the comfort that must be found in the knowledge that Baskerville had entered into glory. He then gave the final benediction and the boys sang "There Is a Happy Land" in Turkish.

When the song was over, Sattar Khan walked up to Samuel Wilson and expressed great sorrow for the young man's death. "So costly a sacrifice upon the altar of freedom," he said.

Sattar gave Wilson the rifle Baskerville had held in his hands when he was shot. The Feda'i had etched his name on it, along with a single line in Persian describing how he had been killed in the cause of liberty. He hoped Wilson would send it to his mother in South Dakota. The two men held each other, and wept.

Afterward, Annie returned home to find Baskerville's steamer trunk had been delivered to the house. It was unlocked. Inside, she found a pair of his shoes and the clothes he wore when he died. Someone had washed them; they were folded and placed next to his cartridge belt. In the corner of the trunk was a class picture, taken when he had first arrived in Tabriz. He stood next to his students in the suit he had just been buried in, a broad smile on his clean-shaven face. Annie decided to keep the photograph rather than send it home. She wanted it displayed in the American Memorial School so the students would never forget who he was and what he did.

"The people say of Mr. Baskerville: He was a sacrifice for us," she wrote his mother, when her grief finally allowed it. "His holy blood ended the war."

The following day, April 22, 1909, twenty-five hundred pounds of wheat arrived in the city via the opened Jolfa Road.

Howard Baskerville's tomb in Tabriz. Strangely, both his date of birth and
date of death are incorrect. He was born April 13. He died April 20. The discrepancy
is likely due to the conversion from the Iranian solar calendar to the Gregorian calendar.

CHAPTER NINETEEN

The Seed of Better Things

KONSTANTIN NIKOLAEVICH SMIRNOV was relaxing with the crown prince in his quarters when news arrived that the capital city had been surrounded. It was July 12, 1909, not three months since the siege of Tabriz had ended. Three months was all it took for Tabriz's victory to reignite the revolution. The flames jumped from city to city, consuming the shah's support. People came out of their homes like prisoners released. They kissed their neighbors, slapped each other on the back. One by one they took up the cry, *Long Live the Constitution!* until it grew into a deafening chorus. And then, when the hugs and handshakes were over, they turned toward Tehran, burning with vengeance.

They came from Rasht and Qazvin, Isfahan and Gilan. They were bolstered by Bakhtiyari tribesmen and a contingent of Armenian soldiers. Among the fighters were clerics from Qom and merchants from Mashhad. And pulling up the rear, like a mad coachman driving a team of raging horses, were the Tabrizis themselves. Collectively, they became known as the Nationalist Force. And they had just reached the capital.

The shah knew they were coming, which is why he had fled Bagh-e Shah for his smaller, more fortified palace at Saltanat Abad, in the northernmost tip of Tehran. His entire court had been transferred to the cramped, two-story structure, fronted by fields and a shimmering pool, and buttressed from behind by Mount Damavand, Persia's tallest peak. His wife and sons and advisers, his royal guards and servants— some five hundred people in all—had been packed inside the crowded palace for weeks, awaiting the end.

Smirnov had tried to make the best of it. He continued his lessons with Ahmed, though the young prince was understandably distracted. He may have been a terrible student, but he'd learned enough history to know how popular uprisings usually end. The shah's guards had boosted the palace defenses and set up watch posts all along the perimeter. But no one could say for certain if these would keep the people at bay. In the meantime, there was little to do but carry on. Smirnov roamed the halls with Ahmed, practicing the day's lessons, or took walks across the sprawling grounds, stopping every now and then to crane his neck at the massive, white-capped mountain towering over the palace.

Mount Damavand looms large in Persian mythology. This is the place where, according to the great Persian epic, the *Shahnameh*, the villainous serpent-king Zahhak was chained for all eternity—a just punishment for plunging ancient Persia into the abyss of darkness. Smirnov knew the story well. Zahhak, it was said, ruled over Persia for centuries. Every day he sacrificed two of Persia's children to feed the vile serpents that sprang from his shoulders. Then, one day, a simple blacksmith named Kaveh dared to raise his voice. He ripped off his leather apron and brandished it as a flag to rally the people, launching a revolution that would finally free Persia from the grip of the serpent-king.

Smirnov must have shaken his head at the irony. Here was Mohammed Ali Shah, choosing to make his last stand at the foothills of a mountain that all Persians viewed as the supreme symbol of resistance against tyranny and despotism.

Not that the shah was considering surrender. He still refused to restore the constitutional order, despite repeated pleas from Smirnov, who believed it was the only way for him to keep his head. Instead, the shah ordered the Cossack Brigade under Colonel Liakhov's command to stop the revolutionaries from entering the capital at any cost. Liakhov, who in Smirnov's telling had grown ever more aloof and imperious since the loss of Tabriz, seemed positively unconcerned with the fate of the shah. He complained that he didn't have enough troops to adequately confront the Nationalist Force, not with his men scattered across the country, trying to tamp down fires everywhere. Nevertheless, he obeyed the order and took three hundred fifty men with him to meet the Nationalist Force on the road to Qazvin.

For three days the two sides exchanged bullets. The nationalists had the numbers, but Liakhov had the Maxim guns. Still, there were just too many revolutionaries to kill. They came at the Cossack Brigade in wave after wave, pinning Liakhov's men to their barricades, until there was no choice but to fall back to Saltanat Abad—"to protect the royal family," Smirnov dutifully reported to the Russian embassy, though he seemed skeptical of the excuse. The Russians believed that as long as they could safeguard the shah, he would keep the throne. They were wrong.

With the Cossack Brigade having abandoned the battlefield, the nationalists entered Tehran with little further resistance. They made their way as a unit to the ruins of the parliament building, where, on July 15, 1909, they unilaterally announced an end to the reign of Mohammed Ali Shah.

Sattar Khan joined them there. He pulled into Tehran on horseback, Baqer once more at his side. *The heroes of the revolution!* the people cried. *The liberators of Tabriz!*

Only, Tabriz had not really been liberated. After the initial shipment of wheat arrived on April 22, the shah struck a deal with the Russian and British governments to fully lift the siege over the coming days. But then he abruptly changed his mind. The roads would remain closed, he declared.

At that point, Russia had finally had enough of Mohammed Ali's dithering. Contrary to the terms of the Anglo-Russian Convention, but with the tacit blessing of Britain, three thousand Russian troops crossed the Aras River and made their way toward Tabriz, ostensibly to secure the safety of Russian nationals in the city. But that was just a pretext for invasion and occupation.

For Tabrizis, foreign intervention was the one fate worse than the shah's tyranny. With the Russians only a few days' march away, the Tabriz Anjoman sent an urgent telegram to Tehran. "The Shah is like the father and the people are like the children," the telegram read. "If father and children [are] angry with each other, the neighbors ought not to intervene. . . . May His Majesty immediately order that the way be opened for food and supplies so that there be no grounds for Russian troops to be stationed on Iranian soil."

Even Sattar Khan, the People's Commander, was open to negotiating with the shah, if it meant avoiding Russian occupation. "Get along with Mohammed Ali Mirza and do not worry about me," he told the Feda'i. "I will mount my horse and escape Iran by highway and byway and head for Najaf."

The shah got the message. He agreed to an immediate ceasefire and ordered the Prince to open all roads in and out of Tabriz at once. He even announced a general amnesty for all the nationalists in the city. But it was too late. On April 29, Russian troops entered Tabriz.

The city was freed from starvation, but it was now under Russian control. The revolutionaries were forcibly disarmed. All Russian subjects in the city were arrested and sent back to St. Petersburg to be punished for taking part in Persia's revolution, though most had already managed to escape with the help of Tabrizis. They snuck back across the Aras River and rejoined their Bolshevik allies who were, at that moment, prepping for another go at bringing down the tsar.

Sattar and Baqer were untouchable, of course. But the Russians, fearing unrest if the heroes of the revolution remained in Tabriz, compelled the anjoman to force them both out of the city—"in the interest of the people," they said. Sattar didn't mind. He was eager to join the revolutionaries who were then marching toward Tehran. He wanted to be there when the shah was pulled from his throne. He had given everything to the cause. His bullet-marked body bore the story of the Persian Constitutional Revolution. He was not about to miss its final chapter.

Sattar's entry into Tehran that July caused a great commotion. Most residents had never set eyes upon him, though they'd memorized his features from the postcards they kept hidden in their homes: the dark face, the elegant mustache, the dapper clothes. They had been told he was a giant, a monster, a ghost. The shah's mullahs called him the devil. But here he was, just a man: tired and grizzled, his face flushed with drink.

Sattar's presence on parliament grounds lent an air of legitimacy to the actions of the Nationalist Force. Never before in Persian history had the people successfully dethroned a shah. There was simply no blueprint for it. Even some staunch constitutionalists were wary of what it would mean for the future of the constitutional monarchy they had envisioned when they launched the revolution four years earlier. Many of the younger, more radical nationalists were calling for an end not just to the shah's reign but also to the monarchy altogether. Now was the time to put the past behind them and begin anew with a Persian Republic.

Sattar Khan played the role of moderator. His endorsement of the shah's forced abdication not only gave the action credibility; it calmed the people's nerves, filling them with a sense of hope and optimism for Persia's future.

When word came to Saltanat Abad of what the nationalists had done, the shah grew desperate. He was agitated, unable to keep still, lashing out at anyone within reach. His advisers kept pushing him to negotiate surrender, but he refused. He continued to insist that the throne was his by divine right, that he could not surrender it even if he wanted to. Only Smirnov could soothe him. His son's tutor had unexpectedly become his chief adviser and confidante. "My job, in essence, was to put the Shah in a good mood and remind him that the trifling matter soon will end," Smirnov confessed, many years later.

Despite everything that had transpired, Smirnov had recently decided to renew his contract with the shah for another three years. Even he recognized the folly of that decision. In his memoirs, he bluntly asks himself why he would choose to accompany the Royal Family to Saltanat Abad, knowing that the end was near. "In a word, my salary was good," he answers.

But the truth was that Smirnov had come to love the crown prince. Ahmed was now twelve years old. He was still arrogant and uncharitable, but he no longer cried so easily, and he had ceased his habit of burning the servants' ears with a pair of pliers he would heat on the stove. Smirnov truly believed that, under his guidance, the crown prince could develop the prudence, poise, and political sense necessary to become a fine king. "His mild character is not the stuff of tyrants," he reported to his superiors in St. Petersburg. And so, he had made the decision to stay with the boy no matter what happened.

Now he found himself shadowing the anxious monarch through the hallways, listening to his crazed ramblings, trying his best to steer him to reason. The shah had sent royal emissaries to St. Petersburg to beg for the tsar's help, but Nicholas was no longer willing to prop up his fellow monarch on a throne that was already lost.

"What should I do?" the shah kept asking.

Smirnov proposed taking refuge at the Russian embassy. He and his family would be taken in; they'd be safe from harm. Of course, that would mean the end of his reign. But it didn't have to mean the end of the dynasty. If he left now, it's possible the nationalists would let his son take the throne. That way his legacy would endure. But if he stayed, it's likely he and his family would be hung from a tree.

The shah, however, had a different proposal in mind. He wanted Smirnov to reach out to the Russian embassy and get its blessing to commence "the bombardment of Tehran from without." The shah still had a contingent of loyal Russian officers stationed in Kermanshah. They could roll the necessary artillery to the outskirts of Tehran by dawn and begin bombing the city at first light.

Smirnov was stunned. The shah was asking for the assistance of a foreign country to bomb his own capital? Perhaps if the lives of Russians were being threatened by the revolutionaries, the proposal would be considered. But there was no reason to fear violence against foreigners. Smirnov had to grudgingly admit that, thus far, the conduct of the Nationalist Force had been exemplary. There had been no reports of looting or revenge killings. Indeed, the conquest of Tehran had been practically bloodless.

The shah was not interested in such facts. He ordered Smirnov to deliver the message to the Russian embassy and inform the Russian officer in charge in Kermanshah—a Captain Perebinosov—to prepare to attack the city at dawn. It was late; he was tired. He was going to sleep. He expected an answer by morning.

Although he did not agree with the bombardment of Tehran, Smirnov sent the request to his superiors anyway. The response came quickly: Russia could not countenance Tehran's bombardment, given the risk of injuring the lives and interests of Russian nationals in the city.

Smirnov woke the shah at 5:00 a.m. the following morning and delivered the news. His Majesty accepted it without comment. Strangely, he seemed relieved.

Meanwhile, no one in the palace could find Colonel Liakhov. He usually met with the shah twice a week, but he had not been seen in days, not since the Cossack Brigade was forced to retreat back to Saltanat Abad. The last time Smirnov spoke to him, Liakhov had flatly confessed that the situation was hopeless: there was no way to avoid

Tehran's occupation by the revolutionaries. Rumors were circulating at court that he had surrendered to the nationalists. Smirnov refused to believe it. But it was true.

Liakhov had ridden his horse to the ruins of the parliament building—the building that he himself had ruined—and personally negotiated "a declaration of peace between the Nationalists and the Cossack Brigade." In exchange for a pardon and safe passage back to St. Petersburg, Colonel Vladimir Liakhov handed command of the brigade to the Nationalist Force, which then, remarkably, recommissioned the soldiers back into service, placing them in charge of securing the capital that had just been taken from them.

It was a shrewd bid for self-preservation on Liakhov's part, and it worked marvelously. His surrender would, in the weeks to come, be heralded by the Western press as a masterstroke of military diplomacy, recasting Liakhov's legacy from the "Butcher of Parliament" to "Persia's Savior."

"Hero of the hour!" declared the *Washington Post*. "[His surrender] saved Persia from mob rule and preserved the lives of Europeans in that country."

Before the month was over, Liakhov would be back in St. Petersburg, promoted by the tsar for his "honorable role" in Persia. But when the men of the Cossack Brigade learned what their commanding officer had done, they were infuriated. Smirnov called Liakhov "a swindle," and declared his pursuit of negotiations with the nationalists without the shah's knowledge to be "depraved" (the two men would not see each other again until the launch of the Great War, when both were sent to the Caucasian Front to battle the Ottoman army).

The shah, however, seemed unsurprised by Liakhov's surrender. He simply gave Smirnov "a bitter grin" and called for the crown jewels to be packed for travel. Without the Cossack Brigade there was no sense in continuing the fight. He would ask the Russian embassy for refuge.

The royal carriage arrived at the Russian ambassador's house at 8:30 a.m. on the morning of July 17, 1909. Mohammed Ali was escorted into a charming white bungalow and locked inside. Attached to the house was a small verandah overlooking a delightful little Persian garden. As he stepped out to take in the view from his temporary home, the former shah was forced to pass beneath a set of British and Russian flags suspended just above the door. The flags were ceremonially crossed, a symbol of the enduring cooperation between the two nations when it came to Persian affairs.

The press picked up the image. Not long after, a satirical cartoon was published in one of the Persian papers, depicting a timid Persian Lamb squeezed between a stately English Lion and a mighty Russian Bear. The cartoon was meant to serve as history's final judgment on Mohammed Ali Shah—the wretched, bumbling monarch who foolishly relied on foreign powers to protect his reign, only to see those powers abandon him at the end. But it was also a foreshadowing of what was to come, as the democracy that so many Persians—and one American—had fought for, would, over the next decade, be squeezed to death by those same two foreign powers.

❖

ELECTIONS WERE HELD in November 1909, with the new parliament in session before the end of the year. The first order of business was to pardon all the shah's prisoners and to declare a national amnesty for anyone who fought against the constitution. Only five people were tried for "crimes against the martyrs of the revolution," most prominently, the old, ill-tempered ayatollah, Fazlullah Nuri, who was sentenced to death by hanging.

The execution of an ayatollah was an unprecedented act in this majority Shi'ah country, but it was meant to signal the new reality in democratic Persia: no citizen—whether cleric or king—would henceforth be above the law. Nuri, wearing a noose around his neck, was dragged before a large crowd. Given the chance to speak, he cast his role in the revolution as nothing more than a personal rivalry between him and his fellow ayatollahs. "Neither was I a 'reactionary,' nor [were] Sayyid Abdollah [Behbehani] and Sayyid Mohammad [Tabatabai] 'constitutionalists,'" he said. "It was merely that they wished to expel me, and I them, and there was no question of 'reactionary' or 'constitutional' principles."

Although there was heated debate in parliament over whether or not to continue the monarchy, the delegates eventually agreed to place the twelve-year-old crown prince on the throne. When Ahmed heard the news, he ran away and hid. He had to be dragged to Golestan Palace by force, all the while crying, "I don't want to be king! I want my Shah Baba!"

Smirnov managed to calm him down. The Russian counseled the new shah to be steadfast, to keep quiet, and, above all, to maintain a neutral stance on everything—the nationalists, the Russians, the British, his father—until the political winds in Tehran subsided. He would be there to guide him through the storm.

Parliament, however, preferred not to have any more Russians at court. It was decided that Ahmed Shah should be educated solely by Persians. Smirnov received a polite letter informing him that his contract had been annulled. It was time for him to go home.

Smirnov tried to fight the decision. He filed a formal complaint with the Russian embassy citing breach of contract. But the complaint was ignored. His superiors told him they had no interest in taking up his case. Parliament was free to choose whomever it wanted to instruct the new shah. An angry Smirnov responded that the embassy seemed to be confusing him for "a common tutor." But, in the end, he had no choice but to accept the decision and leave Persia. The young shah wept at his departure.

All three Russians at court had now been expelled. Shapshal was back in Crimea, living quietly on his estate near Theodosia, sending the new shah lavish gifts in a bid to regain the good graces of the court.

Liakhov was in St. Petersburg, being showered with medals and rising up through the military ranks. And Smirnov was in Dagestan, bitter and disgraced, writing books about his life and experiences in the Land of the Lion and the Sun.

With most matters of immediate concern having been settled, parliament turned its attention to Howard Conklin Baskerville. One by one, the delegates from Tabriz paid tribute to the American missionary who gave his life to free Persia. The head of the Azerbaijan delegation took the podium and gave an emotional speech, describing in detail the young man's actions during the terrible siege, and vowing that Persia would never forget his sacrifice. The carpet-weavers union had constructed a massive carpet made of cotton and wool, with Baskerville's face woven into the center; it would be prominently displayed in the newly established Constitution House in Tabriz so that future generations would always remember his name.

On the other side of town, however, the American legate, John B. Jackson, was doing his best to forget all about Howard Baskerville and the trouble he had caused. Jackson had finally managed to rid himself of William Doty, reassigning him to the Russian city of Riga, in modern-day Latvia (Doty would bounce around from one posting to another until his retirement in Newcastle, England; he died in Southport on April 9, 1963). The unexpected, and thoroughly unwelcomed, victory of the revolutionaries over the shah had forced a complete overhaul of America's foreign policy priorities in Persia. But at least the legate didn't have Howard Baskerville to worry about anymore.

"His death, regrettable as it may have been, simplified matters," Jackson wrote his superiors in Washington.

The State Department closed the file on Baskerville and sent copies of all pertinent documents and dispatches concerning the young man's actions to the Presbyterian Board of Foreign Missions in New York, along with an explicit warning to make sure nothing like this ever happens again. Robert E. Speer responded with a personal letter, saying he

THE SEED OF BETTER THINGS

was deeply embarrassed by Baskerville's "interference in the civil strife which is going on in Northwest Persia" and promising to do a better job of keeping the missionaries he sent out into the world "entirely free from all entanglements in [such] affairs."

"Our view of the impropriety of missionary interference in politics are [*sic*], we believe, in entire accord with the views of the Government, and our missionaries throughout the world are under strict instruction in the matter," Speer wrote.

The Presbyterian Board of Foreign Missions agreed with the State Department that it would be in the best interest of everyone involved to simply forget the entire affair. That was easier said than done in Tabriz.

Baskerville's death cast a pall over the West Persia Mission. The American Memorial School, which had always managed to speak with one voice, found itself bitterly divided between those who viewed his actions as admirable—even necessary—and those who condemned them as a violation of his sacred calling. Sarah Wright's father, John, was severely critical of Baskerville's decision to join the revolution. He wrote a letter to Robert Speer pinning the responsibility for Baskerville's death directly upon the faculty and students of the American Memorial School, which, in his words, had become a "hotbed for revolutionary activity."

"It seems to me most of this station are so deeply in sympathy with the Revolutionalists that their talk unconsciously influenced Mr. B. to take the step that he did," Wright complained to Speer. "And now that Mr. B. has gone, most of our circle seem (to me) swept away by an impulsive sentiment. . . . Some hold him up as the ideal missionary and want to call him a martyr for Christ!"

That is exactly how Annie Wilson understood Baskerville's actions. She wrote her own letter to Speer, pushing back on Wright's criticism and explicitly casting young Howard as having sacrificed himself for the people of the city. "Whether you can approve of Mr. Baskerville's action or not, its motive was noble," she wrote. "We may hope that many Persians will remember it and that his blood will be the seed of better things. Such an example of devotion has stirred all hearts."

The Russian occupation of Tabriz only widened the rift at the school, pitting the Wilsons and the Jessups, both of whom became more vocal in their support for Persian sovereignty, against the Pittmans and the Wrights, who welcomed the Russians as a potentially stabilizing force that could bolster their evangelical work in the city. The rift never healed.

Less than a year after Baskerville's death, the Wrights abandoned the West Persia Mission. The Pittmans followed soon thereafter. Eventually, even the Wilsons left. In 1912, Samuel and Annie named Frederick Jessup the school's new headmaster and, together with their two youngest children, boarded a steamship bound for New York. Agnes was already at Vassar, and Rose had just joined her there as a freshman. Both girls were waiting for them at New York Harbor, waving from the crowded docks.

The Wilsons moved into a large unfurnished house, their sole décor two massive Persian carpets they had carried with them all the way from Tabriz. Yet, as with Justin Perkins, Samuel could not remain disentangled from missionary life for long. When the Great War began, he felt called to return to Persia. He crossed the Aras River via a brand new railroad built by the Russians and entered Tabriz to a rousing reception from the faculty and students at the American Memorial School.

A few months later, Annie received a cablegram in New York: "Dr. Wilson in hospital—Typhoid."

Samuel Graham Wilson was buried in the Tabriz Cemetery, next to the three children he and Annie had lost in Persia. Frederick Jessup placed a stone over his grave, carved with a simple inscription: "He that loseth his life for my sake shall find it" (Matthew 10:39).

Alone without her husband for the first time in thirty years, Annie relocated to Southern California, where she founded the Presbyterian Church of Pasadena and taught courses in the Bible at Occidental

College in Los Angeles, just a few blocks from where I now live. She retired some years later and moved to a small house in San Jose, a few blocks from where I grew up. She died there on February 1, 1952.

As I write these final words, I can't help but think how strange it is that I spent years walking the same streets that Annie Rhea Wilson walked, stopping at the same cafés, strolling through the same parks. My family moved to San Jose not long after we arrived in the United States. Like Annie, we came in the wake of a revolution, fleeing the chaos and violence that ultimately transformed Iran's repressive monarchy into an equally repressive Islamic Republic. We settled in San Jose in the midst of the Hostage Crisis—444 days in which Americans were held captive inside the US embassy in Tehran. That event and its aftermath created an unbreachable chasm between Iran and America, and I found myself, over the following years, caught in the void: both American and Iranian, yet made to feel neither.

How I wish I'd known the full story of Howard Baskerville then! How different my childhood would have been had I been aware of Baskerville's response when he was told he could not fight for another country's freedom: "The only difference between me and these people is the place of my birth," he said, "and that is not a big difference."

By the time I fully discovered who Howard Baskerville was and what he had done, he'd been dead nearly a century. But that death, and the life that preceded it, continues to drive me today. It serves as a reminder that we must not be slaves to "the bigotry of creeds" or "the prejudice of nationality"; that our obligations to one another go beyond the particular religion we subscribe to or the citizenship we've been assigned; that the suffering of any person anywhere is the responsibility of all peoples everywhere. The lesson to be learned from the epic life and tragic death of Howard Baskerville is that the markers of identity we rely on to separate ourselves into different tribes serve only to mask the humanity we all hold in common.

"I am Persia's," the young American declared a few weeks before his death.

Annie understood what Baskerville meant. Like me she was both Persian and American. Born in Seir, she spent decades living and serving in the land of my birth. She watched five shahs sit on the throne. She laughed and cried, suffered and celebrated alongside people who did not look like her, who spoke different languages, practiced different faiths, and carried different nationalities. So when, at the end of her life, she sat down in that tidy home in San Jose to record her memories of the years she'd spent in Persia—the children she buried there, the school she and Samuel built together in Tabriz, the revolution that upended their lives, and the young man from South Dakota who died defending their city—she wanted to make certain none of us would ever forget what Baskerville had done, and why.

She was the actor portraying Husain in the Taziyeh, circling the stage at the end of the drama, staring hard into each of our faces, asking us a simple question: How will we choose to honor the memory of Howard Conklin Baskerville?

Annie's choice is clear. This book is mine.

What is yours?

The twelve-year-old Ahmed Shah Qajar, the seventh and final king of the Qajar Dynasty.

EPILOGUE

ON DECEMBER 6, 1925, the Qajar royal carriage—the one Mohammed Ali had been riding in when someone lobbed two handmade bombs at his motorcade; the one that had transported him to the Russian embassy, thus ending his reign—pulled up to a large circular amphitheater not far from Golestan Palace in Tehran. Some three thousand people, including diplomats from England and the newly formed Soviet Union, had gathered there in anticipation of a historic announcement. In the center of the amphitheater was a hastily built stage—empty, save for a table and chair. A brood of dour old men in turbans were huddled at the foot of the stage, grumbling among themselves. There were soldiers spread across the perimeter, their backs stiff with expectation, their faces full of menace.

The royal carriage came to a stop a few feet from the amphitheater entrance. The door swung open, and out stepped Reza Khan Savadkuhi—"Sixty-Bullet Reza"—the low-born, barely literate, Cossack Brigade soldier from the hills of Mazandaran. Tall, unshaven, and heavy-bodied, he had been talked into wearing his dress uniform for the occasion: shiny, knee-high boots; blue, fur-lined cloak; sword and dagger clipped to his belt. He kept pulling at his collar, as though it were trying to strangle him.

With an air of strained confidence he strode up to the stage, hesitated for a moment, took a wrong turn, corrected himself, and then climbed the short flight of steps. He saluted the military, then pulled out the chair before changing his mind and tucking it back under the table. He would stand. From his coat pocket he removed a neatly folded piece of paper and began reading it slowly, in a low, rumbling voice. He had memorized the words; until a year before, he could barely read or write. Fortunately, the speech was short and to the point.

By order of parliament, and with the full-throated support of the Soviet and British governments, Reza Khan Savadkuhi was hereby declaring an end to the Qajar Dynasty and the beginning of a new royal line in Persia—*his*.

Henceforth, he would be known as Reza Shah.

The story of how a penniless orphan became the "Shadow of God on Earth" is also the story of how the promise of postrevolutionary democracy in Persia was shattered by more than a decade of political infighting, foreign interference, and, of course, "a war to end all wars."

❖

THE PARLIAMENT THAT was resurrected in the wake of Tabriz's victory over the shah, though almost wholly composed of nationalists and former revolutionaries, was nevertheless riven by factionalism and personal feuds. A political divide quickly formed between the so-called moderates, who made up the largest voting bloc and who advocated for maintaining the status quo—a strong constitutional monarchy held in check by the firm hand of parliament—and the younger, more aggressive Social Democrats, who wanted to replace the monarchy with a republic and carry out a wide-ranging program of economic and social reforms, including women's rights.

It did not take long for the political debate to spill out of parliament, with rival factions shooting each other in the streets. At first, both sides looked to Sattar Khan for support. But the vagaries of postrevolutionary politics were beyond the skills of the People's Commander. He tried his best playing the role of peacemaker, at one point physically placing himself between the two sides in the middle of a street fight. He got a bullet in the leg for his trouble. After that, Sattar Khan simply gave up. Unable to return to Tabriz, which was still occupied by Russian troops, he begrudgingly settled in Tehran. He died on November 9, 1914— bitter, angry, and drunk. Ironically, he was buried in the shrine of Shah Abdol Azim, the same place where Ayatollah Nuri and his followers had taken sanctuary at the height of the Constitutional Revolution.

Meanwhile, parliament had come to a complete standstill. The people were starting to realize how difficult it is to get things done when everyone gets a vote. Without Sattar on the scene, there was no singular, charismatic voice to rally everyone together under a common cause. The new Qajar king, Ahmed Shah, displayed little interest in ruling. He may have taken his old tutor's advice to remain neutral a little too seriously. He was, in the words of one historian, "a timid procrastinator who regarded his constitutionality as one of cynical non-action."

Persia's clergy had already begun to abandon politics after the execution of Fazlullah Nuri. But then, in 1910, the great revolutionary ayatollah, Abdollah Behbehani, who had become a vocal supporter of the moderates in parliament, was assassinated by none other than "Haydar the Bomb Maker," the same man who was tried, imprisoned, and eventually released for trying to assassinate Mohammed Ali Shah. After Behbehani's murder, his revolutionary ally Ayatollah Tabatabai retired from politics, living out the last years of his life in quiet seclusion, and the rest of the clerical establishment more or less retreated back to the mosques.

The postrevolutionary vacuum of power in Persia paved the way for the British Lion and the Russian Bear to pursue their own military and economic interests in the country without hindrance. The Russians, in particular, began making absurd demands of the fractured parliament. Their occupation of Tabriz had become an unmitigated disaster. Russian troops rounded up and executed anyone they viewed as a threat to their military presence. They murdered residents without fear of consequence and destroyed the city's most cherished monuments, including the Citadel—that enduring symbol of Tabriz's fortitude and perseverance. A short-lived resistance movement, led by Howard Baskerville's favorite student, Sadeq Rezazadeh Shafaq, put up a fight for a brief while. But the movement was easily crushed and Sadeq himself forced to flee to Europe (he returned to Persia in 1923 with a PhD in Western philosophy).

By 1912, there were more than twenty thousand Russian troops stationed across the entirety of Persia's northern territories. And yet, the Russian government had the gall to demand parliament compensate it for "the expense of its present dispatch of troops." Under threat of a full-scale invasion, it forced the Persian government to cover the cost of its own foreign occupation. The Russians even tried to restore Mohammed Ali, then exiled in Odessa, back onto the throne, helping him raise a small army that was quickly routed when it crossed from Russia into Persian territory (Mohammed Ali died in 1925 while living in exile in Italy).

While Russia plundered Persia's north, Britain launched its own military occupation of the south, deploying its "Indian Army" (the Sepoys) into cities such as Isfahan and Shiraz, ostensibly to protect their assets from governmental unrest. But that was a convenient lie. The truth was that Britain had unexpectedly discovered oil in the southwest province of Khuzestan. The troops were meant to secure the area so the British could ship barrel after barrel of freshly pumped crude back to the United Kingdom, in urgent preparation for a war that everyone knew was coming.

When the First World War finally broke out in 1914, the Persian parliament wisely declared neutrality, hoping to be spared the consequent devastation. But it made no difference: Persia became an active battlefield between Russian and Ottoman troops. During the four-year conflict, the city of Tabriz changed hands between the two armies eight times! At one point, Ottoman soldiers broke into the American Memorial School and demanded that Frederick Jessup, the school's headmaster, hand over the relief funds he had collected to help the suffering residents of the city. Jessup refused and was beaten and imprisoned for forty-four days as a result. He never fully recovered. He died of pneumonia on December 1, 1919, at the age of 43.

When the war finally ended, Persia was left in ruins. The disruption of supply lines had already caused enormous hardship for the population. But a series of droughts over the next few years plunged the country into a deep economic depression. Famine and disease ran rampant. The influenza pandemic of 1918—perhaps the war's most devastating legacy—wiped out nearly a tenth of Persia's entire population. With the country partitioned between Russia in the north and Britain in the south, parliament had no means to adequately respond to the humanitarian disaster. Thousands of children died from malnutrition. The hungry ate dogs and rats. Women held their starving babies out to strangers. It seemed that Persia had lost more than its sovereignty; it had lost its *farr*. The people felt abandoned by God. The mullahs blamed democracy.

Persia received a measure of reprieve with the Russian Revolution of 1917. The Bolsheviks, buoyed by some of the same Russian fighters who had defended Tabriz against the shah, seized the Winter Palace and executed Tsar Nicholas II and his entire family. The new Communist regime removed all troops from Persia, canceled all loans and concessions, and, for the first time since 1909, allowed the county to fulfill its own destiny without foreign interference . . . but only in the north. The south was still occupied by British forces. Indeed, the removal of Russian troops from Persia encouraged Britain to further flex its military power over the country. London became the new benefactor of the Cossack Brigade, replacing the Russian officers with British ones. To cement its hold over Persia, Britain signed a sweeping agreement with the cash-strapped parliament, promising to share financial and military assistance in exchange for unfettered access to the southern oil fields.

However, Britain's plans for Persia would only be realized if the country could be stabilized. The British argued that the postrevolutionary chaos only proved what they believed all along: Persia was not ready for democracy. It needed another strong leader to guide the country. Not the present shah, of course; these days Ahmed seemed to spend more time shopping in Paris than ruling in Persia. What the country required was someone who could calm the waters and restore order throughout the land, by force if necessary: someone whom the people could trust, and Britain could control.

That someone, it turned out, was Reza Khan Savadkuhi.

After the Cossack Brigade's surrender to the Nationalist Force, Reza Khan not only chose to remain in uniform, he also swiftly rose to the rank of brigadier general. As a military leader, Reza was charismatic and ruthless, but with a surprising propensity for organization and management. His general distrust of Russia had, after the Russian Revolution, morphed into a blind hatred for the Bolsheviks—the result, quite possibly, of having faced their fighters in battle at Tabriz. When Britain took control over the Cossack Brigade, Reza's anti-Communist proclivities quickly earned him the trust of his British superiors, and he was tapped to lead the force.

Historians still disagree over whose idea it was—Britain's or Reza's—but on February 21, 1921, Reza Khan, with the full backing of the British government, marched his Cossack Brigade into Tehran and declared a military coup. The Persian Constitution was suspended, all newspapers shut down, public gatherings banned, taverns and theaters closed, and government services temporarily put on hold. There was little resistance. The people were tired and hungry and afraid. Frustrated by a lack of social and economic progress, fractured by the never-ending squabbles in parliament, and fearful that the country might be falling apart, Persia's population simply surrendered to the new order.

Reza declared himself commander-in-chief of the armed forces and named his political ally, a journalist by the name of Sayyed Zia, the new prime minister. But after a few months, Zia was shunted aside and Reza became prime minister himself. Having now taken charge of both the military and the parliament, Reza Khan put forth a bill abolishing the Qajar Dynasty and vesting provisional leadership over the country in the prime minister. Ahmed Shah was in France at the time and, given the anti-Qajar sentiment in Persia, thought it best to just stay there; he died in 1930, in a posh neighborhood just outside of Paris.

Reza's bill passed parliament by a wide margin. Less clear was what should replace the Qajar Dynasty. Reza made a public show of preferring a Persian Republic, in the mold of the Turkish Republic recently founded by his fellow military commander, Kemal Atatürk. This was a clever bit of political theater from the simple soldier turned politician. Reza knew that by siding with the Social Democrats, who had for years been clamoring for a republic, he would curry their favor as a fellow "progressive." But he also understood that Persia's clergy had no tolerance whatsoever for the aggressively secular policies being put forth in Turkey. His vocal support for a republic ended up mobilizing the conservative elements in the country, pulling the mullahs out of the mosques again, and creating such chaos in parliament that people began publicly calling for a strong, authoritarian hand.

The final nail in the coffin of republicanism in Persia took place on March 3, 1924, when the Turkish Republic abolished the Islamic Caliphate. That action made the idea of a republic synonymous with "atheism" among conservative Persians, giving fuel to the argument of those who favored a continuation of the constitutional monarchy, but with a new monarch. And who better to sit on the throne than the man who was already in charge of both the parliament and the military?

❖

REZA SHAH'S OFFICIAL coronation took place on April 25, 1926—seventeen years, almost to the day, when he or someone under his command fired a bullet through the back of Howard Baskerville in an orchard near Qaramalik. All of Tehran was strung with electric lights for the coronation. Horsemen carrying banners paraded through the streets. Bright, colorful carpets were hung end to end on the walls of homes and buildings, so that the whole of the city appeared made not of brick and plaster, but of wool and fabric, "like a great and sumptuous tent open to the sky," wrote one European observer.

Inside Golestan Palace, the throne room was packed with dignitaries from all over the world, everyone silent with anticipation. At last, there came a stirring in the back, as the doors opened and a little boy appeared, alone and dressed in military uniform. This was the shah's son, Mohammed Reza, the crown prince of Persia. He shuffled uncertainly to the front of the room and found his place on the lowest step of the throne, awaiting his father's entrance.

Reza Shah entered wearing a blue cloak encrusted with jewels. Escorted by his generals, he strode to the throne and took a seat, the crown prince visibly shaking at his feet. The new shah had commissioned a new throne to be built for the occasion, a gaudy reproduction of the famed Peacock Throne that had been captured from India in 1793. He had also commissioned a new crown—a dazzling tiara fronted by a golden sun and arrayed with diamonds and pearls. Every aspect of his reign was meant to signal a break from the Qajar past. Indeed, he would even change the country's name, formally requesting Woodrow Wilson's League of Nations to begin referring to the country as *Iran* (meaning "Land of the Aryans") in all official documents and correspondences.

When the time came for one of the senior-most clerics in the room to lift the crown and place it on the new shah's head, Reza plucked it from the old man's hands and, following the example set by Napoleon, crowned himself. That may have been the moment the mullahs realized they'd been played. After goading the clerical establishment into supporting his ascension to the throne (lest Persia become another Turkey), Reza Shah's new dynasty—the Pahlavi Dynasty, it would be called—would spend the next five decades beating Persia's mullahs into silent submission.

Soon after his coronation, Reza Shah instituted an aggressive "modernization" program that included bans on all head scarves for women and laws requiring all men to wear "Western clothes" in public. He made female education compulsory and mandated the mingling of the sexes in schools, restaurants, and theaters. The constitution he had fought against as a Cossack soldier was swiftly discarded, and parliament was completely defanged; the shah simply got rid of elections and instead packed the National Consultative Assembly with his own hand-picked delegates. He abolished the free press, filled government ministries with members of the military, and executed anyone who betrayed any hint of opposition to his rule.

All of these actions could be ignored—even encouraged—by Reza's British benefactors, as long as London believed he could be controlled. But Reza Shah never had any intention of being placed under the thumb of a foreign power. The new shah unilaterally canceled the British oil concession and started making friendly overtures to Turkey and Germany, the latter eventually growing into Iran's largest trading partner. When he refused Britain's invitation to join the Allies in the run up to the Second World War, the Soviets and British, citing his friendly overtures toward Nazi Germany, invaded and reoccupied Iran. Britain had placed Reza on the throne, and it reserved the right to remove him from it. On September 16, 1941, Reza Shah was forced into exile and the crown placed on the head of his son, Mohammed Reza Pahlavi, whom we last saw as a young boy quivering at his father's feet.

This is the shah that I grew up with, a man who furthered his father's policy of brutal repression but had none of his father's strength or charisma. What Mohammed Reza Shah did have, however, was a wealthier and far more powerful benefactor than any previous shah could have imagined: the United States.

The Second World War left the British Empire cash-strapped and overextended. It no longer had the means to maintain its occupation of foreign lands. It therefore ceded control over Iran to the United States, which was more than willing to step in and help prop up the shah in exchange for access to Iran's oil fields and the purchase of millions of dollars of American military equipment.

When, in 1953, a second popular revolution forced Mohammed Reza Shah from his throne, America simply swooped in and placed him right back on it. Bolstered by his CIA-trained secret police force, the SAVAK, which tortured, disappeared, and murdered tens of thousands of Iranians during his reign, the shah managed to hold onto power for another two and half decades, until 1979, when the same coalition of merchants, intellectuals, and revolutionary clerics who had come together to topple the Qajar Dynasty seventy years earlier did the same to the Pahlavi Dynasty.

This time, the United States was unable to reverse the will of the people. However, as happened in 1909, the coalition that sent the shah into exile could not hold in his absence. And into yet another postrevolutionary vacuum of power stepped the Ayatollah Ruhollah Khomeini, who rallied the pious masses to his side and seized control of the country for himself, transforming Iran into a totalitarian state ruled by a corrupt clerical class and backed by a ruthless military.

Reading this brief history, should we then conclude that the Constitutional Revolution was an abject failure? That, in effect, Howard Baskerville died for nothing? That would be shortsighted and naïve. The Constitutional Revolution created profound social and cultural shifts in Iranian society. From its acclaimed public education system to its world-renowned health care and its illustrious tradition of art and cinema—so much of what Iranians rightly celebrate today as their nation's proudest achievements were rooted in the goals of Persia's nationalists. The very concept of Iranian nationalism—the belief that the country is one people composed of different ethnicities and religions yet united by a singular national identity—was born from the blood of the martyrs who died trying to establish democracy in Persia a century ago.

Whatever else was achieved by the multiracial, multilingual, multireligious coalition that forced Mohammed Ali Shah from his throne, that remarkable success set the precedent for the exercise of people power in Iran, creating one of the most robust protest cultures in the world. And if this vibrant people's movement has yet to achieve the freedom that all Iranians deserve—despite three revolutions and countless strikes, uprisings, and street demonstrations—it is not because the people are too weak or the government too strong. It is because the country remains, to this day, a pawn in the hands of global powers. A tyrant stays in power by isolating his people from the rest of the world. In the case of Iran, the world has done the tyrant's work for him.

No matter. For more than a century the people of Iran have been told—by foreigners and talking heads, by their own political and religious leaders—that "resistance is equal to suicide." For more than a century they have continued to resist. Driven by the same belief that led Tabriz to victory against the shah—that people should be masters of their own fate; that they should be free to act and think without coercion; that they should have a say in the decisions that rule their lives—they have never stopped beating on freedom's door. Now, that door is cracking ever so slightly, as a government whose chief duty is to feed and protect its citizens has proven utterly incapable of doing either. Just a little more nudging and the door will break open. And woe to those who thought they could keep it closed forever.

ACKNOWLEDGMENTS

THIS BOOK COULD not have been written without the support of my research assistant, Ehsan Siapoush, who provided much of the primary research material and translated all Persian texts and documents. Further research was provided by Farzam Farrokh and by the good folks at the Baskerville Institute in Salt Lake City, Utah. I am grateful for the time and energy given to the manuscript by my fabulous editor, Alane Mason, at W. W. Norton and my wonderful literary agent, Elyse Cheney. I also want to thank my wife and best friend, Jessica Jackley, as well as my beautiful children—Cyrus, Jaspar, Asa, and Soraya—for putting up with my wild mood swings over the three years it took to write this book.

NOTES

INTRODUCTION

The prominent writer and activist who wondered what would happen if Baskerville were alive today was the incomparable poet and novelist Reza Baraheni, writing in *The Nation*: "No Wreath for Mr. Baskerville: America in Cahoots with the Shah," March 12, 1977. Those interested in Baraheni's work should read my anthology of contemporary Middle East literature, *Tablet & Pen* (New York: W. W. Norton, 2011).

PART ONE

The Saadi poem is from his masterwork *Golestan* and is my own translation from the original Persian.

CHAPTER ONE

The formal name of the board was the Board of Foreign Missions of the Presbyterian Church in the USA (established 1837); we refer to it throughout as the Presbyterian Board of Foreign Missions.

The exact timing of Howard Baskerville's departure to Persia is impossible to know for certain. The American Memorial School began its fall session in early October. The journey from New York to Persia could take anywhere between four and six weeks. My assumption, therefore, is that he would have boarded a steamship sometime in August. We don't know which ship he took or his exact destination—Liverpool and Glasgow are merely the two most obvious. I have done my best, in these early chapters, to re-create Baskerville's long, arduous journey to Persia by scouring through documents left behind by those who made a similar journey at around the same time. My main source was the travelogue of Abraham V. W. Jackson, *Persia Past and Present* (New York: Macmillan, 1906). Jackson was a student at Columbia University who was given leave for a year of travel as part of his research on "Zoroaster and the ancient faith of the Magi." He left New

York in 1906 and spent considerable time in Tabriz, boarding at the home of the Wilsons just before Howard Baskerville arrived.

Edward A. Steiner described the horrors of steerage class aboard the SS *Kaiser Wilhelm II* in his book *On the Trail of the Immigrant* (Toronto: Fleming H. Revell, 1906). Between 1890 and 1914, roughly fourteen million European migrants made the crossing to the United States. During this 25-year period, approximately 87 percent traveled in steerage. See Drew Keeling, "Oceanic Travel Conditions and American Immigration, 1890–1914," MPRA (June 2013).

By the time Howard Baskerville left for Tabriz, his father, Henry, had moved the family once again to New London, Minnesota, where they stayed until a year after Baskerville's death. They then moved again to Princeton in 1911, where the family remained until Henry's death on June 30, 1912, at the age of 63.

Woodrow Wilson's "progress of civilization" quote is from his address at the University Club of Chicago. See W. Barksdale Maynard, *Woodrow Wilson: Princeton to the Presidency* (New Haven, CT: Yale University Press, 2008), 51–52. For more on Wilson's religious beliefs see Patricia O'Toole, *The Moralist: Woodrow Wilson and the World He Made* (New York: Simon & Schuster, 2018). Paul Robeson is quoted in his memoir, *Here I Stand* (London: Cassell, 1988), 11.

Wilson's avowed racism is well documented, but it has only recently become known to the wider public. "Wilson was not just a racist. He believed in white supremacy as government policy, so much so that he reversed decades of racial progress," writes Gordon J. Davis in "What Woodrow Wilson Cost My Grandfather," *New York Times,* November 24, 2015. See also Neville K. Meaney, "Arthur S. Link and Thomas Woodrow Wilson," *Journal of American Studies* 1, no. 1 (1967): 119–26.

Wilson's pedagogy at Princeton is outlined by Hardin Craig in *Woodrow Wilson at Princeton* (Norman: University of Oklahoma Press, 1960); his quote regarding the usefulness of general education is from page 80 of the book.

"Princeton in the Nation's Service" is the title of a famous oration Woodrow Wilson delivered at the sesquicentennial celebration, when Princeton looked back to its founding in 1746. Wilson's quote regarding popular sovereignty as the moral judgment of God is pulled from Arthur S. Link, "A Portrait of Wilson," *Virginia Quarterly Review* 32, no. 4 (1956): 524–41; 529.

The missionary dispatches from China and Japan are taken from *The North China Mission of the Methodist Episcopal Church* (New York: Methodist Episcopal Church, 1905), 2, and A. Gosman and L. W. Eckard, *Historical Sketches of the Missions in Japan, Korea* (Philadelphia: Woman's Foreign Missionary Society of the Presbyterian Church, 1891), 3, respectively. See also Matthew M. Davis, "Evangelizing the Orient: American Missionaries in Iran, 1890–1940" (PhD diss., Ohio State University, 2001).

Frances Packard quoted in his memoir, *The Story of Our Missions in Persia* (Philadelphia: Board of Foreign Missions, 1920), 25. Justin Perkins's quote is from his memoir, *A Residence of Eight Years in Persia, Among the Nestorian Christians; With Notices of the Mohammedans* (Andover, MA: Allen, Morrill & Wardwell, 1843), 149–50. John Macdonald Kinneir's *A Geographical Memoir of the Persian Empire* (London: John Murray, 1813), which had become an essential companion for missionaries stationed in Persia since its publication, describes the entirety of the Persian population as "totally devoid of many estimable qualities, and profoundly versed in all the arts of deceit and hypocrisy. They are haughty to their inferiors, obsequious to their superiors, cruel, vindictive, treacherous and avaricious, without faith, friendship, gratitude or honor."

CHAPTER TWO

Herman Melville is quoted in his *Redburn: His First Voyage* (Cambridge, UK: Press Syndicate of the University of Cambridge, 1983). You can get a wonderful glimpse of what the Liverpool docks would have looked like to Baskerville from Ian Collard's *Liverpool Landing Stage Through Time* (Stroud, UK: Amberley Publishing, 2011).

Although this was his first trip abroad—his first trip anywhere, really—Howard was not the first Baskerville to set foot on the isle. That honor was claimed by his ancestor Martels de Baskerville, who sailed to England alongside William the Conqueror, at the head of a 700-ship invasion fleet launched from Normandy in the year AD 1066. Martels bled with William as they broke through the English lines at the Battle of Hastings. He marched with William to London, burning everything along the way. And he was there at Westminster Abbey when William was crowned king on Christmas Day. For his help in seizing the English crown, the nobleman born in a small village in the parish of Baskerville (now *Bacqueville*), in northern France, was rewarded with lands and titles and, most valuable of all, *legacy*. "The family of Baskerville is one of the most ancient and honorable in England," wrote John Burke in his *Genealogical and Heraldic History of the Landed Gentry*, published a century and a half after William's invasion. "It has ever maintained the highest rank among the gentry, and it can boast of the blood of the *Plantagenets*."

There is a small town in France named Dives-sur-Mer, at the mouth of a river by the same name, where William assembled his fleet. At an old-timbered inn called L'Hostellerie Guillaume le Conquerant, above an open courtyard with carved rafters and sculptured reliefs is a large mural containing the names and coats-of-arms of the knights who conquered England. Among them is the name *Baskerville*, next to a white shield emblazoned with a thin red banner and three blue circles. More on the Baskerville legacy can be found in Patrick Hamilton Baskerville, *Genealogy of the Baskerville Family and Some Allied Families, Including the English Descent from 1266 A.D.* (Richmond, VA: W. E. Jones' Sons, 1912). A hand-drawn design of the Baskerville coat of arms done by a friend of the author can be found on page 48.

Barbara Tuchman is quoted from her excellent exploration of the First World War, *The Guns of August* (New York: Macmillan, 1962), 18. There was a growing sense among some in the German high brass that, if a great war was indeed coming, it would be best to just get it started, and on Germany's terms. "War is a biological necessity of the first importance, a regulating element in the life of mankind which cannot be dispensed with," wrote the German general Friedrich von Bernhardi, in trying to convince the German Empire to confront the triple alliance of England, France, and Russia. Friedrich von Bernhardi,

Germany and the Next War (London: Arnold, 1914), 18. See also Peter Hart, *The Great War* (Oxford: Oxford University Press, 2013).

Woodrow Wilson's speech to Congress is quoted in A. Scott Berg, *Wilson* (New York: Simon & Schuster, 2013), 437.

"PERSIA HAS A PARLIAMENT," *The Independent*, August 16, 1906.

"PARLIAMENT FOR PERSIA: Merchants and Mullahs Compel the Shah to Grant Reforms," *New York Times*, January 23, 1906.

The Constitutional Revolution in Persia encompassed a broad spectrum of ideas and objectives, reflecting diverse intellectual trends, social backgrounds, and political demands. But it was unquestionably an indigenous movement and not a simple parroting of European political thought. During the nineteenth century, demands for political reform were prominent in the writings of popular Persian thinkers such as Mirza Malkom Khan (d. 1908), who crafted the earliest known systematic exposition in Persian of a constitutional system; Mirza Fath-Ali Akhundzada (d. 1878), who wrote tracts calling on the people to throw of the yoke of both political and religious tyranny; Mirza Yusuf Mostashar ad-Dawla (d. 1895), who advocated a distinctly Islamic form of modernism; and, of course, the great pan-Islamic modernist thinker and activist, Sayyid Jamal ad-Din Asadabadi ("al-Afghani"; d. 1897), about whom much more will be written in Chapter Five of this book. Their writings were popularized through a surge of newspaper, pamphlet, and book publications at the end of the nineteenth century, which also led to a wave of translations and adaptations of Western works of political philosophy published in Persian for the first time. All of this helped shape the ideology that led to the Persian Constitutional Revolution of 1905.

Morgan Shuster is quoted in his book, *The Strangling of Persia* (New York: Century Company, 1912), xviii. The judgment of Mohammed Ali as "the most perverted, cowardly, and vice-ridden monster that had disgraced the throne of Persia in many generations" is also Shuster's.

E. G. Browne's most comprehensive book about the events of the Constitutional Revolution is *The Persian Revolution of 1905–1909* (Cambridge, UK: Cambridge University Press, 1910). See also Hasan Javadi, "E. G. Browne and the Persian Constitutional Movement," *Iran* 14 (1976): 133–40. The sniffy British minster was James M. Balfour, and his quote about Persians and constitutionalism is from *Recent Happenings in Persia* (Edinburgh: W. Blackwood and Sons, 1922), 54.

Aleksandr Izvolskii is quoted in Firuz Kazemzadeh, *Russia and Britain in Persia: Imperial Ambitions in Qajar Iran* (London: I. B. Tauris, 2003), 488. The term "Great Game" is attributed to British intelligence officer Arthur Conolly and was popularized by Rudyard Kipling in his 1904 book *Kim*. See also Ishtiaq Ahmad, *Anglo-Iranian Relations 1905–1919* (Bombay: Asia Publishing House, 1937).

On the topic of the Berlin-Baghdad railway and its role in precipitating the First World War, I suggest Edward Mead Earle, *Turkey, the Great Powers, and the Baghdad Railway: A Study in Imperialism* (New York: Macmillan, 1923), and Sean McMeekin, *The Berlin-Baghdad Express: The Ottoman Empire and Germany's Bid for World Power, 1898–1918* (New York: Penguin, 2011).

Christopher Clark provides a deep psychological dive into Wilhelm in *Kaiser Wilhelm II: Profiles in Power* (London: Longman, 2000). Wilhelm's comments concerning the plight of Muslims in occupied lands is taken from Virginia Cowles, *The Kaiser* (London: Collins, 1963), 164–65. His words regarding Saladin are taken from Wolf von Schierbrand, ed., *The Kaiser's Speeches: Forming a Character Portrait of Emperor William II* (New York: Harper & Brothers, 1903), 320–21. The kaiser had, in fact, already begun formulating a secret strategy to inflame existing anti-British and anti-Russian sentiments among Muslim populations so as to encourage them to rise up against their foreign masters. The strategy would be formalized with the creation of the Orient Intelligence Bureau, the purpose of which was to persuade Muslims living under British, French, and Russian rule that Germany was the friend of Islam and to spur them to think of the conflict in Europe through the lens of holy war. To this end, the bureau worked hand in hand with the Ottoman sultan's imams (Muslim clergy) to compose fatwas (religious proclamations) declaring jihad against "the West." The fatwas were translated into multiple languages and distributed widely in all occupied Muslim lands. It was a cunning maneuver on the part of the kaiser, one that would have catastrophic consequences in the century to come.

For insight into the Anglo-Russian Agreement see Rose Louise Greaves, "Some Aspects of the Anglo-Russian Convention and Its Working in Persia, 1907–14," *Bulletin of the School of Oriental and African Studies* 31, no. 1 (1968): 69–91.

Missionary orientations usually came in the form of what was known as "magic lantern lectures," meant to provide prospective missionaries with an introduction to the daily life, occupations, religion, culture, and even physical features of the lands they were about to serve. The magic lantern was an early slide projector of sorts. It used an oil lamp and a concave mirror to direct light through a small, rectangular, wood-framed sheet of glass that was either etched or painted with images. One by one these images would be projected onto a screen (usually just a white sheet tacked to the wall) while a "lecturer" read an accompanying script; a thump on the floor would inform the lantern operator that it was time for a new slide. The Presbyterian Board of Foreign Missions published a number of magic lantern lectures covering regions such as India, China, Persia, Syria, and Africa and distributed them across the United States at a cost of 15 cents each. The lectures served as a kind of multimedia missionary manual. Each set contained some seventy or eighty slides, a map of the country, a closing hymn or two (the words projected on the wall so everyone could sing along), and an accompanying text to be read aloud by a designated lecturer. The magic lantern itself had to be secured locally. See Donald Simpson, "Missions and the Magic Lantern," *International Bulletin of Missionary Research* 21 (1997): 13–15. The words quoted in the text are from *Magic Lantern Lectures of Foreign Mission Lands: Syria* (New York: Board of Foreign Missions of the Presbyterian Church in the USA, 1880–1900).

CHAPTER THREE

Woodrow Wilson's views on the French Revolution are discussed by Allen Lynch, "Woodrow Wilson and the Principle of 'National Self-Determination': A Reconsideration," *Review of International Studies* 28, no. 2 (2002): 419–36. Lynch notes that while the precise term "national self-determination" did not become current until the First World War, the concept had been in the air since the time of the French Revolution.

For constitutionalism in Mexico and China, see Charles A. Hale, "The Civil Law Tradition and Constitutionalism in Twentieth-Century Mexico: The Legacy of Emilio Rabasa," *Law and History Review* 18, no. 2 (2000): 257–80; and Egas Moniz Bandeira, "Political Reforms in a Global Context: Some Foreign Perspectives on Constitutional Thought in Late Imperial China," *Contemporary Chinese Political Economy and Strategic Relations: An International Journal* 3, no. 1 (2017): 139–85.

For more on the Young Turks, I suggest Kemal H. Karpat, ed., *Social Change and Politics in Turkey: A Structural-Historical Analysis* (Leiden: E. J. Brill, 1973). The Young Turk movement began in 1889 when five medical students in the military academy of Constantinople secretly formed an organization that they named the Ottoman Society for Union and Progress. Two characteristics of this movement must be noted. First, the Young Turks were a small group, at times numbering no more than perhaps a few members. Second, although it is debatable whether or not the Young Turks could be classified as members of the elite, it is a fact that they frequented the same social circles as the ruling elite and maintained personal contacts with the men they opposed politically. See Bernard Lewis, *The Emergence of Modern Turkey* (London: Oxford University Press, 1968).

Nader Sohrabi provides an informative comparison between revolutionary Turkey and Persia in *Revolution and Constitutionalism in the Ottoman Empire and Iran* (New York: Cambridge University Press, 2011); and in "Historicizing Revolutions: Constitutional Revolutions in Ottoman Empire, Iran, and Russia, 1905–1908," *American Journal of Sociology* 100, no. 6 (1995): 1383–447. Sohrabi notes the importance of the role played by the Social-Democratic Party, an organization founded in 1905 by Persian emigrants in Transcaucasia with the help of local revolutionaries, during the Constitutional Revolution. Members of the organization maintained close links with the Hemmat Party, a radical democratic party organized by Transcaucasian revolutionaries of both Muslim and non-Muslim origins. Close ties were also maintained with the Baku and Tbilisi committees of the Russian Social-Democratic Workers Party.

Sohrabi makes another important point regarding the contribution of the French Revolution to these calls for constitutionalism around the world, noting that the influence may have been more subtle than is often assumed. It is impossible to imagine that all actors were aware of the French Revolution and that they attempted to emulate that revolution at every step. Historical evidence does not support such an argument. Nor was the revolutionaries' major demand, a call for a constitutional system, seen to be peculiar to France alone. By the early twentieth century, constitutionalism had taken a strong hold in all of western Europe, and the constitutionalists idealized the system of rule throughout Europe rather than the one particular to France. Nevertheless, the fact remains that in Iran, Russia, and Turkey, France occupied a privileged position in the constitutionalist consciousness. See also Bruce Mazlish, "The French Revolution in Comparative Perspective," *Political Science Quarterly* 85, no. 2 (1970): 240–58.

Ronald Dworkin defines constitutionalism as "a system that establishes individual legal rights that the dominant legislature does not have the power to override or compromise." That is why constitutionalism is considered to be the foundation of any democracy. See Ronald Dworkin, "Constitutionalism and Democracy," *European Journal of Philosophy* 3, no. 1 (1995): 2–11.

The best book I know of regarding the Russian Revolution remains Orlando Figes, *A People's Tragedy: A History of the Russian Revolution* (New York: Penguin Random House, 1998). The peasants who marched on the Winter Palace were convinced that, as the embodiment of the nation, the tsar personally knew each of their names. He understood and empathized with their problems, no matter how small. As one of his royal biographers put it: "Thousands of invisible threads centre in the Tsar's heart, and those threads stretch to the huts of the poor." A. G. Elachaninov, *Tsar Nicholas II* (London: Hugh Rees, 1913), 2–3. See also Robert D. Warth, *Nicholas II* (Westport, CT: Praeger, 1997).

Vladimir Dzhubkovsky is quoted in Richard G. Robbins, *Overtaken by the Night: One Russian's Journey Through Peace, War, Revolution, and Terror* (Pittsburgh: University of Pittsburgh Press, 2017), 107.

It bears mentioning that Tsar Nicholas II was convinced the uprising against his throne was caused by "the Jews"—a favorite scapegoat of his—and so actively encouraged their massacre on the streets as an act of patriotism to the country and loyalty to his reign. Nicholas was, of course, a virulent anti-Semite. A copy of the *Protocols of the Elders of Zion*, which was first published in St. Petersburg in 1902, was found among his possessions after his death in 1918; see Figes, *A People's Tragedy*, 197, 242.

Tsar Nicholas II's advice to Mohammed Ali Shah is quoted in Leon Novar, "The Great Powers and Iran, 1914–1921" (PhD diss., University of Chicago, 1958).

The Nord Express was operated by France's International Sleeping-Car Company (Compagnie Internationale des Wagons-Lits), which had made a name for itself linking together vast swaths of Europe through a series of opulent train services. These included the Sud Express, from Paris to Lisbon, and, most famous of all, the Orient Express, which ran between Paris and Constantinople. Such trains provided well-to-do Europeans with the opportunity to personally experience the far-flung corners of the continent from the comfort of a spacious, private compartment.

CHAPTER FOUR

Technically, the first American Protestant missionary in Persia was James Lyman Merrick. The independent American Board of Commissioners for Foreign Missions (ABCFM), established in 1810 as the first Protestant missions society in the United States, commissioned Merrick at about the same time as it did Justin and Charlotte, but with the express task of evangelizing to Muslims. For a short time, ABCFM's mission efforts in Persia were bifurcated between the more formalized program of the Perkinses' outreach to Nestorian Christians and another strand addressing Muslims that Merrick pursued almost independently. Yet Merrick was soon recalled by the church because of his combative style and his refusal to abide by the ABCFM's orders, and the program aim toward Muslims was temporarily abandoned. See Thomas S. Kidd, *American Christians and Islam: Evan-*

gelical Culture and Muslims from the Colonial Period to the Age of Terrorism (Princeton, NJ: Princeton University Press, 2013).

For more on the early years of Justin Perkins, see the biography written by his only surviving son, Henry Martyn Perkins, *Life of Rev. Justin Perkins, D.D. Pioneer Missionary to Persia* (New York: Fleming H. Revell, 1887), as well as his own memoir, *A Residence of Eight Years in Persia, Among the Nestorian Christians; With Notices of the Muhammedans* (Andover, MA: Allen, Morrill & Wardwell, 1843).

For more on the Second Great Awakening, see Richard D. Birdsall, "The Second Great Awakening and the New England Social Order," *Church History* 39, no. 3 (1970): 345–64; and Joseph Conforti, "The Invention of the Great Awakening, 1795–1842," *Early American Literature* 26, no. 2 (1991): 99–118. Nathan Hatch has argued that the Second Great Awakening is best understood as a democratizing process within evangelical Protestantism that was set in motion by the American Revolution. Nathan O. Hatch, *The Democratization of American Christianity* (New Haven, CT: Yale University Press, 1989).

Regarding the prominence of women in the Second Great Awakening, Nancy F. Cott notes that the term "young women" usually meant unmarried women, since the average age at marriage was about twenty-two years. Cott writes: "In revivals in Plymouth, Torrington, Bristol, and Norfolk, Connecticut, and in Lenox, Massachusetts, in 1798–1799, almost two-thirds of the converts were female. In Canton, Connecticut in 1805–1806, and in Farmington, Connecticut in 1826, the reporting ministers said the conversions occurred 'chiefly' among females . . . three-fifths of the converts in the New England revivals between 1798 and 1826 were female. Young female converts ranged from mill workers to students at selective female academies." Nancy F. Cott, "Young Women in the Second Great Awakening in New England," *Feminist Studies* 3, no. 1/2 (1975): 15–29. See also Anne M. Boylan, "Evangelical Womanhood in the Nineteenth Century: The Role of Women in Sunday Schools," *Feminist Studies* 4, no. 3 (1978): 62–80.

Notably, the first person to receive a copy of Henry Martyn's New Testament in Persian was Fath 'Ali Shah, ruler of Iran from 1797 to 1834. See Joseph L. Grabill, *Protestant Diplomacy and the Near East: Missionary Influence on American Policy, 1810–1927* (Minneapolis: University of Minnesota Press, 1971).

According to William Hutchison, whose parents were missionaries in Persia, the missionary movement there originated "both in Christian zeal for evangelization and a belief in American exceptionalism." American missionaries were primarily interested in saving souls but also believed that Persians could benefit economically and spiritually from American influence. William R. Hutchison, *Errand to the World: American Protestant Thought and Foreign Missions* (Chicago: University of Chicago Press, 1987).

The term *Nestorian* is used here in a historical sense, though the Nestorian community prefers the term *Church of the East*. For more on the Nestorians and other Middle Eastern Christian sects, see Wilhelm Baum and Dietmar W. Winkler, *The Church of the East: A Concise History*, vol. 1 (London: Routledge, 2003). I borrow the analogy of oil and water to describe Nestorian doctrine from Diarmaid MacCulloch, *Christianity: The First Three Thousand Years* (New York: Viking, 2009), 223. Justin and Charlotte's final instructions are pulled from Perkins, *Residence of Eight Years in Persia*, 29. According to their instructions, their first task was to understand who the Nestorians actually were and what they believed. With the exception of the scant information collected by Dwight and Smith, the ABCFM knew absolutely nothing about the Nestorians. They seemed to be wholly unfamiliar with the history and beliefs of the community they were sending these two young missionaries to live among. There were some among them who seemed to think that the Nestorians were descendants of one of the lost tribes of Israel. What they knew for sure was that they weren't evangelicals, and that seemed to be all that mattered. Not only did Justin and Charlotte learn all they could about the Nestorians, they became absolutely enamored with Nestorian culture, so much so that Justin adopted their native dress and began walking around Urmia wearing a two-foot-tall sheepskin hat. He drew lovingly detailed sketches of their men, women, and children that are still celebrated today. He taught himself their native language, Syriac, becoming the first person to create a written script for it. He then taught that script to multiple generations of Nestorian children. Together with Charlotte, he opened the first printing house in Urmia and used it to publish his own Syriac translations of the Old and New Testaments, an absolutely Herculean feat that has been compared to the printing of the Gutenberg Bible.

Dwight and Smith quoted in John Elder, *A Brief History of the Iran Mission of the Presbyterian Church in the USA*. This is an unpublished manuscript written some time in the 1950s and housed in the Presbyterian Historical Society (Record Group 189, The Elder Family Papers, Box 1, File 2).

Judith's story is told in Joseph G. Cochran, ed., *The Persian Flower: A Memoir of Judith Grant Perkins* (Boston: American Tract Society, 1853). An avid reader and accomplished musician, Judith Perkins was mature for her age, fiercely independent, and delightfully skeptical. "Oh that I were a Christian!" she wrote in a letter. "How happy I should be! Would it not be pleasing to God? Why am I not one?" More on Judith can be found in Gordon Taylor, "Deep Waters: Life and Death in the Perkins Family, 1834–1852," *Journal of Assyrian Academic Studies* 23 (2009): 64–73.

Dietrich Bonhoeffer quoted in *Dietrich Bonhoeffer: Witness to Jesus Christ*, edited by John de Gruchy (Minneapolis: Fortress Press, 1991), 292.

PART 2

Hafez translated by Daniel Ladinsky, *The Gift by Hafez* (New York: Penguin, 1999).

CHAPTER FIVE

The constitutionalists called Shapshal, "Shapshal *Khun*" (*khun* is the Persian word for "blood"), a sobriquet the Russian would earn for the zeal with which he persecuted the revolutionaries during the shah's coup.

Parliament's letter to the Tabriz Anjoman telling them to get back to their jobs is pulled from Janet Afary, *The Iranian Constitutional Revolution, 1906–1911: Grassroots Democracy, Social Democracy, and the Origins of Feminism* (New York: Columbia University Press, 1996), 93. The story of the prostitute march is also from Afary's absolutely indispensable book.

Iranian Azerbaijan, or East Azerbaijan, is a province of Iran that borders Armenia in the north. It is nationally (though not ethnically) distinct from the Republic of Azerbaijan, which declared its independence from the Soviet Union in 1991.

Najaf's grand ayatollah is quoted in Abdul-Hadi Hairi, "Why Did the 'Ulamā Participate in the Persian Constitutional Revolution of 1905–1909," *Die Welt des Islams* 17, no. 1/4 (1976–1977): 127–54; 146. In fact, as early as 1902 the four grand ayatollahs of Najaf had written letters to the Persian court demanding the establishment of a chamber of representatives. Hairi writes that "as far as personal motives are concerned one may argue that the three top mujtahids of Najaf, that is, Tihrani, Khurasani, and Mazandarani, together with their assistants and co-thinkers, such as Na'ini and Mahallati, were very concerned with the welfare of the people and their being treated with justice. During the period of Qajar rule, justice did not exist, and the people's lives were at the governors' mercy; therefore, these 'ulamai felt religiously responsible to support the movement which aimed at the removal of such a rule. For this reason, supporting the movement was considered equivalent to fighting a Holy War under the command of the Hidden Imam and any opposition to it was as waging a war against him." See also Nikki R. Keddie, "Iranian Politics 1900–1905: Background to Revolution," *Eastern Studies* 5, no. 1 (1969): 3–31. Keddie notes that the pro-constitutional preachers not only emphasized the compatibility of Islam and the constitution but also introduced modern ideas and explained the viewpoints of the constitutionalists in an understandable way. They constantly spoke of the benefits of constitutionalism to the people and reminded them of the "tragedies and ugliness of the tyrannical era."

Nuri's famous line—"Freedom is heretical to Islam"—is from Afary, *Iranian Constitutional Revolution*, 111.

Ahmed Kasravi's three-volume account of the Constitutional Revolution is my primary source for what was happening in Tabriz during the war and will be frequently cited in this book as it not only records his eyewitness account but also compiles the accounts of other participants of the revolution in Tabriz. Ahmed Kasravi, *History of the Iranian Constitutional Revolution*, 3 vols. (Costa Mesa, CA: Mazda, 2006 and 2015).

The word *farr* is also attested to as *farnah* or *farrah* in Middle and Old Persian. See http://www.iranicaonline.org/articles/farrah.

Abbas Amanat quoted in his wonderful biography of Nasir ad-Din Shah, *Pivot of the Universe: Nasir Al-Din Shah Qajar and the Iranian Monarchy, 1831–1896* (Berkeley: University of California Press, 1997), 7. Amanat's *Iran: A Modern History* (New Haven, CT: Yale University Press, 2017) has also been a valuable and much referenced resource throughout this book.

Regarding the legacy of the tobacco protests, the historian Hamid Algar writes: "The immediate consequence within Iran of the successful conclusion [of the tobacco protest] was a noticeable increase in clerical power." The ulama won a decisive victory over the state and the dynasty, a victory that awakened them to the immense political power they could muster by espousing the anti-imperialistic, democratic demands of the people; this power was to be tested and used again during the Constitutional Revolution with even greater success and would peak with the Iranian Revolution of 1979. Hamid Algar, *Religion and State in Iran 1785–1906: The Role of the Ulama in the Qajar Period* (Berkeley: University of California Press, 1980), 218.

The tsar's threat is from Leon Novar, "The Great Powers and Iran, 1914–1921" (PhD diss., University of Chicago, 1958).

CHAPTER SIX

Marco Polo quoted in *The Travels of Marco Polo: The Venetian* (New York: G. Bell & Sons, 1854), 44. See also Maryam Mir-Ahmadi, "Marco Polo in Iran," *Oriente Moderno* 88, no. 2 (2008): 1–13. The connection of Tabriz to Europe is ancient. In Edward Gibbon's *The Decline and Fall of the Roman Empire*, we read the following itinerary to *Taurus*, ancient name of Tabriz: "From Constantinople to Trebizond, with a fair wind, four or five days; from thence to Erzerom, five; to Erivan, twelve; to Taurus, ten; in all, thirty-two. Such is the itinerary of Tavernier who was perfectly conversant with the roads of Asia."

Eric Hobsbawm, in his seminal work, *Bandits*, focuses on social banditry in rural societies, but some of his findings are applicable to the Persian looti in its urban context. Bandits, Hobsbawm says, are potential rebels, because they "resist obedience, are outside the range of power, are potential exercisers of power themselves." Sometimes, bandits join revolutionary movements when they consider the motives to be just. Then, they demonstrate their trustworthiness by their personal behavior, showing self-sacrifice and devotion to their cause. See Eric Hobsbawm, *Bandits* (London: Weidenfeld & Nicolson, 1969). See also Asghar Fathi, "The Role of the 'Rebels' in the Constitutional Movement in Iran," *International Journal of Middle East Studies* 10, no. 1 (1979): 55–66.

Annie Rhea Wilson's unpublished memoir is titled "My Memories" and was written as a gift to her family. Thankfully, it has been preserved by her descendants as it provides a wonderful account, not only of her many years in Persia, but also of the events of the Constitutional Revolution and of the tragic death of Howard Baskerville. Samuel Wilson's many books include *Persia: Western Missions, Modern Movements Among Muslims*, and *Baha'ism and Its Claims*. But the most helpful to our investigation is his classic text, *Persian Life and Customs: with scenes and incidents of residence and travel in the land of the Lion and the Sun* (Edinburgh & London: Oliphant, Anderson & Ferrier, 1896). The book provides vivid descriptions of western Persia, and in particular Tabriz, at the turn of the twentieth century. I pull most of my descriptions of Tabriz during Baskerville's time from it.

The number of students at the American Memorial School in Tabriz is taken from an interview with Annie and Agnes Wilson in the *Ellsworth American*, February 14, 1912.

Michael P. Zirinsky writes: "Mathematics and science held a special place of central importance in the Presbyterian curriculum. The mission believed arithmetic, algebra, and geometry had great practical value, that they helped in the study of the physical sciences, and that they had 'a high degree of disciplinary value, [helping] to develop accuracy and logical reasoning, two things sadly needed in this country.'" Michael P. Zirinsky, "A Panacea for the Ills of the Country: American Presbyterian Education in Inter-War Iran," *Iranian Studies* 26, no. 1/2 (1993): 119–37.

To quote a former Tabriz mission school student whose parents and grandparents had also been mission educated: "Our schools were multilingual. English was started at the third grade. From the 7th grade all subjects were taught in English except languages which were French or Russian (optional), Armenian for Christian students only and Persian. School started at 8:00 and ended at 4:00. There were no optional courses except languages, consequently students who lasted and graduated were very well educated. Courses taught were as follows: algebra, Bible, agriculture, geometry, ethics, French, solid geometry, sociology, Persian, cot geometry [short for cotangent geometry], astronomy, Armenian, accounting, botany, physics. . . . A diploma from Tabriz Memorial School was given the same value as two years of college by the New York Board of Regents. My brother, after finishing high school and with only five months of college in Iran came to the U. S. in 1943 and was accepted into the third year of Worcester Polytechnic Institute and later on completed a masters degree from M. I. T. and Carnegie Institute. So you see the schools were top notch and I believe superior to present day American high schools." Quoted in Linda Colleen Karimi, "Implications of American Missionary Presence in 19th and 20th Century Iran" (PhD diss., Portland State University, 1975), 72.

Karimi notes: "Because no financial distinctions were made at the mission schools, they served as equalizers in society. There were students of all financial and social levels attending. Each was accepted as an individual on his own merits. Students of the nobility and landholding class, as well as sons of slaves and peasants, were represented. They all slept in the same rooms, ate at the same table and did chores assigned to all. Former students and teachers attest to this and indicate that the dignity of labor and worth of the individual were an important part of the missionary legacy."

Sadeq Rezazadeh Shafaq's *Howard Baskerville: The Story of an American Who Died in the Cause of Iranian Freedom and Independence* (Cambridge, MA: Ty Aur Press, 2008) is the closest thing ever written to a biography in English of Howard Baskerville, though it is simply the published version of a speech Shafaq gave in Baskerville's honor for the fiftieth anniversary of his death in 1959.

About Hassan Sharifzadeh, the newspaper of the Tabriz Anjoman records that, "Nationalist fervor and zeal, humanist mentality, high-mindedness, and unsullied morals were among his characteristics and all his life, he dedicated himself to reform the national imperfections. Poverty couldn't prevent his innate passion and inherent devotion from progress, and despite his father's disapproval, who was one of the ulamas of Tabriz, he was steadfast in his purpose" (*Anjoman-e Tabriz*, Year 3, No. 3). Kasravi maintains that Sharifzadeh was among those activists "who could understand the country's situation as well as the situation of European countries and wish for the dismantling tyranny"; see Ahmed Kasravi, *History of the Iranian Constitutional Revolution*, vol. 3, 149. Karim Taherzadeh-Behzad calls Sharifzadeh a "genius" and a "noble politician" who showed "superiority over Mujahedin [the revolutionaries]"; see Karim Taherzadeh-Behzad, *Qiyam-e Azerbaijan* [Azerbaijan uprising during the Iranian Constitutional Revolution] (Tehran: Eghbal, 1956), 150–51. Mehdi Mojtahedi notes that Sharifzadeh knew some French but went to the American Memorial School to learn English fluently. Soon he became "Fazil" and erudite. "Ultimately," Mojtahedi writes, "he became a teacher at that school and tried his best to amplify good virtues and conscience in his students. He was a compassionate teacher. All his students worshipped him. In Taqizadeh's words, his students were in fact his disciples and had strong faith in him. He was a leader to the young intelligentsia, I must say"; see Mehdi Mojtahedi, *Rejal-e Asr-e Mashrutiat* [Eminent men of Azerbaijan during the constitutional period] (Tehran: Zarrin, 1997), 208.

On the goal of missionary education, see Zirinsky, "A Panacea," 122–27. The statement regarding all actions of the American Memorial School being predicated on furthering "the diffusion of Christian ideas and influences, the conversion of pupils, and the development of the Christian community" is pulled directly from "Statement of Educational Policy of East Persia Mission," drafted in the 1918 Annual Meeting of the Presbyterian Board of Foreign Missions and submitted by C. H. Allen, chairman of the Educational Committee (Presbyterian Historical Society, Record Group 91, Box 14, File 8).

On Tabriz as the ideal place for missionary endeavors, see Christoph Werner, *An Iranian Town in Transition: A Social and Economic History of the Elites of Tabriz, 1747–1848* (Wiesbaden: Otto Harrassowitz Verlag, 2000), 92. Werner clarifies that there was only a "limited presence of foreigners in Tabriz," and that in the 1830s and 1840s their number would not have exceeded "fifty individuals." However, he suggests, "their presence in Tabriz was a constant reminder that the town was now in close contact with the larger outside world, and became a symbol for the growing influence of European powers and the continuous influx of Western culture in Iran." Tabriz's importance as a city stemmed from its population, commercial importance, links to the ruling Qajar Dynasty, and geographic proximity to Turkey and Europe. See also Joel Feurt Hanisek, "From the Domain of Certitude to the Relational Realm: U.S. Missions in Iran and the Politics of Piecemeal Social Change" (PhD diss., Trinity College, Dublin, 2019).

For more on the Bab, see Peter Smith, *The Baha'i Faith: A Short History* (Oxford: One World, 1996). It should be mentioned that Tabriz was also the birthplace of perhaps the greatest Sufi mystic who ever lived, Shams-e Tabriz, beloved friend and mentor to the poet Jalal ad-Din Rumi.

Instructions to missionaries to "put aside their concern for the civil and temporal conditions" of the communities in which they served come from Andrew Wilcox, *Orientalism and Imperialism: From Nineteenth-Century Missionary Imaginings to the Contemporary Middle East* (London: Bloomsbury Academic, 2018), 151–53. This may explain why there is no record of any one else from any other mission—whether in Tabriz or anywhere else in Persia—having taken an active role in the Constitutional Revolution, save for Howard Baskerville.

Baskerville's missionary efforts are outlined in a letter written by Annie Wilson to Baskerville's mother after his death. Baskerville's lack of success as a missionary is sometimes cited by modern commentators as proof that he wasn't really a missionary after all, that he had come to Persia solely as a teacher (see Chapter Seventeen). That argument is belied by the fact that the American Memorial School was built and run exclusively as a missionary school: its primary purpose wasn't to teach math and geography; it was to convert students to Christianity. Every single American who taught at the school was a Christian. Every single American teacher was employed by the Presbyterian Board of Foreign Missions. And every single American, Baskerville included, was there, first and foremost, to save souls.

CHAPTER SEVEN

Tabriz's first US consul general, William Doty, was born in Brooklyn in 1870. He received degrees at both Princeton University and Princeton Theological Seminary. He served as a US Senate page for two years before joining the Foreign Service in 1900. His first post was as consul general in Tahiti in 1902. He served there until 1906 when he was transferred to Tabriz.

John B. Jackson, the American legate, was appointed minister to Persia on July 1, 1907, and served until July 3, 1909. State Department memos regarding the viably of the Constitutional Revolution are pulled from Kaymar Ghaneabassiri, "US Foreign Policy and Persia, 1856–1921," *Iranian Studies* 35, no. 1–3 (2002): 145–75.

Henry Harris Jessup is quoted from his book *The Mohammedan Missionary Problem* (Philadelphia: Presbyterian Board of Publications, 1879). For more on Henry Jessup, see Steven Fink, "Fear Under Construction: Islamophobia Within American Christian Zionism," *Islamophobia Studies Journal* 2, no. 1 (2014): 26–43.

Nazemol Eslam Kermani provides a concise history of the secret societies in his *Tarikh-e Bidari-yi Iraniyan* [History of Iranian awakening], edited by Ali Akbar Saeedi Sirjani (Tehran: Bonyad-e Farhang, 1968), 161. Kermani was himself a founding member of a secret society.

The most prominent secret society founder was Karbalai Ali Monsieur (1879–1910). Sometimes called the "pulse of the revolutionary movement in Tabriz," he was a well-regarded member of the Social-Democratic Party, an intellectual, and a well-traveled merchant who, among other things, cofounded and headed Tabriz's Secret Center during the first period of the Constitutional Revolution. During the war over Tabriz, Ali lost all three of his sons, and his house was repeatedly looted. After the occupation of Tabriz by the Russian army, Ali Monsieur ended up as a penniless fugitive, but his legacy as one of the intellectual leaders of the revolution survived.

The telegram in which the Tabriz Anjoman calls the shah an oath-breaker is pulled from Ahmed Kasravi, *History of the Iranian Constitutional Revolution*, vol. 3, 612; the collective statement is pulled from Janet Afary, *Iranian Constitutional Revolution, 1906–1911: Grassroots Democracy, Social Democracy, and the Origins of Feminism* (New York: Columbia University Press, 1996), 136. You can read the entire Persian Constitution including all articles of the Supplementary Fundamental Laws in Edward G. Browne, *The Persian Revolution of 1905–1909* (Cambridge, UK: Cambridge University Press, 1910).

CHAPTER EIGHT

What we know about Sattar Khan's early years are detailed by Anja Pistor-Hatam, "The Iranian Constitutional Revolution as *lieu(x) de mémoire*: Sattar Khan," in *Iran's Consti-*

tutional Revolution: Popular Politics, Cultural Transformations and Transnational Connections, edited by H. E. Chehabi and Vanessa Martin (London: Bloomsbury, 2010), 33–44.

Note that almost all of Sattar Khan's quotes in this book are pulled from Mohammad Hassan Pedram, *A Collection of Aphorisms and Sayings of Sattar Khan* (Tabriz: Akhtar, 2010), with my best attempt to link his words to the context in which he spoke them.

Archeologists in Qaradagh have found rock carvings that go back thousands of years, including pictographs and mythographs representing real or imaginary objects, animals, and humans with suns for heads. See Jalal Rafifar, "Some Indications of Shamanism in Arasbaran Rock Carvings," *Documenta Praehistorica* 34 (2007): 203–13. More general information on Iranian petroglyphs can be found in Ebrahim Karimi, "The Petroglyphs of Domab in the Central Plateau of Iran," *Near Eastern Archaeology* 81, no. 2 (2018): 128–40.

The Shahsevan trace their lineage to the Safavid Shah Abbas I (1571–1629). As Richard Tapper notes: "Evidence for the existence of a tribal group bearing this name is lacking until sometime after Abbas's reign, and it is unlikely that a tribal confederation under the name Shahsevan was formed before the eighteenth century." See Richard Tapper, "Raiding, Reaction, and Rivalry: The Shahsevan Tribes in the Constitutional Period," *Bulletin of the School of Oriental and African Studies* 49, no. 3 (1986): 508–31; 509. As the story goes, early in his reign, Shah Abbas was faced with a revolt from within his kingdom. In desperation, he sent out a call to all loyal supporters to come to his aid and help him defeat his enemies. Those tribes who answered the call were ultimately given the name "Shahsevan," meaning "those who love the shah." The epithet stuck. Over the centuries the Shahsevan maintained their allegiance to the shahs, regardless of who actually sat on the throne. See also Abbas Amanat, *Iran: A Modern History* (New Haven, CT: Yale University Press, 2017), 343.

Of note regarding Sattar Khan's spiritual transformation in Tabriz is that it occurred under the guidance of one of the city's most revered religious figures: a fiery, activist cleric named Mirza Ali Aqa Tabrizi, known to everyone in Persia as *Seqat ol-Islam*. A wildly popular scholar with a passion for democratic values, Seqat ol-Islam wrote dozens of books about everything from Muslim-Christian relations and the pernicious role of European markets on the Persian economy to the Spanish Inquisition and the history of the Iberian Peninsula. As the leading constitutionalist cleric in Tabriz, he received the highest number of parliamentary votes among the ten delegates from Azerbaijan. But rather than go to Tehran and serve in parliament, he decided to stay in Tabriz and continue his work and ministry. That was probably a smart move on his part. For while he was an enormously influential figure in Tabriz, he was deeply controversial most everywhere else. That's because Seqat ol-Islam was a *Shaykhi*, a member of a mystical sect of Shi'ah Islam that was viewed with skepticism if not downright hostility by most Persians.

The Shaykhis believed that salvation was achieved not through the performance of religious obligations (prayer, fasting, and so forth) but rather through an inward, intuitive experience of the sacred. Although founded in the mid-eighteenth century, it remained a popular form of Islamic spirituality in Persia, particularly among younger clerics and seminarians who longed for something more than just academic study and empty theologizing. The movement split in 1844, when one member of the Shaykhi sect—a merchant from Shiraz with no clerical credentials named Sayyed Ali Muhammad—had an inward spiritual experience that led him to believe he was "the Bab." That's how Babism was born, and from it, Baha'ism. Shaykhism survived the split, however, transforming into a small, independent, and popular spiritual movement that was, like so many other alternative spiritualities in Persia, centered in Tabriz.

There are numerous sources for the story of the girl dressed as a man in the field hospital. I read it in Houshang Ebrami, *Sattar Khan, Sardar-e Melli* [Sattar Khan, national commander] (Tehran: Tous Publishing, 1974).

CHAPTER NINE

Smirnov's memoir is titled *Zapiski vospitatelya persidskogo shaha, 1907–1914 gody* [Memoirs of the tutor of the Persian Shah, years 1907–1914] (Tel Aviv: Ivrus, 2002). Although there is no English version of the book, pertinent sections were translated for me by Ilya Shevchenko. See also Evan Siegel, "A Review of the Memoirs of Konstantin Nikolaevich Smirnov, Crown Prince Ahmad's Tutor," n.d., http://iran.qlineorientalist.com/Articles/ Smirnov/Smirnov.html.

A prominent scholar of the Orient and an expert on Persia, Smirnov published a number of works on Persian culture and history. But he was also a formidable military character. Four years before being sent to Persia, he had been appointed commander of Russia's most strategic port in Manchuria—Port Arthur—during what would become the longest and most deadly land battle of the Russo-Japanese War. Japan had laid siege to the port for six months. When Smirnov arrived to assume command, he found his orders repeatedly undermined by the port's previous commander, Anatoly Stessel, and Stessel's close comrade, Gen. Alexander Fok. On January 1, 1905, Stessel and Fok suddenly, and without consulting Smirnov, surrendered the port to the Japanese army. Smirnov was incensed. After the war, he filed formal charges against both men, accusing them of cowardice and dereliction of duty. He even testified at their court-martial. Stessel and Fok were ultimately found guilty and sentenced to death, though the sentence was later commuted to ten years in a military brig. Far from being feted as a hero, Smirnov was excoriated by his fellow commanders in the Russian military for testifying against one of their own. Just before Fok began serving his time, he challenged Smirnov to a duel for calling him a coward. Smirnov accepted and was shot in the abdomen, just above his right hip. He took the bullet wound with him to Persia.

Details on Mohammed Ali Shah's assassination attempt and its aftermath are pulled directly from Mehdi Malekzadeh, *Zendegani-e Malek Al-Mutekallemin* [History of the Constitutional Revolution], vol. 3 (Tehran: Elmi and Partners Publishing House, 1946), 620–23; and from "Vaghe-ye Nagovar" [The unfortunate accident], *Soore Esrafil* newspaper, March 13, 1908. The shah's response to the delegates is pulled from Ahmed Kasravi, *History of the Iranian Constitutional Revolution*, vol. 3, 648.

While the role of Shapshal Khan in the attempt on the shah's life has never been fully reported, the mastermind of the act was Haydar Khan, known as *Haydar Amuoghli*, or

"Haydar the Bomb Maker" (Haydar would, years later, manage to successfully assassinate the Ayatollah Behbehani). The bomb throwers were Azerbaijani émigrés from Baku. See Abbas Amanat, *Iran: A Modern History* (New Haven, CT: Yale University Press, 2017), 348. However, the evidence clearly suggests that Shapshal Khan, as a Russian agent, had advance knowledge of the attempt on the shah's life. He even may have helped plan it.

Born in 1873 in Crimea as Serayah b. Mordekhay Sapsal, Shapshal Khan was a member of the Karaism, a small but ancient Jewish sect that rejects all sources of Jewish law save for the Torah. You can (and should) learn more about the incredible life of Shapshal Khan by reading Dan D. Y. Shapira, "A Jewish Pan-Turkist: Seraya Szapszał (Şapşaloğlu) and his work '*Qirim Qaray Türkleri* (1928) (Judaeo-Türkica XIII)," *Acta Orientalia Academiae Scientiarum Hungaricae* 58, no. 4 (2005): 349–80. The source for Shapshal's income as the shah's tutor comes directly from Edward G. Browne, *The Persian Revolution of 1905–1909* (Cambridge, UK: Cambridge University Press, 1910), 198.

There is eyewitness testimony of the takeover of Tehran by Liakhov recorded in Ahmad Tafreshi Hosseini, *The Journal of the Constitutional News and the Revolution of Iran*, edited by Iraj Afshar (Tehran: Amir Kabir, 1973), 120. "On Friday evening of 26 June [1908] the government announced a warning everywhere that nobody is allowed to gather in Bazaars, mosques and houses and if they do so, they will be in trouble and taken to prison. Another thing was that people shouldn't carry their guns while out and about, and if ordinary people come to contact with the military forces, the latter have the right to attack and strike. The Palkonik [Liakhov] is now responsible for order in the city. God help us ordinary people, if a mere soldier tells us to get naked or if they rush to your house at night you have to surrender immediately and let go of whatever you have and if a thief comes at night, one doesn't dare to defend with one's heart in one's mouth as the thief might be from the forces of order. To cut a long story short, we are in deep trouble. God damn those who did this to us. Made us look malicious people in the eyes of Shah and stripped us of our respect in his eyes and robbed us of safety and security. One wishes that we should have died ten years ago in 'good times' to not see such days."

CHAPTER TEN

The *tar* and the *tanbur* are traditional stringed instruments. The *daf* is a Persian frame drum held vertically in one hand and struck with the other.

While we have no idea who the source for the rumor about Howard and Agnes was, the State Department report was compiled by Augustin W. Ferrin, the American consul in Tabriz, on September 19, 1927, and titled "Death of American Citizen in Constitutional Disturbances of 1909."

The name of the village Maragheh is demonstrative of the region's historic past as the birthplace of Zoroastrianism, the ancient Iranian religion founded by the prophet Zarathustra (known to the Greeks as Zoroaster). More than three thousand years ago, Zarathustra walked this very ground, preaching his radical vision of a sole, singular God called Ahura Mazda, or "the Wise Lord." Zoroastrians view the natural elements, fire especially, as divine agents of ritual purity. The ruins of dozens of ancient fire temples can still be seen across the region; in Maragheh, there is a subterranean chamber with a fire temple inside where residents say Zarathustra himself once worshipped (the most famous fire temple in Iran lies in the city of Yazd, where the sacred ritual fire has been kept burning since AD 470). It is unclear exactly when Zarathustra preached his faith. Dates range from the purely mythical (8000 BC) to the eve of the Iranian kingdom (seventh century BC). I believe the most logical date for the birth of Zoroastrianism is ca. 1100–1000 BC, and I explain why in my article, "Thus Sprang Zarathustra: A Brief Historiography on the Date of the Prophet of Zoroastrianism," *Jusur* 14 (1998–1999): 21–34. For Maragheh fire temples, see Abraham V. W. Jackson, *Persia Past and Present* (New York: Macmillan, 1906), 61. In Europe and America, modesty required women to ride sidesaddle, but that was a completely unfamiliar position in Persia. The first time Annie Wilson went riding in Persia, she passed a group of boys who took one look at the sunburnt woman seated sideways on her horse and screamed, "Here's a woman with only one leg!"

Regarding the role and status of women in the Constitutional Revolution, it should be noted that they had been at the forefront of the revolution from the start—literally. In the early days of the protests, they had formed human barriers at the head of marches, knowing the shah's soldiers would hesitate before firing upon mothers and daughters. They organized boycotts against European-made textiles and fabrics and established women's anjomans across the country. By 1910, they had established some fifty girls' schools in Tehran alone.

"The growing telegraphic communications throughout Iran's major cities made it possible for protesters in the capital to transmit the constitutional message of the movement and to coordinate their efforts with cohorts in Tabriz, the true center of radical activism, and elsewhere." Abbas Amanat, *Iran: A Modern History* (New Haven, CT: Yale University Press, 2017), 334.

The London *Times* article about the shah surreptitiously purchasing and distributing rifles is headlined "The Persian Crisis: A Dark Outlook," and dated June 19, 1908.

The story of Sharifzadeh at the Telegraph House is from Karim Taherzadeh-Behzad, *Qiyam-e Azerbaijan* [Azerbaijan uprising during the Iranian Constitutional Revolution] (Tehran: Eghbal, 1956), 136–40. The glowing profile of Sattar Khan is from *The Times* (London, UK), September 23, 1908.

CHAPTER ELEVEN

For more on the great Bolshevik robbery, see Nadezhda K. Krupskaya, *Reminiscences of Lenin* (Honolulu: University Press of the Pacific, 2004), and Simon Sebag Montefiore's prologue in *Young Stalin* (New York: Random House, 2007).

Joseph M. Hone and Page L. Dickinson provide a detailed account of Liakhov's time in charge of the Cossack Brigade in *Persia in Revolution, with Notes of Travel in the Caucasus* (London: T. F. Unwin, 1910). Liakhov's comment about the Cossack Brigade being "the only force in Persia which can be called a military force," is from the *Washington Post* article titled "Was Persia's Savior: Col. Liakhoff Tells of His Brigade's Deeds," September 12, 1909.

The events surrounding the bombardment of parliament are pulled almost entirely from Ahmed Kasravi, *History of the Iranian Constitutional Revolution,* vol. 3, 686–89. The delegate's foolish boast about clearing the gunmen from parliament is pulled from Kasravi, *History,* vol. 3, 691. Kasravi also notes that the day before the coup, the shah sent an ominous message to all the provincial governors: "This Majlis [Parliament] stands in violation of the Constitution. Whoever disobeys our orders from now on commits a transgression and is to be severely punished." Kasravi, *History,* vol. 3, 727.

Out of nearly one hundred twenty different provincial anjomans whose members had been recruited to help protect parliament, only two anjomans defied Ayatollah Behbehani's request to disperse from parliament grounds and chose to remain: an independent anjoman representing a liberal faction in Tehran; and, of course, the anjoman from Tabriz. Everyone else promptly departed the scene, allowing Liakhov's men to take the perimeter with ease. See Mehdi Malekzadeh, *Zendegani-e Malek Al-Mutekallemin* [History of the Constitutional Revolution], vol. 3 (Tehran: Elmi and Partners Publishing House, 1946), 260–61.

"I think . . . that the Russian officers were purposely never fired on," wrote the British charge d'affairs in Tehran to Sir Edward Grey. "Persians all say that special injunctions were issued to that effect and M. de Hartwing volunteered to me the statement that such was the impression of one Russian officer. Were it otherwise it seems incredible, considering the short range and excellent cover which the popular party enjoyed, that they should have escaped. . . . Colonel Liakhoff in particular could have been killed at almost any moment . . . they owed their lives to the general conviction that their death would bring about Russian intervention." Parliamentary Papers, 1909, "Correspondence, Affairs of Persia," p. 155.

The text of Liakhov's proclamation can be found in Edward G. Browne, *Letters from Tabriz: The Russian Suppression of the Iranian Constitutional Movement* (Washington, DC: Mage Publication, 2008), 211.

It bears repeating that, in the view of John B. Jackson, the destruction of parliament and the slaughter of the elected delegates inside was the fault of both sides. "That His Majesty's action is not in accord with the Constitution can of course not be denied," Jackson wrote in a letter to the State Department, "but the action of the political societies [anjomans] has been no more constitutional."

Edward Grey is quoted in *Cambridge History of British Foreign Policy, 1783-1919,* vol. III (Cambridge, UK: Cambridge University Press, 2011), 415. The shah's comment on reconquering the country by the sword is from Kasravi, *History,* vol. 3, 711. The story of Shapshal Khan strangling the prisoners is from Elena Andreeva, *Russian Travelers to Iran in the Nineteenth and Early Twentieth Centuries and Their Travelogues* (New York: New York University Press, 2001), 321–22.

There is a fascinating eyewitness account of the aftermath of parliament's destruction by a Russian travelogue writer named N. P. Mamontov, who just happened to be in Tehran at the time. Mamontov states in his travelogue that he has no personal interest in the revolution and so can be trusted to provide an objective account of events. "I am not a diplomat, not an officer of the Cossack Brigade of His Majesty the Shah—I am someone who is absolutely uninterested in Persian affairs; an ordinary traveler, one who has personally seen most of the events I describe," he writes. Nevertheless, Mamontov passionately defends Liakhov from the accusation of "illegal actions" and depicts him as a hero who came to the rescue of the lawful ruler of Iran, who was very grateful to him for "saving [his] shaken throne." At the end of his account, Mamontov writes: "While the Russian officers are in the Brigade, they cannot let die the unit they have created, and for which they are responsible, and the Shah who has blindly trusted them. The [Russian] press is fiercely attacking Colonel Liakhov, accusing him of various transgressions of the law. I don't know if my poor notes have helped somewhat to restore the truth, but I am absolutely convinced that any honest military officer would do the same in [Col. Liakhov's] place. . . . Anyway, if we consider involvement of the Russian officers in the internal disturbances in Persia, we have to immediately raise the question of recalling the whole Russian Military Mission from Tehran." N. P. Mamontov, *Ocherki sovremennoi Persii* (St. Petersburg: Tipografiia Kirshbauma, 1909), 8.

CHAPTER TWELVE

Note that Sattar Khan's ward, Amirkhiz, is the only major nationalist ward that lies on the northern banks of the Mehraneh River. The shah's secret message to the Rahim Khan is quoted in Ahmed Kasravi, *History of the Iranian Constitutional Revolution*, vol. 3, 779–80.

Hooman Estelami has written an excellent primer on the Urmia mission titled *The Americans of Urumia* (New York: Bahar Books, 2021). William Ambrose Shedd, the legendary head of that mission, was born on January 24, 1865, to missionary parents in Seir, the same mountain village that Annie Wilson was born in. He died of cholera during the First World War and was buried in Tabriz. His wife, Mary Lewis Shedd, wrote a personal biography of him titled *The Measure of a Man: The Life of William Ambrose Shedd, Missionary to Persia* (New York: George H. Doran, 1922). The book's introduction was written by none other than Robert E. Speer.

In a letter to his friend, Seyed Hossein Khan Edalat (journalist and women's rights activist), Hassan Sharifzadeh elaborates on his depression during this time. "Up until noon, I preoccupied myself with reading some books and newspapers. Right after noon, a kind of sadness and heart distress inflicted on me which doesn't fade away at all. I cannot read nor have I any desire for the newspaper. I'm seeing an abundance of emotions within myself that I had never saw before. I sit, then I stand up, I pace up and down the room, sometimes I lie down, but all these movements occur without me instigating them. I'm longing for a comrade and companion in my alone time but I'm left with not a soul to talk to. Except two-three people, no one knows my place. Everyone who comes to me thinks I despise companionship because I'm not able to offer proper hospitality. I have no desire for food nor my sleep is under control. I struggle to lay back and deceive myself that it's only the beginning, but it is not effective. The distress of friends, now and then, is being embodied before my eyes and then I imagine the collapse of the real Kaaba of Iranians, the National Assembly." See Evan Siegel, "Seyed Hassan Sharifzadeh: Member of the Tabriz Secret Center and the Friend of Howard Baskerville," *Mahd-e Tamaddon* 1, no. 16 (2014): 66–67.

The text of the royalist fatwas mandating jihad is from Mohammad Bagher Vijuyeh, *Tarikh-e Enghelab-e Azarbaijan va Enghelab-e Tabriz* [History of the revolution of Azerbaijan and the riots of Tabriz] (Tabriz: Ibn Sina, 1969). See also Janet Afary, *The Iranian Constitutional Revolution, 1906–1911. Grassroots Democracy, Social Democracy, and the Origins of Feminism* (New York: Columbia University Press, 1996), 213.

The Tabriz Anjoman's newspaper published the shah's telegram to Rahim Khan, along with a brief sarcastic reply—"O King! All oral instructions and telegrams remained sterile and Liakhov's plan was not implemented in Azerbaijan"—followed, of course, by a few lines of poetry from Saadi: "God will take the ship wherever He wishes / even if the captain tears off his clothes."

The story of the bathhouse attack is taken from Afary, *Iranian Constitutional Revolution*, 214. The story of the Muslims protecting the Jews from Rahim Khan is from Pierre Oberling, "The Role of Religious Minorities in the Persian Revolution, 1906–1912," *Journal of Asian History* 12, no. 1 (1978): 1–29; 10.

At the start of the Constitutional Revolution, the shah distributed flyers across Tabriz, ostensibly written by the Baha'i community, claiming that the revolution was actually a Baha'i uprising and that anyone who did not convert to Baha'ism would be killed. "We are Baha'i and we do these things in order to publicly practice our faith. Iranians must become Baha'i and if not, they will all be massacred." The shah had even sent letters addressed to specific nationalists in Tabriz thanking them for "their efforts in spreading Baha'ism." See Kasravi, *History*, vol. 3, 658.

Regarding the teachings of the Baha'i and the Constitutional Revolution, Moojan Momen writes: "The Baha'i community in Iran were enacting an ambitious social program including establishing modern schools, the advancement of the social role of women and the elation of local representative councils—all of which were also part of the program of the constitutionalists and reformers." Moojan Momen, *An Introduction to Shi'i Islam* (New Haven, CT: Yale University Press, 1987), 344.

According to comments made to me by Nader Saiedi, professor of Near Eastern Languages and Culture at UCLA, while Abdul Baha supported the fight for parliamentary democracy in Persia, he was opposed to what he viewed as certain "undemocratic" elements in the constitutional movement. His main objection was the clerical leadership, which he viewed as enemies rather than supporters of democracy. In general he believed that until Persians were liberated from the cultural despotism of the clerics, no real success against political despotism would be possible. Abdul Baha was also critical of the adversarial relation between parliament and the shah. He wanted the two pillars of the country to unite in the face of foreign interference from the Russians and British, instead of fighting with each other. Finally, Abdul Baha believed that both the royalists and the nationalists were prejudiced toward the Baha'i, and that both were seeking to institutionalize religious bigotry by establishing Shi'ism as the state religion and accepting only Jews, Christians, and Zoroastrians.

It should be mentioned that the charge of Babism stuck particularly well to Sattar Khan because of his Shaykhi tendencies. Recall that the teachings of the Bab arose out of Shaykhism.

The story of the assassination attempt by Sattar's servant, Abbas, is pulled from Kasravi, *History*, vol. 3, 798. The story of Pokhitonov is pulled from Vijuyeh, *Tarikh-e Enghelab-e Azarbaijan* [History of the revolution of Azerbaijan], 28.

The text of the telegram to the shah announcing the impending victory over Tabriz was written by Moqtadar od-Dowle, the royalist acting governor, and is quoted in Kasravi, *History*, vol. 3, 794–95.

CHAPTER THIRTEEN

The text of the Nationalist Manifesto is pulled from Angus Hamilton, *Problems of the Middle East* (London: E. Nash, 1909), 145. Lenin is quoted in Janet Afary, *The Iranian Constitutional Revolution, 1906–1911. Grassroots Democracy, Social Democracy, and the Origins of Feminism* (New York: Columbia University Press, 1996), 211. See also Abbas Amanat, *Iran: A Modern History* (New Haven, CT: Yale University Press, 2017), 357.

E. G. Browne writes about Sattar's Khan's leadership over the Feda'i at this time, noting that, despite his exalted status, Sattar never claimed superiority over his fellow fighters. He was a sympathetic commander who had a habit of asking military and strategic advice from even the lowliest soldier. He always consulted the other commanders before launching an operation and established close relationships with the rank-and-file men and women who served under him. "Whenever his followers beseeched him not to expose himself in battle, Sattar would laugh and reply that he did not understand such subtleties of command. He was a simple soldier. His place was in the firing line." Edward G. Browne, *The Persian Revolution of 1905–1909* (Cambridge, UK: Cambridge University Press, 1910), 441–42. Brown's quote about England's "Indian Empire" is from page 430.

There were, at the time, some 20,000 Persian expatriates and refugees living in the Ottoman Empire. They became the unofficial ambassadors of the revolution, raising cash, making speeches, and writing articles in support of their countrymen back home.

This is how the London *Times* described the Prince's force on September 23, 1908: "The occasional signs of tarnished magnificence in the uniforms of regular soldiers, and stray tatters of the panoply of war brought vividly to the writer's mind the bridal processions of some broken-down Indian princelet, who clings to the tarnished relics of a dead magnificence, in the empty hope that the present state of decay may be confused in the wraith of the past pretensions. . . . The regular troops were beyond contempt. It was evident that they were just village yahoos, caught, dressed, and armed for the occasion. But individually the Shahsevan horsemen were good material. . . . It is depressing to think that a government that Downing-street treats with on terms of international equality could only exert its authority over its own subjects by inviting a horde of professional brigands to combine in the pillage of the its chief trading centre."

Sattar's humorous letter to the Prince is quoted in Esmail Amirkhizi, *Qiyam-e Azerbaijan va Sattar Khan* [Azerbaijan uprising and Sattar Khan] (Tehran: Tehran Bookshop, 1978), 197. The negotiations between the Prince and Tabriz is pulled from Ahmed Kasravi, *History of the Iranian Constitutional Revolution*, vol. 3, 830.

Mehdi Mojtahedi writes: "As soon as the news of the Nationalists' victory reached the hearts of Russian and Ottoman liberators and adventurers, a number of Turks of Caucasus and Ottomans, Armenians and Georgians came to Tabriz and joined the rank and file of Azerbaijani Mujahedin [the Feda'i]. While they helped Sattar Khan, [they also] added to the chaos of the city and also talked about Social-Democracy (in a Russian form) and Pan-Turkism. Once Seyyed [*sic*] Hassan Sharifzadeh uttered words of criticism, the Mujahedin killed that young honorable man who was the spokesperson of the Bazar." Mehdi Mojtahedi, *Rejal-e Asr-e Mashrutiat* [Eminent men of Azerbaijan during the constitutional period] (Tehran: Zarrin, 1997).

Evan Siegel argues in "A Review of the Memoirs of Konstantin Nikolaevich Smirnov, Crown Prince Ahmad's Tutor" that Mojtahedi's words are not reliable and that Sharifzadeh was killed because he simply wasn't in favor of unnecessary conflict and was critical of the radical tendencies of some of the revolutionaries in Tabriz.

Mohammad Bagher Vijuyeh gives a detailed account of the assassination of Sharifzadeh and argues that he wasn't killed by revolutionaries at all but rather by agents of Mir Hashem's Islamic Anjoman. He says that Sattar Khan interrogated the assassins and learned that they had been given 700 tomans by the Islamic Anjoman to kill seven people, including Sharifzadeh. Mohammad Bagher Vijuyeh, *Tarikh-e Enghelab-e Azarbaijan va Enghelab-e Tabriz* [History of the revolution of Azerbaijan and the riots of Tabriz] (Tabriz: Ibn Sina, 1969).

Karim Taherzadeh-Behzad disagrees with Vijuyeh, asking why, if the assassins were from the Islamic Anjoman, they would have run to the house of Sattar Khan instead of Mir Hashem for protection. Taherzadeh-Behzad believes that Sharifzadeh was simply killed by men in a drunken state who were disgruntled by Sharifzadeh's insensitive words. That may be the most mundane explanation for Sharifzadeh's murder, but it also appears to be the most accurate. Karim Taherzadeh-Behzad, *Qiyam-e Azerbaijan* [Azerbaijan uprising during the Iranian Constitutional Revolution] (Tehran: Eghbal, 1956).

In a letter to Edward G. Browne on April 8, 1910, Rev. William Ambrose Shedd writes about how Sharifzadeh's murder activated Howard Baskerville to join the revolutionary cause: "In the [Memorial] School were naturally young Persians of the progressive class, and one of the Persian teachers was Mirza Husayn [Hassan] Sharif-zada, who became one of the most trusted and best of the Nationalist leaders in Tabriz. Sometime during 1908 he was assassinated in the streets of Tabriz by some men of the opposite party. These circumstances, as well as the inevitable sympathy of a young and enthusiastic American with the popular cause, led [Baskerville] to take an interest in the movement, and also made him acquainted with the leaders." Browne, *Persian Revolution*, 440.

PART THREE

Tahirih, it should be mentioned, was more than just a celebrated poet. Born Fatimeh Baraghani to a family of nobles in the city of Qazvin, Tahirih was a prominent member of the Baha'i faith, one of the first followers of the Bab (he gave her the title *Tahirih*, meaning "the Pure One"), and a fierce advocate of women's rights who was executed by Nasir ad-Din Shah in 1852 for refusing to renounce her beliefs. This poem is titled "Proclamation" and is translated by Ahbieh Hussein and Hillary Chapman in *The Calling: Tahirih of Persia and Her American Contemporaries* (Maryland: Ibex, 2017).

CHAPTER FOURTEEN

The story of the crows and a list of witnesses to their attack on the flags at Golestan, along with the poem excerpt, are recounted in Ahmed Kasravi, *History of the Iranian Constitutional Revolution*, vol. 3, 983. The Russian politician's criticism of Liakhov is quoted in Janet Afary, *The Iranian Constitutional Revolution, 1906–1911. Grassroots Democracy, Social Democracy, and the Origins of Feminism* (New York: Columbia University Press, 1996), 236.

In a marginal note in his memoirs, Smirnov declared that he believed the whole Tabriz insurgency would end in Azerbaijan's separation from Iran. "The Persians and the Azerbaijanis are different in spirit and have long despised one another. The impetuous, arrogant Azerbaijani considers the submissive Persian a coward, while the Persian considers the Azerbaijani insolent. After the [destruction of parliament], they forgot about their pretensions." Smirnov envisioned Iranian Azerbaijan uniting with the Ottoman Empire as an Azerbaijani province of the Armenian-Kurdish province. That was decidedly not the case. The revolutionary movement in Tabriz never developed into an ethnic separatist movement. There was no widespread resistance to a perceived ethnic Persian domination. Rather, the resistance was focused solely on restoring the constitution over all of Persia.

In his great biography of Reza Shah, Reza Niazmand confirms that Reza Khan was indeed among the Cossacks assembled at Bagh-e Shah by Colonel Liakhov. Reza Niazmand, *Reza Shah az Tavalod ta Saltanat* [Reza Shah from birth to monarchy] (Tehran: Donya-ye Ketab, 2004).

CHAPTER FIFTEEN

For more on the Taziyeh, see Stephen Blum, "Compelling Reasons to Sing: The Music of Ta'ziyeh," *TDR* 49, no. 4 (2005): 86–90.

Prior to his arrival in Tabriz, Arthur Moore had made a name for himself as a highly respected international journalist, traveler, and adventurer. Though born in Newry, in Northern Ireland, he came from a long line of Liverpudlians, most of whom toiled in the shipyards of the Mersey docks. After graduating from Oxford in 1904, he had gone off to the Balkans to write about the plight of the Christian population in the Ottoman Empire. From there he traveled to Macedonia to report on the Young Turk revolution. His dispatches home, printed in numerous papers, caught the attention of E. G. Browne, who encouraged Moore to go to Persia and report the truth about what was taking place there. See Keith Haines, *William Arthur Moore (1880–1962)*, available online at http://www.bagenalscastle.com/documents/William%20Arthur%20Moore%20(1880%20-%201962).pdf.

John B. Jackson's memo to the State Department complaining about William Doty's nationalist proclivities is dated June 29, 1909. The Najaf fatwas are quoted in Ahmed Kasravi, *History of the Iranian Constitutional Revolution*, vol. 3, 834–36. An absolutely exhaus-

tive analysis of Persia's revolutionary flags can be found here: https://www.kavehfarrokh
.com/news/the-lion-and-sun-motif-of-iran-a-brief-analysis/.

The story of Mirza Ansari's torture and murder is told by Esmail Amirkhizi, *Qiyam-e
Azerbaijan va Sattar Khan* [Azerbaijan uprising and Sattar Khan] (Tehran: Tehran Bookshop, 1978), 250–51. Ansari was killed at the hands of a ruthless, blood-thirsty royalist
named Samad Khan, who is yet another of the great historical characters of the Constitutional Revolution that I simply do not have the space to cover in this book. Born Shoja'
od-Douleh sometime around 1858, Samad Khan belonged to a well-off family in Maragheh. During the reign of Nasir ad-Din Shah, Samad Khan was the chief of Moqaddam
horsemen. He was appointed governor of Maragheh in 1890 and was a close companion
of Mohammad Ali when the latter was crown prince in Tabriz and was one of Mohammad
Ali's most loyal disciples when he became shah. In 1908, the shah sent Samad Khan to
Maragheh to raise a force against Tabriz. He was ruthless toward the population of Maragheh, killing men women and children and tossing their bodies over the city wall. After
the war he was appointed governor-general of Azerbaijan. In the last years of this life, he
moved to Russia, where he died of cancer in 1917, just before the Russian Revolution.

Sattar Khan's reply to the 48-hour reprieve is quoted in Kasravi, *History*, vol. 3, 872.
Kasravi calls Sattar's sortie on the Jolfa Road "a major battle" but notes it was "not recorded
in the newspapers and we do not know on what day it occurred, and we only see that in the
blue book it says that it happened on Monday 22 February." Kasravi, *History*, vol. 3, 951.

CHAPTER SIXTEEN

The shah's comments regarding a million soldiers spent is quoted in Ahmed Kasravi,
History of the Iranian Constitutional Revolution, vol. 3, 864. The story of the March 5
incursion can be found in Kasravi, *History*, vol. 3, 959. Baskerville's actions during the
incursion are recorded in Sarah Wright's diary, dated March 5, reiterated in a letter sent
to Robert E. Speer by Sarah's father, John (see Chapter Nineteen for more on that letter).

Frederick Jessup's letter to the Presbyterian Board of Foreign Missions is pulled from
Firoozeh Kashani-Sabet, "American Crosses, Persian Crescents: Religion and the Diplo-
macy of US-Iranian Relations, 1834–1911," *Iranian Studies* 44, no. 5 (2011): 607–25.
William Shedd quoted in *Agents of Imperialism*, 151.

On April 5, 1909, the assistant secretary of state, Huntington Wilson, wrote the
following report regarding Baskerville's use of the consulate library to research bomb-
making techniques: "In January last, Mr. Baskerville was reported to be investigating the
question of explosives for the benefit of the revolutionists and endeavoring to obtain private information from them secretly. The Consulate in Tabriz warned him that the United
States is neutral in the civil conflict in Persia and that it would compromise the American
government and the interests of the Presbyterian Mission and of American citizens in Persia for an American to assist either side." The conversation between Doty and Baskerville
at the barracks is pulled directly from Shafaq's account: Sadeq Rezazadeh Shafaq, *Howard
Baskerville: The Story of an American Who Died in the Cause of Iranian Freedom and Independence* (Cambridge, MA: Ty Aur Press, 2008), 12–13.

There is some confusion in the historical records over whether Baskerville actually surrendered his passport. Kasravi and Shafaq both report that he did (Kasravi, *History*, vol. 3, 998; Shafaq, *Howard Baskerville*, 12–13). But according to the 1927 consular investigation by Augustin W. Ferrin, Baskerville refused, "asserting that as an American citizen he had the right to serve in the army of the nationalists," which he was expressly and repeatedly told he did not have the right to do. The confusion seems to rest on a memo Doty sent to John B. Jackson, in which he writes: "Thereupon I sought to have him surrender to me his passport in order no longer to compromise the American Government, and to announce himself as a man without a country, but he claims that he as an American citizen has the right to serve in the army of the Nationalists." Doty does not specifically say that Baskerville refused to hand the passport over, only that he disagreed with Doty's interpretation regarding what he was doing in Tabriz, and whether it was, in fact, a violation of American law.

Baskerville's speech to his class is from Shafaq's account, but the timing of the speech, as reported by Shafaq, cannot be correct. In Shafaq's account, the speech takes place before Hassan's death, which is simply not possible. The city wasn't even under siege at that time.

Baskerville's final resignation letter to Wilson is dated April 2, 1909. If Sarah Wright is correct, that is just around the time that Doty went to see him on the parade grounds, which in her diary takes place on April 1. Thus the order of events I present in my book, in which the conversation with Doty happens before Baskerville resigns from his classes.

CHAPTER SEVENTEEN

Baskerville's entrance into church dressed as a soldier is pulled both from Sarah Wright's diary, dated April 4, 1909, and from Annie Wilson's letter to Mrs. Emma Baskerville, dated April 20, 1909.

Doty's words to Baskerville quoted by John B. Jackson in a memo sent to Philander C. Knox on April 30, 1909. Doty's own memo to Jackson, requesting that he contact the Presbyterian Board of Foreign Missions, is dated April 5, 1909.

Regarding the British consulate's threat to arrest any British citizen joining the Feda'i, it should be remembered that Arthur Moore was Irish and so his activities fell beyond the responsibilities of the British consulate.

Jackson's request to reassign Doty can be found in his memo dated February 25, 1909. Robert E. Speer's memo denying Baskerville's status as a missionary is dated April 6, 1909. It should be noted that when we contacted the Presbyterian Historical Society for clarification on this matter, we were told by one librarian that, as far as she knew, Baskerville had applied to be a missionary but that his application had been rejected, and that, as a result of the rejection, he had reapplied to the school as a teacher. However, multiple searches through the archives by multiple researchers found no record that Baskerville's application had been rejected. Nor could we find his application to be a teacher. What we did find was a copy of his missionary application stamped "RECEIVED" on March 5, 1907, by Speer himself.

As to the notion that Baskerville couldn't have been a missionary because he was a teacher, it is important to note that most of the missionaries connected to the West Persia Mission had more than one job, including Wilson, Jessup, and all the other teachers at the American Memorial School. Among Doty's surviving documents are the files of numerous American missionaries in Tabriz who were in the country under multiple professions. One man, Dr. John Sergis, was "acting as a missionary in Persia" while also employed there in the occupation of dentistry. Another, Marcus Daniel, was one of a handful of American citizens in Urmia engaged "as missionaries and merchants."

In our research we unearthed a Fiftieth Commemoration Document of Baskerville's death titled, "Iranians Commemorate Death of American School Teacher," in which someone at the Presbyterian Historical Society had crossed out the words "School Teacher" and had hand-written "Mission Teacher" instead. And perhaps, in the end, that is the best way to think of Howard Baskerville: as a mission-teacher. His job was to teach. His mission was to covert souls.

Huntington Wilson's response to Knox is from a memo dated April 30, 1909. Jackson's response to Knox is from a memo dated April 30, 1909. It is unclear whether by "an individual missionary" Jackson was referring to Samuel Wilson, but that is what I assume. Apparently, the meager compensation at the school was an issue of much contention among the missionaries. A letter dated November 8, 1907, from Robert Speer's cousin (his name is illegible in the letter) to Speer in New York records the complaints from the mission-teachers at the American Memorial School over their low wages: "the demand for larger salaries is insatiable and no matter what we give they ask for more. At this rate it will soon be cheaper to have young men like M. B. and Votier [sic] who are in Tabriz come out [to Tabriz rather] than employ native teachers. The College teachers here are now getting 300 toman with house and garden and much dissatisfied at that." It's obvious young missionary teachers such as Baskerville would have come cheap. After Baskerville's death, William Doty reports that his "estate" was estimated at a mere $200.

Regarding the law against fighting in a foreign country, there is, of course, a long history of US citizens fighting in foreign wars, from the Abraham Lincoln Brigade, which fought against Francisco Franco during the Spanish Civil War, to the countless American Jews who continue to serve in the Israel Defense Forces. However, 18 US Code §959 clearly states that "Whoever, within the United States, enlists or enters himself, or hires or retains another to enlist or enter himself, or to go beyond the jurisdiction of the United States with intent to be enlisted or entered in the service of any foreign prince, state, colony, district, or people as a soldier or as a marine or seaman on board any vessel of war, letter of marque, or privateer, shall be fined under this title or imprisoned not more than three years, or both."

Joshua Keating explains in an essay in *Foreign Policy* dated September 2, 2011: "In the 1967 case *Afroyim v. Rusk*, the Supreme Court ruled that under the 14th amendment, U.S. citizens cannot be involuntarily stripped of their citizenship. (That case involved a dual U.S.-Israeli citizen who had his U.S. citizenship revoked after voting in an Israeli election, but the precedent applies to military service as well.) Since then, the government has had to prove that an individual joined a foreign army with the intention of relinquishing his or her U.S. citizenship. The army in question must be engaged in hostilities against the United States or the individual must serve as an officer." Baskerville's letter to Doty explaining his actions and why the laws against fighting in foreign wars do not apply to his actions is dated April 1, 1909.

For more on the history of martial Christianity, see Arthur Cushman McGiffert, "Christianity and War: A Historical Sketch," *American Journal of Theology* 19, no. 3 (1915): 323–45. McGiffert notes that, to those who counter with the words of Jesus that "he who uses the sword, perishes by the sword," St. Thomas Aquinas replies: "he who uses the sword . . . out of zeal for justice . . . does not take the sword of himself, but uses it as committed to him by another." What matters, in other words, is why one picked up the sword in the first place.

Robert Speer's thoughts on the role of the missionary in the world is pulled from his book *Missionary Principles and Practice* (New York: Fleming H. Revel, 1902), 552. After he returned from his trip to Tabriz, Speer liked to tell a story about how he had asked a young Persian convert how to help Persia, and the man replied in English, "By preaching Christ in the crucified style." See Robert Speer, *The Unfinished Task of Foreign Missions* (New York: Fleming H. Revel, 1926), 351.

Wilson's letter to Speer is dated April 19, 1909. Jackson's complaint to Knox about Doty having become Russian in his sympathies is dated June 29, 1909.

A report in the *New York Times*, published April 5, 1909, reads: "The situation here is serious. All the bakeries are closed, and there have been many deaths from starvation. The women of Tabriz are today demonstrating on the streets against the continuance of the situation. Sattar Khan, however, has reiterated his firm resolution never to surrender, and he declares untrue the reports that he welcomes Russian intervention."

Writing from Tabriz in April 1909, Frederick Jessup notes that, despite the shortage of food, "the city is holding out and the people talk as though they were determined not to yield. They know that to fall into the hands of . . . the other troops of the Shah would be far worse than the present distress, and as the champions of the constitution, they are determined to hold out to the bitter end." Jessup continues: "The king is hard up for the sinews of war and practically the whole of Persia is up in arms against him. All the sympathy of liberty-loving and of thinking people must be on the side of the nationalists. This is not really a revolution but a stand for the rights of the people to the Constitution which was granted by the late Shah and which this king has many times solemnly sworn to uphold. The way he has upheld it has been by seeking in every way to destroy it, by blowing up the Parliament with a cannon, by killing all the most liberal minded patriots he could lay hands on, and beseiging [*sic*] and bombarding Tabriz because she has stood for the defence [*sic*] of the Constitution." Jessup quoted in Firoozeh Kashani-Sabet, "American Crosses, Persian Crescents: Religion and the Diplomacy of US-Iranian Relations, 1834–1911," *Iranian Studies* 44, no. 5 (2011): 607–25.

It is worth noting, as Jessup does in his letter, that in the midst of the civil war, the "missionary" aim of American Presbyterians assumed secondary importance. Jessup appreciated the struggle between liberalism and despotism and the aspirations of Iranian nationalists to implement their hard-won constitution. He implores Speer: "Do not cease to pray for poor Persia that she may be delivered from all these distresses and enter upon a new era of liberty."

The letter from the women of Tabriz to the Prince is quoted in Janet Afary, *The Iranian Constitutional Revolution, 1906–1911. Grassroots Democracy, Social Democracy, and the Origins of Feminism* (New York: Columbia University Press, 1996), 195.

Sattar's thirty-seven captured men were put in chains and brought before a great feast that the Prince's troops put together for the occasion of their upcoming torture and execution. But as the soldiers were fattening their bellies for the promised entertainment to come, the captured men managed to dig a hole in the wall of their cell and escape back to the city. Tabriz celebrated their return—until it was realized they had brought no wheat back with them.

Edward G. Browne records a letter sent to him by someone in Tabriz regarding Sattar's demise during the last few weeks of the siege: "From information supplied to me from several trustworthy sources since my account of the siege of Tabriz was in print, I fear there is no doubt that Sattar Khan deteriorated sadly during the latter part of the siege and afterwards. The following is from a correspondent in whose judgement I have great confidence, and who was well placed for forming an opinion. I quote it with great regret, but since the aim of the historian should be the truth only, I feel that I have no right to suppress it."

The correspondence is as follows: "With regard to Sattar Khan, I hope you will be moderate in your praises of him in your Constitutional History. I went to Tabriz a fervent admirer of Sattar, and I came away with another lost illusion. Sattar is an illiterate, ignorant Qara-daghi horse-dealer, who has no more idea of what a Constitution means than Rahim Khan. He was a sort of luti [*sic*] in Tabriz, and had enrolled himself amongst the Fidayees before the coup d'etat of June, 1908. When the fighting began in Tabriz, he shewed considerable courage, and a certain spirit of leadership which enabled him to assert his supremacy over the lutis [*sic*] of his quarter. He has something in him of a Claude Duval, a chivalrous brigand, not without a love of theatrical effects. This character undoubtedly led him to act well in adversity, and, as much as anyone, I am ready to acknowledge the great debt Persians owe to him. . . . But success spoiled him. He began to rob inoffensive citizens; his house was full of spoils; eleven stolen pianos decorated his drawing-room; he took to heavy drinking; he took unto himself many wives; he was no longer seen in the firing rank, but rested on his laurels in slothful ease." Edward G. Browne, *The Persian Revolution of 1905–1909* (Cambridge, UK: Cambridge University Press, 1910), 441–42.

CHAPTER EIGHTEEN

According to Ahmed Kasravi, Tabriz was willing to surrender to the shah only under the following five conditions: (1) the shah must accept the Persian Constitution; (2) a general amnesty called for all fighters; (3) all royalist troops removed from the city's perimeter and dispersed; (4) the Feda'i be allowed to keep the rifles and weapons they had; (5) the people be informed about who is to be sent as governor to the province of Azerbaijan. Ahmed Kasravi, *History of the Iranian Constitutional Revolution*, vol. 3, 994.

Sattar's reply to Sadeq regarding the cannon quoted in Kasravi, *History*, vol. 3, 999. Baskerville's letter home is dated April 11, 1909.

A question remains regarding Arthur Moore's actions during the war—whether he was merely an observer or whether he actually fought himself. Moore says he fought in the final battle, with Baskerville's troops attacking Qaramalik from the right, the Armenians attacking from the left, and his group taking the center. Kasravi and other Persian eyewitnesses at the time call this a bald-faced lie. "This man [Moore] himself writes a long story in which he says that 350 rifle men have been assigned to him and counts himself among the leaders and that most of them did not come that night but abandoned him. He made himself out to be of equal stature with Baskerville in this battle and calls the Tabrizis 'cowardly' and gives himself over to criticizing them. But this was all lies and everyone knows that this Englishman never fought or fired a bullet at the enemy. The only claim he could stake was that he had accompanied Baskerville in drilling and instructing. He withdrew from activity that night [April 19–20]." Kasravi, *History*, vol. 3, 999–1000.

Kasravi quotes the account of one of Baskerville's students who took part in the final fight: "By night, when we were to have gathered at the municipality, of those who had taken the oath only 11 came. The others were either frightened and turned back themselves or had been stopped from going by their mothers and fathers when they found out what Baskerville intended. But of the rest, a large group gathered. . . . We were led to a mosque to rest there for a few hours. Baskerville did not rest for a moment and got us all to drill and exercise, even in the mosque. They say that Sattar Khan would come and the assault would begin before first light. But Sattar Khan came late and it was already first light and the sky was half aglow when we set off. At the same time, bands of mojaheds were advancing, each along the different route. The sun has not yet risen when we approach the enemy. We took Orchard Lane and advanced. On each side of us there were orchards. At the end of Orchard Lane was a vast field. At the other end of the field was a Cossack cannon barricade, around which the Cossacks were standing guard. We saw them from afar. One was twirling a charcoal brazier and he obviously did not see us. As soon as we got to the end of Orchard Lane, we approached the opening to the field and Baskerville ordered, 'Run,' and, with him in the lead, we ran to the Cossack barricades." Kasravi, *History*, vol. 3, 1000.

Baskerville's funeral recounted in Kasravi, *History*, vol. 3, 1002–1004; and in Annie Wilson's letter to Emma Baskerville.

CHAPTER NINETEEN

The final days of the shah are recounted in Smirnov's memoir, *Zapiski vospitatelya persid-skogo shaha, 1907–1914 gody* [Memoirs of the tutor of the Persian Shah, years 1907–1914] (Tel Aviv: Ivrus, 2002). There is an interesting footnote in Smirnov's account. Apparently he had suggested the shah place Persia under Russian protection: "Due to the confidentiality at that time, I did not write in my notes what exactly the 'matter' was. Now, that Emperor Nicholas II has already left the stage and Russia collapsed, it is possible to mention this: I was encouraging Mohammad Ali Shah more or less to turn to the Tsar with a request to take Persia under his protection, meaning to be in the same relationship to Russia as the Emir of Bukhara. It is clear that Mohammad Ali Shah's telegram was a very risky document, but apparently the secret was kept well, since I have never heard, from any of the officials of the Ministry of Foreign Affairs, any hint of this fact that took place. This definitely proved to me that the plans of the Russian Government did not include an increase in territory at the expense of Persia, about which Russia's ill-wishers and those who were hostile to us were constantly alarmed."

The telegram from the Tabriz Anjoman to the shah is quoted in Ahmed Kasravi, *History of the Iranian Constitutional Revolution*, vol. 3, 1009.

The Russian travel writer, N. P. Mamantov, writes this about Ahmed Mirza: "the love of the Crown Prince of Iran Ahmad Mirza to possessions, in particular clothes and jewelry, is already evident. Although the Crown Prince is only a child, he likes the courtiers to bow to him when he passes by, otherwise he gets angry. And often with his childish thoughts he tries to punish people. The Crown Prince's tutor [Smirnov] has worked hard for a long time to correct his nasty traits and reprehensible habits. Prior to arrival of Smirnov to the court, the Crown Prince often made inappropriate jokes, which are unfortunately common in the Iranian court. For example, he burns the ear of an innocent person that happened to pass by with a pair of hot pliers that he had fried in the stove, and then nastily laughs at the poor guy. The juvenile Crown Prince has three distasteful qualities: love of money, absolute jealousy, belief in extraordinary authority. He always manifests these qualities." N. P. Mamontov, *Ocherki sovremennoï Persii* (St. Petersburg, 1909). This is our English translation of the Persian translation of the book that was published under the title *The Government of the Tsar and Mohammad Ali Mirza*, by Sharafoddin Mirza Ghahremani (Tehran: Ettaalat Newspaper Publication, 1929), 34–35.

"WAS PERSIA'S SAVIOR: Col. Liakhoff Tells of His Brigade's Deeds," *Washington Post*, September 12, 1909. See also "AN EXCITING INCIDENT: COLONEL LIAKHOFF'S SUBMISSION 'BRAVO LIAKHOFF,'" *Manchester Guardian*, July 17, 1909.

Hassan Taghizadeh in *The History of the Early Days of the Constitution* writes: "the Committee sent by the Majles [Parliament] to discuss the power transition with Mohammad Ali [Shah] raised the issue of Ahmad Shah's reign and demanded that the new king, who lives in Zargandeh with his parents, return to the royal palace. Mohammad Ali Mirza and Malakeh Jahan never wanted to separate from Ahmad Mirza. Eventually, after hours of negotiations, his parents agreed to allow Ahmad Mirza to return to the royal palace as the king of Iran. Nevertheless, the main problem was that Ahmad Mirza did not want to be separated from his parents at all, he clung to his parents' skirts and asked "Shah Baba" not to let them take him away. Everyone present was crying for a child who did not want to give up his mother's lap, but ultimately he was literally dragged out of Zargandeh by force, while shouting that "I want my Shah Baba and don't want to be king." He was transferred to the summer palace of Qajar kings in Sultanabad. Nizam al-Mulk and Ala al-Douleh, Russian Capt. Smirnov, and a number of Russian soldiers, accompanied him and practically handed him over to the viceroy Azedolmolk."

Taghizadeh continues: "The young king, even after being transferred to the capital and the royal palace in Tehran with honor and respect and was officially elected to the throne of Iran, was not at peace and was looking for an opportunity to rejoin his parents. One day, he was riding a donkey out of sight of the guards to secretly go to Zargandeh and rid himself of the royal ceremonies, but the guardian courtiers were informed in time and returned him to the royal palace in the middle of the way." Hassan Taghizadeh, *A Glimpse into the History of the Early Days of the Revolution and Iranian Constitutionalism* (Tehran: Mehregan, 1959), 86.

John Wright's letter to Robert Speer complaining about the American Memorial School is dated April 22, 1909. Annie's letter to Robert Speer is dated April 26, 1909.

Matthew Davis writes: "Although the anti-constitutionalist missionaries were not in favor of reestablishing royal despotism in Iran, they were highly contemptuous of the constitutionalists, who, in their view, could not understand, much less implement, a Western constitution. The anti-constitutionalist missionaries were highly critical of their pro-nationalist colleagues. Indeed, one missionary [John Wright] called the Memorial School in Tabriz where Baskerville taught a 'hotbed for revolutionary activity' and blamed Baskerville's death on pro-nationalist sentiments among the missionaries. Both the pro- and anti-constitutionalists among the missionaries were motivated by the same ideology of mission; the pro-constitutionalists, however, were more optimistic about the prospect of Iranians being able to reform themselves." Matthew Davis, "Evangelizing the Orient: American Missionaries in Iran, 1890–1940" (PhD diss., Ohio State University, 2001), 184.

In his book on the Persian Constitutional Revolution, E. G. Browne cites the following words by William Shedd, which imply a sense of detachment in the way the missionaries ultimately viewed Baskerville's actions: "I think that there is no doubt whatever of Mr. Baskerville's worthiness to be ranked as a martyr, perhaps the more so as he found a good deal to disappoint him and still held on. The Mission, of course, is precluded by its position from espousing a political cause, and Mr. Baskerville's act was a private one." Edward G. Browne, *The Persian Revolution of 1905–1909* (Cambridge, UK: Cambridge University Press, 1910), 441.

EPILOGUE

The description of Reza Khan's announcement in Tehran is taken from Vita Sackville-West, *Passenger to Teheran* (London: Hogarth Press, 1926), 142–49.

Sattar Khan had been offered the governorship of Ardabil, but he was forced to step down from his post after only two months in office. Apparently, he proved to be a drunken and aggressive governor who didn't know how to behave in peacetime.

Reza Shah's coronation story is taken from the eyewitness account of Percy Loraine found in G. Waterfield, *Professional Diplomat: Sir Percy Loraine of Kirkharle Bt. 1880–1961* (London: Murray, 1973), 121–29.

For more on the legacy of the Persian Constitutional Revolution, see Abbas Amanat, *Iran: A Modern History* (New Haven, CT: Yale University Press, 2017), 383–85.

BIBLIOGRAPHY

(compiled by Ehsan Siapoush)

Abrahamian, Ervand. *Iran Between Two Revolutions*. Princeton, NJ: Princeton University Press, 1982.

Adamiyat, Fereydoun. *The Idea of Social Democracy in the Iranian Constitutional Movement*. Tehran: Agah, 1975.

Afary, Janet. *The Iranian Constitutional Revolution, 1906–1911. Grassroots Democracy, Social Democracy, and the Origins of Feminism*. New York: Columbia University Press, 1996.

Afshari, Mohammad Reza. "The Pishivaran and Merchants in Pre-Capitalist Iranian Society: An Essay on the Background and Causes of the Constitutional Revolution." *International Journal of Middle East Studies* 15 (1983): 133–55.

Ahmad, Ishtiaq. *Anglo-Iranian Relations, 1905–1919*. Bombay: Asia Publishing House, 1937.

Amanat, Abbas. *Pivot of the Universe: Nasir Al-Din Shah Qajar and the Iranian Monarchy*. Berkeley: University of California Press. 1997.

———. *Iran: A Modern History*. New Haven, CT: Yale University Press, 2017.

Amirkhizi, Esmail. *Qiyam-e Azerbaijan va Sattar Khan* [Azerbaijan uprising and Sattar Khan]. Tehran: Tehran Bookshop, 1978.

Aslan, Reza. *No God but God: The Origins, Evolution, and Future of Islam*. New York: Random House, 2005.

———. *God: A Human History*. New York: Random House, 2017.

———, ed. *Tablet & Pen: Literary Landscapes from the Modern Middle East*. New York: W. W. Norton, 2011.

Avery, Peter. *Modern Iran*. London: E. Benn, 1967.

Balfour, James M. *Recent Happenings in Persia*. Edinburgh: W. Blackwood and Sons, 1922.

Bandeira, Egas Moniz. "Political Reforms in a Global Context: Some Foreign

Perspectives on Constitutional Thought in Late Imperial China." *Contemporary Chinese Political Economy and Strategic Relations: An International Journal* 3, no. 1 (2017): 139–85.

Baraheni, Reza. "No Wreath for Mr. Baskerville: America in Cahoots with the Shah." *The Nation,* March 12, 1977.

Baskerville, Patrick H. *Genealogy of the Baskerville Family and Some Allied Families, Including the English Descent from 1266 A.D.* Richmond, VA: W. E. Jones' Sons, 1912.

———. *Additional Baskerville Genealogy: A Supplement to the Author's Genealogy of the Baskerville Family of 1912; Being a Miscellany of Additional Notes and Sketches from Later Information, Including a Study of the Family History in Normandy.* Richmond, VA: W. E. Jones' Sons, 1917.

Benson, Louis F. *The English Hymn, Its Development and Use in Worship.* New York: Hodder and Stoughton, 1915.

Berg, A. Scott. *Wilson.* New York: Simon & Schuster, 2013.

Birdsall, Richard D. "The Second Great Awakening and the New England Social Order." *Church History* 39, no. 3 (1970): 345–64.

Blincoe, Robert A. *Missions in Kurdistan, 1668–1990: With Missiological Considerations.* Pasadena: Fuller Theological Seminary, School of World Mission, 1997.

Bonhoeffer, Dietrich. *Dietrich Bonhoeffer: Witness to Jesus Christ,* edited by John de Gruchy. Minneapolis: Fortress Press, 1991.

Boylan, Anne M. "Evangelical Womanhood in the Nineteenth Century: The Role of Women in Sunday Schools." *Feminist Studies* 4, no. 3 (1978): 62–80.

Browne, Edward G. *The Persian Revolution of 1905–1909.* Cambridge, UK: Cambridge University Press, 1910.

———. *Letters from Tabriz: The Russian Suppression of the Iranian Constitutional Movement.* Washington, DC: Mage Publication, 2008.

Burke, Bernard, and Peter Townend. *Burke's Genealogical and Heraldic History of the Landed Gentry: Volume One.* London: Burke's Peerage, 1965.

Chardin, Jean. *Voyages Du Chevalier Chardin En Perse Et Autres Lieux De L'orient: 5.* Paris: Lecointe, 1830.

Chehabi, H. E., and Vanessa Martin. *Iran's Constitutional Revolution: Popular Politics, Cultural Transformations and Transnational Connections.* London: I. B. Tauris, 2010.

Clark, Christopher M. *Kaiser Wilhelm II.* London: Longman, 2000.

Cochran, Joseph G. *The Persian Flower: A Memoir of Judith Grant Perkins, of Oroomiah, Persia.* Boston: American Tract Society, 1853.

Collard, Ian. *Liverpool Landing Stage Through Time.* Stroud, UK: Amberley Publishing, 2011.

Conforti, Joseph. "The Invention of the Great Awakening, 1795–1842." *Early American Literature* 26, no. 2 (1991): 99–118.

Cott, Nancy F. "Young Women in the Second Great Awakening in New England." *Feminist Studies* 3, no. 1/2 (1975): 15–29.

Cowles, Virginia. *The Kaiser.* London: Collins, 1963.

Craig, Hardin. *Woodrow Wilson at Princeton*. Norman: University of Oklahoma Press, 1960.

Davis, Gordon J. "What Woodrow Wilson Cost My Grandfather." *New York Times*, November 24, 2015.

Davis, Matthew M. "Evangelizing the Orient: American Missionaries in Iran, 1890–1940." PhD diss., Ohio State University, 2001.

Du Bois W. E. B. *Black Reconstruction in America: An Essay Toward a History of the Part Which Black Folk Played in the Attempt to Reconstruct Democracy in America, 1860–1880*. New York: Russell & Russell, 1935.

Dworkin, Ronald. "Constitutionalism and Democracy." *European Journal of Philosophy* 3, no. 1 (1995): 2–11.

Earle, Edward Mead. *Turkey, the Great Powers, and the Bagdad Railway: A Study in Imperialism*. New York: Macmillan, 1923.

Entner, Marvin L. "Russia and Persia, 1890–1912." PhD diss., University of Minnesota, 1963.

Estelami, Hooman. *The Americans of Urumia*. New York: Bahar Books, 2021.

Fathi, Asghar. "The Role of the 'Rebels' in the Constitutional Movement in Iran." *International Journal of Middle East Studies* 10, no. 1 (1979): 55–66.

Figes, Orlando. *A People's Tragedy: The Russian Revolution, 1917–24*. New York: Penguin Random House, 1998.

Fisher, Gabriel. "Princeton and the Fight Over Woodrow Wilson's Legacy." *New Yorker*, November 25, 2015; available online at https://www.newyorker.com/news/news-desk/princeton-and-the-fight-over-woodrow-wilsons-legacy.

Flynn, Thomas. *The Western Christian Presence in the Russias and Qajar Persia, C. 1760–C. 1870*. Leiden: Brill, 2017.

Fraser, David. *Persia and Turkey in Revolt*. London: William Blackwood & Sons, 1910.

Ghaneabassiri, Kamyar. "U.S. Foreign Policy and Persia, 1856–1921." *Iranian Studies* 35, no. 1–3 (2002): 145–75.

Gnoli, G. 1999. "Farr(ah)." *Encyclopaedia Iranica*, 1999; available online at https://iranicaonline.org/articles/farrah.

Grabill, Joseph L. *Protestant Diplomacy and the Near East: Missionary Influence on American Policy, 1810–1927*. Minneapolis: University of Minnesota Press, 1971.

Grothe, Hugo. *Wanderungen in Persien: Erlebtes Und Erschautes*. Berlin: Allg. Verein für Dt. Literatur, 1910.

Gwynn, Stephen. *The Letters and Friendships of Sir Cecil Spring Rice: Vol. 2*. London: Constable, 1929.

Hairi, Abdul-Hadi. "Why Did the 'Ulamā Participate in the Persian Constitutional Revolution of 1905–1909?" *Die Welt Des Islams* 17, no. 1/4 (1976–1977): 127–54.

Hale, Charles A. "The Civil Law Tradition and Constitutionalism in Twentieth-Century Mexico: The Legacy of Emilio Rabasa." *Law and History Review* 18, no. 2 (2000): 257–80.

Hamilton, Angus. *Problems of the Middle East*. London: E. Nash, 1909.

Hanisek, Joel Feurt. "From the Domain of Certitude to the Relational Realm: U.S. Missions in Iran and the Politics of piecemeal social change." PhD. Diss., Trinity College, Dublin, School of Religion, 2019.

Hart, Peter. *The Great War: A Combat History of the First World War.* Oxford: Oxford University Press, 2013.

Hatch, Nathan O. *The Democratization of American Christianity.* New Haven, CT: Yale University Press, 1989.

Hone, Joseph M., and Page L. Dickinson. *Persia in Revolution, with Notes of Travel in the Caucasus.* London: T. F. Unwin, 1910.

Jackson, Abraham V. W. *Persia Past and Present.* New York: Macmillan, 1906.

Javadi, Hasan. "E. G. Browne and the Persian Constitutional Movement." *Iran* 14 (1976): 133–40.

Karimi, Ebrahim. "The Petroglyphs of Domab in the Central Plateau of Iran." *Near Eastern Archaeology* 81, no. 2 (2018): 128–40.

Karimi, Linda Colleen. "Implications of American Missionary Presence in 19th and 20th Century Iran." PhD diss., Portland State University, 1975.

Karpat, Kemal H. *Social Change and Politics in Turkey: A Structural-Historical Analysis.* Leiden: E. J. Brill, 1973.

Kasravi, Ahmed. *The 18 Year History of Azerbaijan.* 2 vols. Tehran: Amirkabir Press, 1978.

———. *History of the Iranian Constitutional Revolution.* 3 vols. Tehran: Amir Kabir Publications, 1984. Originally published in 1951.

———. *History of the Iranian Constitutional Revolution,* vols. 2–3. Costa Mesa, CA: Mazda Publishers, 2006 and 2015.

Kazemzadeh, Firuz. *Russia and Britain in Persia: Imperial Ambitions in Qajar Iran.* London: I. B. Tauris, 2013.

Keddie, Nikki R. "Iranian Politics 1900–1905: Background to Revolution." *Middle Eastern Studies* 5, no. 1 (1969): 3–31.

Keeling, Drew T. "Oceanic Travel Conditions and American Immigration, 1890–1914." MPRA Paper No. 47850 (June 2013); available online at https://mpra.ub .unimuenchen.de/47850/1/MPRA_paper_47850.pdf.

Kermani, Nazemol Eslam. *Tarikh-e Bidari-yi Iraniyan* [History of Iranian awakening], edited by Ali Akbar Saeedi Sirjani. Tehran: Bonyad-e Farhang, 1968.

Kidd, Thomas S. *American Christians and Islam: Evangelical Culture and Muslims from the Colonial Period to the Age of Terrorism.* Princeton, NJ: Princeton University Press, 2013.

Kinneir, John M. *A Geographical Memoir of the Persian Empire.* London: John Murray, 1813.

Kondoyanidi, Anita A. "The Prophet Disillusioned: Maxim Gorky and the Russian Revolutions." PhD diss., Georgetown University, 2019.

Krupskaya, Nadezhda K. *Reminiscences of Lenin.* Honolulu: University Press of the Pacific, 2004.

Magic Lantern Lectures of Foreign Mission Lands: Syria. New York: Board of Foreign Missions of the Presbyterian Church in the USA, 1880.

Malekzadeh, Mehdi. *Zendegani-e Malek Al-Mutekallemin* [History of the Constitutional Revolution]. 7 vols. Tehran: Elmi and Partners Publishing House, 1946.

Martin, Vanessa. *Islam and Modernism: The Iranian Revolution of 1906.* Syracuse, NY: Syracuse University Press, 1989.

Maynard, W. Barksdale. *Woodrow Wilson: Princeton to the Presidency.* New Haven, CT: Yale University Press, 2008.

Meaney, Neville K. "Arthur S. Link and Thomas Woodrow Wilson." *Journal of American Studies* 1 (1967): 119–26.

Melville, Herman. *Redburn: His First Voyage.* Cambridge, UK: Press Syndicate of the University of Cambridge, 1983.

Mir-Ahmadi, Maryam. "Marco Polo in Iran." *Oriente Moderno* 88, no. 2 (2008): 1–13.

Mojtahedi, Mehdi. *Rejal-e Asr-e Mashrutiat* [Eminent men of Azerbaijan during the constitutional period]. Tehran: Zarrin, 1997.

Montefiore, Simon Sebag. *Young Stalin.* New York: Random House, 2007.

Mossolov, A. A., and A. A. Pilenco. *At the Court of the Late Tsar: Being the Memoirs of A.A. Mossolov.* London: Methuen, 1935.

Mulder, John M. *Woodrow Wilson: The Years of Preparation.* Princeton, NJ: Princeton University Press, 1978.

Nabokov, Vladimir V. *Speak, Memory: An Autobiography Revisited.* New York: Vintage International, 1967.

Niazmand, Reza. *Reza Shah az Tavalod ta Saltanat* [Reza Shah from birth to monarchy]. Tehran: Donya-ye Ketab, 2004.

North Carolina: A Guide to the Old North State. Chapel Hill: University of North Carolina Press, 1939.

Novar, Leon. "The Great Powers and Iran, 1914–1921." PhD diss., University of Chicago, 1958.

Oberling, Pierre. "The Role of Religious Minorities in the Persian Revolution, 1906–1912." *Journal of Asian History* 12, no. 1 (1978): 1–29.

O'Toole, Patricia. *The Moralist: Woodrow Wilson and the World He Made.* New York: Simon & Schuster, 2018.

Pakizegi, Zarin B. "History of the Christians in Iran" (unpublished manuscript, 1992).

Pedram, Mohammad Hassan. *A Collection of Aphorisms and Sayings of Sattar Khan.* Tabriz: Akhtar, 2010.

Perkins, Henry Martyn. *Life of Rev. Justin Perkins, D.D. Pioneer Missionary to Persia.* New York: Fleming H. Revell, 1887.

Perkins, Justin. *A Residence of Eight Years in Persia, Among the Nestorian Christians; With Notices of the Muhammedans.* Andover, MA: Allen, Morrill & Wardwell, 1843.

Pistor-Hatam, Anja. "The Iranian Constitutional Revolution as *lieu(x) de mémoire*: Sattar Khan." In *Iran's Constitutional Revolution: Popular Politics, Cultural Transformations and Transnational Connections*, edited by H. E. Chehabi and Vanessa Martin, 33–44. London: Bloomsbury, 2010.

———. "Sattar Khan." *Encyclopaedia Iranica*, 1996; available online at https://www .iranicaonline.org/articles/sattar-khan-one-of-the-most-popular-heroes-from-tabr iz-who-defended-the-town-during-the-lesser-autocracy-in-1908–09.

Prazniak, Roxann. "Ilkhanid Buddhism: Traces of a Passage in Eurasian History." *Comparative Studies in Society and History* 56, no. 3 (2014): 650–80.

Raees Niya, R., and A. Nahid. *Two Fighters of the Constitutional Movement*. Tabriz: Ibn Sina Press, 1970.

Rafifar, Jalal. "Some Indications of Shamanism in Arasbaran Rock Carvings." *Documenta Praehistorica* 34 (2007): 203–13.

Robbins, Richard G. *Overtaken by the Night: One Russian's Journey Through Peace, War, Revolution, and Terror*. Pittsburgh: University of Pittsburgh Press, 2017.

Robeson, Paul. *Here I Stand*. London: Cassell, 1988.

Rostam-Kolayi, Jasamin. "From Evangelizing to Modernizing Iranians: The American Presbyterian Mission and Its Iranian Students." *Iranian Studies* 41 (2008): 213–39.

Sackville-West, Vita. *Passenger to Teheran*. London: Hogarth Press, 1926.

Sandlin, Lee. *Wicked River: The Mississippi When It Last Ran Wild*. New York: Vintage Books, 2011.

Shafaq, Sadeq Rezazadeh. *Howard Baskerville: The Story of an American Who Died in the Cause of Iranian Freedom and Independence*. Cambridge, MA: Ty Aur Press, 2008.

Shapira, Dan D. Y. "A Jewish Pan-Turkist: Seraya Szapszał (Şapşaloğlu) and His Work 'Qirim Qaray Türkleri' (1928) (Judaeo-Türkica XIII)." *Acta Orientalia Academiae Scientiarum Hungaricae* 58, no. 4 (2005): 349–80.

Shuster, W. Morgan. *The Strangling of Persia*. New York: Century Company, 1912.

Siegel, Evan. "A Review of the Memoirs of Konstantin Nikolaevich Smirnov, Crown Prince Ahmad's Tutor." n.d.; available online at http://iran.qlineorientalist.com/ Articles/Smirnov/Smirnov.html.

———. "Seyed Hassan Sharifzadeh: Member of the Tabriz Secret Center and the Friend of Howard Baskerville." *Mahd-e Tamaddon* 1, no. 16 (2014), 66–67; available online at http://iran.qlineorientalist.com/Articles/Sharifzade.pdf.

Simpson, Donald. "Missions and the Magic Lantern." *International Bulletin of Missionary Research* 21 (1997): 13–15.

Smirnov, Konstantin N., and Nugzar K. Ter-Oganovi. *Zapiski vospitatelya persidsogo shakha, 1907–1914 godi* [Memoirs of the tutor of the Persian Shah, years 1907–1914]. Tel Aviv: Ivrus, 2002.

Smith, S. A. "Moscow Workers and the Revolutions of 1905 and 1917." *Soviet Studies* 36, no. 2 (1984): 282–89.

Sohrabi, Nader. *Revolution and Constitutionalism in the Ottoman Empire and Iran*. New York: Cambridge University Press, 2014.

Steiner, Edward A. *On the Trail of the Immigrant*. Toronto: Fleming H. Revell, 1906.

Sykes, Percy M. *A History of Persia*, vol. 2. London: Macmillan, 1915.

Tabriz Anjoman Newspaper. Tehran: Iranian National Library, 1995.

Tafreshi Hosseini, Ahmad. *The Journal of the Constitutional News and the Revolution of Iran*, edited by Iraj Afshar. Tehran: Amir Kabir, 1973.

Taherzadeh-Behzad, Karim. *Qiyam-e Azerbaijan* [Azerbaijan uprising during the Iranian Constitutional Revolution]. Tehran: Eghbal, 1956.

Tapper, Richard. "Raiding, Reaction, and Rivalry: The Shahsevan Tribes in the Constitutional Period." *Bulletin of the School of Oriental and African Studies* 49, no. 3 (1986): 508–31.

Taylor, Gordon. "Deep Waters: Life and Death in the Perkins Family, 1834–1852." *Journal of Assyrian Academic Studies* 23 (2009): 64–73.

The Princeton Seminary Bulletin, vols. 7–10. Princeton, NJ: Princeton Theological Seminary, 1913.

Tuchman, Barbara W. *The Guns of August*. New York: Macmillan, 1962.

Vaziri, Mostafa. *Iran as Imagined Nation*. Piscataway, NJ: Gorgias Press, 2019.

Vijuyeh, Mohammad Bagher. *Tarikh-e Enghelab-e Azarbaijan va Enghelab-e Tabriz* [History of the revolution of Azerbaijan and the riots of Tabriz]. Tabriz: Ibn Sina, 1969.

von Bernhardi, Friedrich. *Germany and the Next War*. London: Arnold, 1914.

von Schierbrand, Wolf, ed. *The Kaiser's Speeches: Forming a Character Portrait of Emperor William II*. New York: Harper & Brothers, 1903.

Warth, Robert D. *Nicholas II: The Life and Reign of Russia's Last Monarch*. Westport, CT: Praeger, 1997.

Waterfield, G. *Professional Diplomat: Sir Percy Loraine of Kirkharle Bt. 1880–1961*. London: Murray, 1973.

Werner, Christoph. *An Iranian Town in Transition: A Social and Economic History of the Elites of Tabriz, 1747–1848*. Wiesbaden: Otto Harrassowitz Verlag, 2000.

Wilcox, Andrew. *Orientalism and Imperialism: From Nineteenth-Century Missionary Imaginings to the Contemporary Middle East*. London: Bloomsbury Academic, 2018.

Wilson, Annie Rhea. "My Memories" (unpublished manuscript, 1951).

Wilson, Samuel G. *Persian Life and Customs*. Edinburgh & London: Oliphant, Anderson & Ferrier, 1896.

Zirinsky, Michael P. "A Panacea for the Ills of the Country: American Presbyterian Education in Inter-War Iran." *Iranian Studies* 26, no. 1/2 (1993): 119–37.

INDEX

Page numbers in italics indicate a figure on the corresponding page.